History in Primary Schools

A practical approach for teachers of
5- to 11-year-old children

Joan E. Blyth

City of Liverpool College of Higher Education

McGRAW-HILL Book Company (UK) Limited

London · New York · St Louis · San Francisco · Auckland · Bogotá · Guatemala
Hamburg · Johannesburg · Lisbon · Madrid · Mexico · Montreal · New Delhi
Panama · Paris · San Juan · São Paulo · Singapore · Sydney · Tokyo · Toronto

Published by
McGRAW-HILL Book Company (UK) Limited
MAIDENHEAD · BERKSHIRE · ENGLAND

British Library Cataloguing in Publication Data

Blyth, Joan E.
  History in primary schools.
  —(McGraw-Hill series for teachers)
  1. History—Study and teaching
  2. Education, Elementary
  I. Title
  372.8'9   LB1581.B63

  ISBN 0–07–084128–4

Library of Congress Cataloging in Publication Data

Blyth, Joan E.
  History in primary schools.
  (McGraw-Hill series for teachers)
  Bibliography: p.
  Includes index.
  1. History—Study and teaching (Elementary)
  I. Title. II. Series
  LB1581.B63   372.8'9044   81–11736

  ISBN 0–07–084128–4   AACR2

12345   LT   85432

Printed and bound in Great Britain by
Latimer Trend & Company Ltd, Plymouth

6·95

McGRAW-HILL series for Teachers

Consulting Editor:
Peter Taylor,
School of Education, Bristol University

Blyth: History in Primary Schools
Henderson and Perry: Change and Development in Schools
Holt: Schools and Curriculum Change
Hopson and Scally: Lifeskills Teaching
Hutchcroft: Making Language Work
Rowntree: Developing Courses for Students
Saunders: Class Control and Behaviour Problems

Frontispiece   Lord Cobham and his family at table (reproduced by kind permission of the Marquis of Bath)

To my parents
Clare and Edward Guest

Contents

Preface and acknowledgements   ix

Chapter 1 History in the primary school curriculum   1
1.1 The nature of history   1
1.2 History teaching in the English primary school   4
1.3 The past at the infant stage   8
1.4 Young juniors and history   8
1.5 Older juniors and history   9
References   11

Chapter 2 Background to syllabus planning   12
2.1 Introduction   12
2.2 Basic principles   13
2.3 Trends in syllabus making 1950–1980   14
References   21

Chapter 3 Ideas for constructing a syllabus   22
3.1 Introduction   22
3.2 The beginnings of awareness of the past in the infant years   22
3.3 Some history frameworks for the junior school   29
3.4 Some integrated frameworks for the junior school   37
3.5 Conclusion   61
References   63

Chapter 4 The classroom operation   64
4.1 Introduction   64
4.2 The story lesson, with a contribution from Shirley Makin   65
4.3 Interpreting illustrations   72
4.4 Exposition and questions, with a contribution from John
     Pelling   76
4.5 The essential product: cumulative record making   82
4.6 The organization of individual and group work, with a
     contribution from Beryl Fox   85
4.7 The organization of field work, with contributions from
     Margaret West and Frank Harris   93
4.8 Art work, model making, and visual displays, with a
     contribution from Claire Parker   104
4.9 Time charts, with a contribution from John West   112
4.10 Conclusion   123
References   124

Chapter 5   Sources and resources   **126**
5.1   Introduction   126
5.2   First order resource—the teacher   127
5.3   Second order resource—the written and spoken word, with
       contributions from J. M. Salt, Carol Wilson, Ken May, and
       Susan Lynn   135
5.4   Third order resource—mechanical aids   184
5.5   Fourth order resource—outside school   188
5.6   Conclusion   198
References   198

Chapter 6   Assessment, evaluation and record keeping   **201**
6.1   Introduction   201
6.2   The infant years: 5- to 7-year olds   202
6.3   Incidental assessment in the junior school   203
6.4   Long-term assessment in the junior school   205
6.5   Evaluation of syllabuses   206
6.6   Evaluation of materials   208
6.7   Record keeping   212
References   214

Some suggestions for using the book   **215**

Further reading   **219**

Index   **222**

Preface

In writing this book, my aim has been to provide ideas, practical help, and encouragement to non-specialist teachers in primary schools, and also to students training to teach history to younger children. The 1978 Primary School Survey emphasized the need for more specific help in the teaching of the past and I hope that this book will fulfil this need to some extent. It is the result of a professional lifetime devoted to the teaching of history in many parts of the country to pupils from the infant stage to Honours degree level, and substantially also to the training of teachers for primary and secondary schools.

The plan of the book follows the needs of teachers in the development of good history teaching. It first considers the place of history in the 5–11 curriculum and then looks at syllabus/content during the last 30 years, before suggesting alternative syllabus frameworks, both for history as a separate subject and as part of an integrated syllabus. The heart of the book is what happens in the classroom and the resources needed to help teachers to improve 'the classroom operation'. The final chapter of the book makes suggestions for teachers to use in checking the effectiveness of their teaching. In order to relate the book to individual schools, I have added ways in which teachers may want to use the separate chapters in their thinking and preparation.

If it helps to make teachers enthusiastic about the past and to show them quick and effective ways of preparing and presenting their historical material, as well as in assessing it, I shall be very satisfied.

Many people have encouraged and helped me during the preparation of this book. Chief among them are Ken Hardcastle of Cheshire LEA and his team of primary teachers, and Michael Bagenal of Cambridgeshire LEA. I am also indebted to practising teachers who have made contributions arising from their own work in the classroom: Beryl Fox, Frank Harris, J. M. Salt, Susan Lynn, Shirley Makin, Ken May, Claire Parker, John Pelling, Margaret West, John West, and Carol Wilson, all of whom have asked me to point out that any opinions expressed are personal and not necessarily those of any LEA, and to Peter Gilliat of Avon LEA for Fig. 3.4, to Jo Hillaby of the University of Bristol for Fig. 3.7, and to the Historical Association for Fig. 3.8.

Finally, my greatest support has come from my husband, Alan Blyth, who scrutinized the whole book and also prepared the section in Chapter 3 on how the 8–13 Schools Council project, *Place, Time and Society*, could be adapted to the 7–11 age range, and contributed substantially to the writing of Chapter 6.

Joan E. Blyth
Liverpool
March 1981

Acknowledgements

The author and publishers wish to thank the following for permission to reproduce material:

C. Morris, *The Journeys of Celia Fiennes*, Gulliver Press; W. R. Stephens, *Teaching Local History*, Manchester University Press; Department of Education and Science, *Primary Education in England*, HMSO.

Discrimination between the sexes

In a book on this subject, it is impracticable to eliminate completely the use of genders and retain a fluent and readable text. The reader is therefore asked to accept that no deliberate distinction between the sexes is implied.

1. History in the primary school curriculum

In thinking about the place of history—if it has a place—in the curriculum of the primary school, we have to clarify the purpose of teaching and learning the subject in the years 5 to 11. Cognitive psychologists emphasize the crucial importance of those years for subsequent academic achievement, an issue which is still too frequently ignored by teachers of older children. In addition, they are years of tremendous physical and emotional development for children. Primary teachers are certainly aware of the vital importance of their work and view their role as being involved in the welfare of all sides of the child's life.

Class teacher organization has emphasized concentration on general concerns, and especially on the linguistic and mathematical side of a child's development since communication, literacy, and numeracy are essential to all human beings. The child below the age of 13 also needs to be taught the basic methodology to understand science and the social subjects, and to appreciate the arts as well as to develop his physical powers. Within social subjects I include morality as well as history, geography and social science. Therefore, the primary school child needs a 'whole curriculum' which at certain times delves more deeply and technically into specific disciplines. In the time at the teacher's disposal this task is a formidable one. Faced with strident demands for other kinds of curricular content, she feels obliged to question the need to include much study of the past or development of the skills of the young historian. The past appears to be only a small part of the social subjects. Yet it is a part of much greater importance than some teachers appreciate. Teachers in the secondary school are educating the 'whole child' in a different way through more structural disciplines but the basic foundations for these disciplines need to have been laid in the primary school.

1.1 The nature of history

Before discussing the aims and purposes of studying history in the primary school it is wise to look at the essential nature of the discipline

1

and find out how children of 5 to 11 will react to it. Many definitions have been made since the institution of Honours degrees in history in the late nineteenth century and they all vary, but from this mine of information five elements become apparent.

In the first place, history is about real people and real events interacting upon each other in the past. The age-old problem of how people and events impinge upon each other is a basic essential of history.

Second, history must be concerned with sequence, time, and chronology. This is unique to the discipline and the most difficult concept to teach and understand. But it is the very essence of history. One well-known modern historian has recently said: 'Freedom to move through time and space is one of the greatest opportunities the historian has'.[1]

A third element is the actual evidence which enables us to know what actually happened in the past. This comes not only from books written by historians (secondary sources) but also from documents written in the past, buildings, landscapes, archaeological remains, reminiscences of older people (oral history), pictures, photographs and films. These primary and secondary sources are the basic material of history but can be difficult to find. The time taken to find the much sought-after recent book in the library, to decipher the faded palaeography (handwriting) of an early document, to travel a distance to look at the relevant building, and to tape record the memories of old people are awe-inspiring tasks for the busy teacher in any school. If and when even some of this information seeking has been done, understanding and interpretation pose their problems. Understanding the meaning of technical terms and seeking advice require diligence and courage. Interpretation will probably involve reading several books (or articles) on the same subject.

A fourth element is the communication of the past to others through talking and writing. Historians using the same sources often interpret them in different ways and from different standpoints, resulting in conflicts of opinion. These conflicts are often only resolved after the discovery of more primary evidence; sometimes, being dependent on irreconcilable approaches to history itself, they are never resolved and we have to be content to accept differing views. Yet controversy and discussion are of the essence of the discipline and help us to a truer view of the subject.

The last element of the discipline of history is the way in which the past affects the present. A knowledge of the past, of individuals and institutions, can help to explain how these people and institutions react and how a chain of events has influenced them.

Primary school children will not be able to understand all these elements, nor for that matter are secondary school pupils or adults able

2

to do so. But they can certainly learn about and try to understand many people in the past, especially children and relatively unsophisticated adults, and can begin to handle simple primary evidence (especially artefacts of the past) and to appreciate that all people and events happen in time, however short a time ago.

Beyond all these separate claims on behalf of history, there is the contention of some philosophers of education such as Hirst, that history is a 'form of knowledge', logically distinct from others such as scientific or mathematical knowledge. If this is so, then the case for including history as such in the curriculum for younger children in an appropriate manner is greatly strengthened. The 'forms of knowledge' approach has itself been subjected to considerable criticism but it is noteworthy that one of the most important recent studies in the teaching of history, by Rogers, appears to give powerful empirical support to Hirst's assertion that children do encounter history as a form of knowledge.

But the views of historians and philosophers are not the only relevant considerations. Nowadays, when considering the place of any subject or activity in the primary school curriculum, teachers are accustomed to hearing how the work of Piaget and his collaborators has thrown light on children's learning. In the case of history, this is less obviously the case. Piaget himself did make a specific study of children's understanding of time, and of moral development, but it has been left to others to delineate the sequence of development in ideas about society, about historical inference, or indeed about person perception. Writers such as Lodwick, Hallam, and Rogers[2] have broken important new ground, but much of it has been at the post-primary level and so in the teaching of younger children it is still substantially necessary to rely on general notions of development, enlivened by the accumulated experience of teachers.

In common with Piaget, the work of Barnes on language in the curriculum is familiar to teachers. This type of research has been extended to the teaching of history through the work of Edwards. He warns teachers of the danger of thinking that the language of history used in the classroom is 'everyday' because the content of the past being studied is about 'ordinary' people. He says that: 'There is an obvious risk of confusion between the "common sense" of then and now.'[3] The language and concepts of past ages need to be taught specifically. A further consideration is the need to be aware of the generalizations made in historical writing; these generalizations are not always clarified by specific factual example and are often too abstract in concept for both teacher and pupils.

Most primary teachers do not feel secure and happy in including

3

historical material in their curriculum unless they are assured of specific assistance. If this is not forthcoming it is only natural that teachers will despair and resort to well-tried areas of the curriculum in which help has been clear, practical, and easily assessed.

1.2 History teaching in the English primary school

The beginnings of history teaching in elementary schools are notoriously difficult to trace. Some light has been thrown on local developments through the very extensive studies carried out by advanced students of education but it is rarely that these have been systematically brought together except by writers such as Bramwell and, more recently, Gordon. The picture which we can now discern is one in which here and there, from surprisingly early in the nineteenth century, some schools touched upon the mainstream of English history, or on the local environment, or both. Historical facts were included, too, in the compendia of information used in middle-class homes and in some of the monitorial and other schools. Some history percolated from the early training colleges down into the elementary schools until the introduction of the Revised Code in 1861 virtually extinguished any form of teaching that did not enable the school to earn its grant. Thus, although Victorian England was a culture which became increasingly aware of its past, and set history firmly in the pattern of its early adult education, the place of history in the elementary, or indeed in the secondary, schools was a variable and insecure one. Talking of social studies in the nineteenth and twentieth centuries, Gordon and Lawton say: 'In this area of the curriculum schools have shown themselves to be highly resistant to change throughout the century' and again: 'Social studies and science . . . have very strong claims but have never been given the prominence they deserve.'[4]

Meanwhile, one celebrated source of information as to how at least some of the upper classes taught their children is the famous *Little Arthur's History of England* by Lady Callcott, first published in 1835 and addressed 'To Mothers'. Lady Callcott presumed that every mother had time and desire to *read* to her children the story of *Britain*'s heritage told in terms of 'heroes' and 'tyrants' (such as William the Conqueror— 'tyrant rather than king'). These stories are exciting, heroic, and heavily biased. They aim to teach morality and greatness.

In 1871, following Forster's Education Act, the 'New Code' allowed an expansion of the elementary curriculum and an opportunity arose to include 'class subjects'. By coincidence, in 1871 and 1873 Oxford and Cambridge universities agreed to introduce Honours history degrees into their curricula. But the gap between the elementary school and the older universities was vast and the new degrees had no direct effect on the training of teachers. History teaching, for most children, thus depended upon the combination of academic content and 'method' prevalent in training college courses. The universities joined in this training after the foundation of day training colleges towards the end of the nineteenth century, but it was not until the beginning of the present century that any official notice was taken of history in elementary schools. The *Suggestions for the Consideration of Teachers and Others Concerned in the Work of Public Elementary Schools* of 1905 saw history as difficult to teach but a subject that should be taught. It should be taught for reasons of morality (compare Lady Callcott); children must know their rights and duties, Britain's heritage must be compared with other nations and the example of 'good men' should be held up to them. Thus, as earlier, history was to be studied for the virtues it *might* develop, not for enjoyment or interest and certainly not for essential, practical reasons.

In 1923 the Board of Education published its first specific suggestions about the teaching of history. It recommended the reading of the good history story books that were being published, as a means of children knowing 'our own national story' and gave an 'alphabet' of 32 dates, events in English history which all children should learn. These ranged from 100 BC to the 1914–18 war. Thus history teaching was for national propaganda and was essentially factual and content based. In his book *Elementary School Work*, Bramwell summarizes the aims of history teaching in the first quarter of the twentieth century as being a school of citizenship involving Britain's heritage from the beginning to the present day and thus encouraging teachers to show pupils historic buildings on their expeditions out of school. In 1927 a *Handbook of Suggestions for Teachers* viewed history as above all an instrument of moral training learnt through good and evil personalities. So by 1927 Lady Callcott's view of over a hundred years earlier still held good.

Confidence in the efficacy of history to transform children and make them 'good citizens' was evaporating by the 1930s. However, the substantial introduction of separate junior schools, 7–11, afforded a new opportunity and in 1931 the Hadow Report proclaimed the belief that children up to the age of 11 could be expected to be able to read a simple story and to understand how history affected 'his everyday life and environment' (vague terms). Although individuals researched and wrote books on the teaching of history in primary schools, few teachers in elementary schools benefited from this work as the training colleges did not consider the subject to be as important as many other subjects for

5

beginner teachers. Yet Fred Clarke's *Foundations of History Teaching* remains a classic for all time, a philosophical and at the same time practical and easily understood basis for all teaching of the past up to the age of 12. This gem of methodology, first published in 1929, contains the arguments of what Rogers and others now call the 'new' history. In criticizing the abortive memorization of facts and dates which are not fully comprehended, Clarke speaks of: 'Children's minds strewn with the debris of a card-catalogue, which they piece together painfully in most unhappy families.' In discussing the difficulties of teaching chronology and time Clarke writes: 'For change, not time, is the historic idea' and goes on to warn of the danger of dates becoming mere telephone numbers. The general ignorance or disregard of little masterpieces such as Fred Clarke's book allowed initiative to come mainly from the Board of Education, through its reports. Yet this was an age when official direction of the curriculum was becoming less acceptable and it is doubtful whether these reports had any effect on headteachers or the majority of children.

After the Second World War and until the cutback of teacher training numbers in the 1970s, considerable interest was taken in history for the 5- to 11-year-olds. This came mainly from enthusiastic individuals but the Ministry of Education did publish a pamphlet in 1952—*Teaching of History*—the cover consisting of small portraits of the sovereigns of England from the beginning to Elizabeth II. As the cover intimates, no very original ideas are voiced for the primary school child. Stories are to be the staple diet with integration of the past into other areas of the curriculum. Shades of Fred Clarke appear with the emphasis on change rather than time. Yet the use of artefacts as evidence and the building up of a class museum point forward to more recent literature.

The 1959 *Handbook* of the Ministry of Education also emphasized the difficulty of teaching history to younger pupils and suggested the 'magic of a well told story' (copied from the words of the 1952 pamphlet!) as the cure for all ills. Yet in addition the *Handbook* grasped the nettle of 'time' and suggested the value of the 'simple illustrated time chart' as a framework into which stories could fit. It is interesting that John West, in his research in the Dudley area (from 1976–80), is finding this use of stories, interrelated with time charts, most effective for the clear understanding of time. The writers of the relevant chapter in the 1967 Plowden Report believed that history should be taught as part of the integrated approach with geography and might be studied topically at intervals instead of chronologically and systematically. Time charts were again recommended. From this time onward the emphasis was on the incidental use of the past as the tool of other more essential disciplines.

The 1960s were also important for the establishment of the Schools Council in 1964. This body financed large and small projects of research for curriculum innovation. One of its first considerations was the curriculum of the primary school, now considered in terms of first (5–8) and middle (8–13) schools. History had some place in three projects: *Environmental Studies 5–13*, *Social Studies 8–13*, and *History, Geography and Social Science 8–13* (Place, Time and Society). They all provided teachers of history with stimulus for thought and encouraged them to formulate their own schemes of work. But the very nature of the projects precluded them from consideration of history in any detail. Recent efforts to initiate a project on history for children between 5 and 7 have proved abortive. In the same way the Schools Council Working Papers Numbers 22 and 55 have generally been concerned with the middle school curriculum. They spend some time on history but, as they are really concerned with the whole curriculum, history is not treated in enough detail. The 8–13 Project was the most constructive of all this effort for the subject of history. It produced a useful analysis of objectives, skills, concepts, and attitudes needed by children in the study of the social subjects. But the very sophistication of the analysis, the freedom allowed to teachers, and work expected of teachers, was likely to cause scepticism in the minds of some colleagues.

In 1978 the Department of Education and Science published *Primary Education in England* for which a survey had been made of history, among other subjects, in a sample of classes in 7–11 schools. The emphasis since 1959 on interest and experiences had tended to divert attention from the structure and sequence of what should be taught. The 1978 Report found history teaching and learning to be very superficial and not stretching enough for the abler children.

Thus the time has come in the development of teaching history in the primary school for a synthesis of the good in all these ideas and stricter guide-lines both in objectives, teaching methods, and content of syllabus. If such guide-lines were produced it would be a significant step towards the improvement of history teaching and, if flexible, could be adapted as the years go by. The fact that 50 per cent of all secondary pupils stop learning history at the age of 14 to concentrate on other disciplines for examination purposes makes the need for this re-thinking and re-writing of history for the years 5–14 the more urgent.

1.3   The past at the infant stage

The professional definition of an 'infant' is a child aged between 4 + and 7. During these formative and crucial years teachers are concerned to socialize their pupils and help them to develop language, number, and physical skills. They have tended to favour an informal, friendly, perhaps unstructured approach, and work beyond the basic number and language tends to be 'one-off' experiences and activities enabling the child to take advantage of content and information in the 7–11 years. Therefore, for most infant teachers the past as 'history' has no place. Authors of books on history teaching and Government reports have also purposely overlooked the place of knowledge of the past in the infant curriculum. It is only recently that work has been done in this area showing that certain topics in the past can play a vital part in the development of young children. Family history, local history and field work, study of artefacts, and dramatization of the past have been found to be suitable topics for this age group to study. All these topics can easily be integrated into the normal infant day and taken up for shorter or longer periods. In a recent book *Children's Minds* a psychologist, Margaret Donaldson, suggested that the intellectual ability of young children has been underestimated, and that thinking about people and events beyond their immediate selves helps them to 'decentre' and 'move beyond the bounds of human sense'. This will form a stronger basis for future intellectual development than heretofore. Therefore, as far as the infant school is concerned history as a discipline is not to be justified, but certain parts of the past, both recent and long ago, have a real part to play in some sort of structured way at certain times in the infant curriculum. How this is to be done will be considered in more detail later.

1.4   Young juniors and history

Having tasted the joys of experiencing the past spasmodically in the infant years, the young junior of 7 years, or the older pupil in the first school, is in a good position to develop this work on more continuous lines. As already mentioned, one overriding justification for studying the past between 7 and 11 is that by 14 in most secondary schools at least half of the pupils drop history or opt for other subjects if they are candidates for any public examination. This may be wise for the majority, as history is known to be a difficult discipline to examine. The years 7 to 14 are free from external examinations, and this allows teachers more scope for exciting and imaginative teaching. Therefore, primary schools are very much justified in giving considerable space in the curriculum to subjects such as history in some form or other. This is even more true than before 7, since many children have begun to master the skills of writing and reading and need new material on which to exercise their new-found talents. History is fortunately a subject which attracts good writers of stories and novels; therefore there are plenty of short and well-illustrated reading books for all levels of ability. Children of 7 and 8 might as well read and write history stories as other stories and their imaginative writing about the past can be as creative and more realistic than much other writing. At this stage of the primary school the able child, who enjoys reading, frequently has little opportunity to satisfy his reading habits, and has soon read all the story books in the class library. Unless his parents have suitable books, his school has a good library, or he can use a good local library, he becomes thwarted and progress tends to stop. The retentive memory of most seven-year-olds makes possible the teaching of continuous interrelated parts of the past. The recording of information in simple diagrams and time charts becomes a growing possibility. Therefore the keeping of a notebook, well illustrated by pupils in one way or another, gives coherence to the past and provides easy reference for discussion in the class. Although history should not be thought of as a 'body of knowledge' to be learnt and memorized for tests, the keeping of a notebook gives the subject a status and importance similar to mathematics and could also form an interest to be shared with parents. In addition, stories of the past can more easily be dramatized at the ages of 7 and 8 than earlier and the subject matter stimulates imagination and active participation. During these early junior years children tend to be less self-conscious than later and eager to participate in acting straightforward roles which can nevertheless involve the stimulation of critical thinking.

Another justification for teaching history during these years is that children of this age range are able physically to participate in field work without becoming too tired. They are beginning to know how to look after themselves and their property without a fuss and to handle clip board, pencils, lunch packs, and mackintoshes a little more effectively. Thus the participation in field work as a usual part of the curriculum is excellent training.

1.5   Older juniors and history

Children of 9 years old are entering a new phase of their career. In some cases they go to middle schools, in others to preparatory boarding schools away from home, and a few may transfer to a local independent school with a junior department. But the majority remain in their primary school and need a more varied diet than previously. By this time, even if streaming is not the norm in a school, it has become apparent to both teachers and pupils which children are quick, slow, able intellectually, or particularly endowed with practical skills. History can provide opportunities for all abilities and interests and all pupils enjoy a well-told story. During these two years more demanding history can easily be introduced. Group work is an excellent social and intellectual experience and 9- to 11-year-olds like it and are good at it. With so many suitable reading books on the market, history is an excellent means for providing this type of experience. Group work on an historical topic also allows leadership to the more able and those with initiative, while others work at collecting information. In addition the children can help each other and take pride as a group in competing with other small groups in the class.

Children of this age range also gain much satisfaction from individual projects in which they choose their own particular topic within the syllabus and refer to many books and other sources of the past. This may be the only time that pupils can enjoy so much time and so much choice in what they do.

Finally, in the later years of the primary school it is possible to begin to introduce written sources of evidence of the past. Children of 6 years can handle artefacts as evidence and talk about them, but by the age of 9 to 11 they can often take pleasure in, for example, the detective pursuit of deciphering seventeenth-century palaeography and coming to conclusions after discussion as to its point of view. The selection of the original material is most important and a dose of too much source material of the wrong sort can discourage the keenest 10-year-old. At this age, also, pupils can undertake quite extensive field work including a residential period. Castles, monasteries, churches, mansions, graveyards, and archaeological remains all provide extensive practical work and use the past, linking class work on books and documents to practical work on a site. Thus it is easy to see that the past has a crucial role to play in the primary years and that this work can be tackled in the way that professional historians undertake it: that is by finding out, observation, reading, and discussion without the anxiety and pressure of an examination at the end of the year.

Teaching history with enjoyment and success depends on conditions in schools, teachers willing to re-think and re-learn and children wanting to be stretched intellectually in the way the past can do it. Conditions in schools are not likely to be improved in the present economic climate but teachers and children can be helped. The purpose of this book in the remaining chapters is to suggest ways in which this can be done.

References

1. Lord Briggs, in a lecture at the National Association of Teachers in Further and Higher Education, History Section, Conference at St Mary's College, Twickenham, July 1978.
2. P. J. Rogers, *The New History*, Historical Association, TH44, 1978.
3. A. D. Edwards, 'The "Language of History" and the communication of Historical Knowledge', in A. K. Dickinson and P. J. Lee, *History Teaching and Historical Understanding*, Heinemann, 1978, p.55.
4. P. Gordon and D. Lawton, *Curriculum Change in the Nineteenth and Twentieth Centuries*, Hodder and Stoughton, 1978, p. 120.

2. Background to syllabus planning

2.1 Introduction

Any book which attempts to help teachers to teach history well must treat three basic issues: syllabus, methods, and resources. The next three chapters of this book are devoted to these three issues. Those facing a class of 30 children or more, all day and every day, are more concerned with what history to teach, how to teach it, and what resources can help them, than why it is taught and how it is assessed.

Of these three important areas this chapter on syllabus/scheme is the most 'sensitive' one. Most experienced teachers know which approaches work for them with their particular children. Most teachers have access to only limited resources and have limited time and energy to accumulate more materials. But the last 20 years in curriculum development have influenced, perhaps unduly, teachers' views of what children can understand and enjoy. Teachers' training 'dies hard', especially with so little opportunity to retrain and many of those in responsible positions have been trained between 1967 and 1977 (i.e., the Plowden era). Some of these teachers view historical content as unimportant and use what suits their chosen 'topic' or 'centre of interest'. In this way, history has been interrelated with geography, literature, R.E., and occasionally science. The DES Primary School Report of 1978 challenged this usual viewpoint and much discussion is now taking place on what to teach. Three extracts from the 1978 Report show this concern:

5.127. Taken as a whole in four out of five of all the classes which studied history the work was superficial.

5.128. A factor contributing to this situation was undoubtedly a lack of planning in the work. Few schools had schemes of work in history, or teachers who were responsible for the planning and implementation of work in this field . . . A framework is required to provide some ordering of the content to be taught. This may be a single path through a chronological sequence or a more complex series of historical topics, which, while not necessarily taught in chronological order, should give a perspective in terms of the ordering of events or by means of comparison with the present day.

I shall analyse some basic 'fundamental truths' about content before suggesting differing frameworks for history, both separate and integrated, and follow this with detailed examples. Any author is bound to have personal preferences and to be unable to disguise this bias, but I have attempted to offer alternative syllabuses to suit a wide range of approaches. The infant years of 5–7 have been considered separately, yet as a preparation for the junior or middle years in the same local area.

Exceptional teachers have experimented most successfully with their own syllabuses and written of their experiences in books and journals. Such enthusiasts as Don Steel and Lawrence Taylor have built up amazing work on family history in selected schools staffed by able teachers. Brendan Murphy of Wigan did similar work in family history with 10- to 11-year-olds, using family trees and family artefacts to learn history backwards. Eric Newton of Everton, Liverpool, used municipal sources to build up a local history syllabus based on models made by children. Pat Raper of Cholsey Infants' School near Wallingford, organized the whole school in celebrating the school's centenary in 1976. John West stimulated 15 schools to work on his syllabus of stories, pictures, and patches of the past. These are only a few examples of very able teachers with a flair for teaching the past and a high motivation in preparing scholarly material. My advice is not intended for such people but for the non-specialist young or older teacher emerging from college having spent too little time on history teaching and with many pressures upon her in the early years of her career. These teachers can only depend upon snippets of their own knowledge, a few 'tips for teachers' on teaching practice (sometimes long ago in schools of 'long ago') and on any textbooks and reading books they can muster. It is for these colleagues, keen to do their best for their children but not necessarily 'sold' on history, that this chapter is really intended. They must be helped to know that they can teach well without spending too much time in preparation.

2.2 Basic principles

In spite of the incongruous situation of teachers feeling strongly about the content of the curriculum yet knowing in their hearts that *how* they teach the material is really more important, headteachers and advisers are looking for some guiding principles to be considered, even if not taken up, in the construction of the history syllabus. Much discussion has taken place during the last two years and a certain consensus of opinion has resulted—'A framework is required'. Consideration of the following basic principles should go some way to help provide this framework.

- There must be *some sort of syllabus* for all teachers—and children—to read; this should be related to the needs of the particular school and therefore reached by common agreement with the staff. Thus history could be treated as a separate discipline at one stage and be used to help an interrelated topic at another in the four years, or it could be entirely separate, or interrelated.
- *Chronology* should be the sequence as far as possible; if strict chronology is not followed, ordering of events, the place of personalities, and sequence may be learnt from the constant use of time charts both around the classroom and in pupils' notebooks. 'History offers organisation of material by time': this is how it was expressed by one historian interested in how younger children learn about the past.
- Content should be *national history* but closely related to local and world history where possible. Modern world history from about 1900 should only be taught in the later years of the primary school since it involves many countries, difficult names, and a facility with the changing map of the world.
- *The history of everyday life* should form the basis of the work but important political events, simple economic trends, and far-reaching cultural changes should be included.
- The syllabus should have room for *varying approaches* so that the patch of history, the line of development, and the important event are introduced at regular intervals. 'In teaching young children . . . it seems clear where the main emphasis should fall—upon the unique event'; this is the view of an historian who has researched on how children learn about the past.

With these basic, though not inflexible, principles in mind they may be applied in more detail to the 5–11 age range on the understanding that most infant (first) schools feed into one junior school, therefore some continuity of approach can be maintained if there is cooperative consultation.

2.3 Trends in syllabus making 1950–80

Those of us who have been interested in books on the teaching of history for many years are pleased with recent developments in this field, particularly in the secondary school area. One favourable sign which points to greater respectability among scholars is the open criticism levelled in a friendly manner by one writer towards another. This will eventually help teachers to reach nearer the truth about teaching history. I am thinking particularly about the work of A. K. Dickinson and P. J. Lee[1] in which they question the value of the concept/objectives taxonomy put forward by J. B. Coltham and J. Fines.[2] There are whispers of this wholesale questioning in the publications from which I am seeking guidance about syllabus construction for 7–11 children.

My selection of books is limited to those specifically concerned with the primary school and to those which courageously address themselves to the question of content. Many valuable books which will be mentioned later are mainly concerned with method and resources, not with syllabus. I have also omitted any articles on research in learned journals. I am treating those that I have selected according to date of publication and this is to some extent an influence on their message. The books fall into three date spans and range from 1950 to 1973. The first in the 1950s are structured and didactic, laying down *one* syllabus for recommendation and, on the whole, adopting the chronological/English history content. During the 1960s the movement towards the integrated curriculum gained momentum. During this period the tendency of the books selected was to favour local history and the study of the environment, with or without geography. Towards the end of the 1960s, the 'topic' approach, popular following the Plowden Report of 1967, took the form of authors offering various approaches and not favouring any one exclusively. With this open-ended approach, which may have led to no history being taught in some schools with the headteacher's agreement and even at her instigation, the late 1970s were reached with the need for a more structured framework.

During the 1930s and 1940s few 'method' books in history were published for the primary age range, an interruption strengthened by the Second World War and lack of paper for printing, as well as lack of time and interest. Three books appeared in the early 1950s all generally advocating a chronological treatment of English history. C. F. Strong's *History in the Primary School* (1950) and R. J. Unstead's *Teaching History in the Junior School* (1956) are seen now by some experts to put the primary syllabus in a strait jacket. In his chapter called 'The four year course' Strong deals with the general framework of 'increasing specialization', the 7–9 years being broad topics, mainly biographical, into which other disciplines may be integrated—'suitable Projects based on centres of interest, which involve other subjects in the curriculum besides History'. The 9–11 age range should study English history 'in neighbourhood, Homeland and Commonwealth' in topics arranged chronologically. In detail his syllabus is worked out as shown in Fig. 2.1.

15

Year

1   Stories from Greek and Roman legend, the Bible and early Christian Europe
    (e.g. King Arthur, St Augustine)

2   Biographies of heroes/heroines up to the present (e.g., Hereward the Wake,
    Richard Lionheart, Roland and Oliver, St Francis, Pocohontas, George
    Washington, Abraham Lincoln)

3   Stories of British history, rural life, and towns (i.e., *social history*)

4   Stories of British history, homeland and Empire, (i.e. *political history*,
    e.g., Magna Carta, Model Parliament, gunpowder plot, Civil War, Church,
    India)

Fig. 2.1   Four-year syllabus by Strong, showing increasing specialization

When the author refers to this very full syllabus as 'the bare bones of a possible syllabus' one wonders what the detailed implementation would be like! He does agree with the introduction of time charts in the fourth year, but it seems to me to be essential to have time charts from the beginning for this syllabus which takes in English history, European history and world history in an 'utter-end-through the ages' (John West) approach. Although most teachers would agree that story and biography are natural approaches and that some effort should be made to reach beyond 1600, yet the diet of political history in the fourth year and the study of Magna Carta, the Model Parliament, the Church and India is far too constipating for both teacher and class. Yet this suggestion was carried out in textbooks written by the same author for children to use and this method book went through at least five editions.

The second book, on similar lines, is R. J. Unstead's *Teaching History in the Junior School* which has tended to be longer lived than Strong's. This book is made more useful by very practical photographs of models made by junior children as well as a detailed bibliography of useful reading books for teacher and taught. Unstead is in no doubt that a chronological treatment of English history across the four junior years is the basis of the syllabus and that local history may be used as illustration rather than in its own right. He believes that the concentric story syllabus (e.g., Strong) involves repetition 'and chronological confusion'. Unstead does not favour time charts, which can help to clear up this confusion. Thus his outline syllabus is as shown in Fig. 2.2.

Year	
1	Early Man, Romans, Saxons, Danes up to 1066
2	The later Middle Ages 1066–1500
3	Tudors and Stuarts 1500–1700
4	Georgian and Victorian Britain 1700–1900 through lines of development (e.g., transport up to 1980)

Fig. 2.2   Four-year chronological syllabus by Unstead

This syllabus is very practically modified by the author for one- or two-teacher schools to cut down teacher preparation, and a very full time chart from year 1 to 1961 is given (for the teacher presumably) and divided into:

Approximate dates	Periods and people	Events	Background

This scheme may try to cover too much but it is definite (no alternatives) and very thoroughly worked out by a practising, enthusiastic, and knowledgeable teacher of history. Many primary schools today which do attempt to teach the past adhere to this through the many textbooks, reading books, and topic books which complement it.

The third publication of the 1950s was a Ministry of Education pamphlet (No. 27) published in 1952: *Teaching of History*. It is mainly concerned with the secondary school but has one chapter on the primary school. As in the case of certain books, this pamphlet is mainly inspirational and does not set out to give a framework. Instead, it suggests historical methods of story-telling and the use of authentic evidence, such as the 'very words' of Mary Stuart and Thomas More just before their executions. The early years (7–9) should concentrate on myths and legends and the later (9–11) on stories of adventure and stories of British history grouped chronologically. Some reference is made to a study of the neighbourhood and interrelated work but the main emphasis is on a well-read teacher stimulating the imagination of her class by well-told and selected stories.

The 1950s books were didactic in most ways and therefore helpful to the majority of non-specialist teachers. The 1960s and 1970s were to bring a more optional and uncertain approach which may have led to the lack of confidence of teachers of history in the 7–11 age range.

The 1960s was a period which saw the effects of the post-war population explosion in the schools, the expansion of teacher training

17

and in-service work, and more opportunities for experiment and re-thinking of the place and purpose of history in the 7–11 curriculum. In all the three books considered here, the influence of the integrated curriculum is shown. In 1965 the lively History Department of Moray House College of Education, Edinburgh, published a pamphlet called *History in the Primary School: a Scheme of Work*. In keeping with 1960s thought the syllabus outline is as shown in Fig. 2.3.

Year

1   Family history

2   The school in its environment: links with other disciplines

3   Line of development on local history—use of evidence

4   Integrated patch of local history and geography

Fig. 2.3 Syllabus for an integrated curriculum (from *History in the Primary School: A Scheme of Work*, Moray House College of Education, 1965)

There may seem to be a repetition in this scheme and too much emphasis on local history at the expense of a wider outlook of national or world history. Yet it bears out the viewpoint of Professor J. S. Bruner that a 'spiral curriculum' involving study of the same material successively in different ways provides the best learning sequence. Many primary schools, helped by active Teachers' Centres and record offices, have pursued this narrow but efficient approach and by now have built up valuable resources for children's activity. This could, even now when resources are scarce, be enlivened by, though not based on, stories from a broader background and found on BBC and/or ITV programmes so ably prepared in actual production and notes for children and teachers. A second individualistic approach appeared in 1966 with John West's *History, Here and Now* (Schoolmaster Publishing Company)—a startling title and a strong plea for younger children to use source material, written or otherwise, and imaginative stories in order to become 'aware' of the past. Therefore, to him, past history lives in the present—'here and now'—and is not irrelevant to the modern child. Like Catherine Firth in the 1920s, John West is the only recent writer who dares to consider the past as a fit study for 'infants'. Catherine Firth recommends stories and pictures of the past grouped according to topic or period. John West suggests the study of artefacts and their relationship to their likely uses and their oldness. He does not actually work out a four-year syllabus but implies that good stories of 'heroes brave and invisible' are vital for one of the years; he suggests that

18

teachers should make a list of 20 heroes and heroines and think out why each one has been included. His own list ranges from Mohammed through Robin Hood and Guy Fawkes to Dave Crockett and Winston Churchill. Somewhere also in the 7–11 years should come a local study and, like Strong and Unstead, he gives a detailed breakdown by weeks of different local studies. He starts with a term's work on environmental studies, then goes on to a term's work on seventeenth-century local history and finally gives a year's work to a study of a village in the thirteenth and nineteenth centuries. All schemes involve use of sources in the record office or library, and field work. It is therefore to be presumed that the local study is for 9–11-year-olds for at least part of their year. As in most books published since 1960 he does not suggest a framework for the four years or the order in which the work should be studied. Time charts are strongly advocated throughout.

The change coming over teachers' attitude to history in the late 1960s is exemplified by *Inside the Primary School* by the former Chief Inspector for Primary Education, John Blackie (1967). In a chapter called 'Exploring the world' he poses the dilemma of the vacuum created by the omission of political history from the primary curriculum. Blackie gives four alternative approaches to be found in schools:

1. History in the integrated scheme with geography.
2. Line of development in social history.
3. Great personalities.
4. Patch of a period of history studied in depth.

None of these supplies the framework now required but suggests approaches of a half-term or term, as the teacher wants. One could adjust Blackie's approaches to junior age level in this way as shown in Fig. 2.4.

Year	
1	Stories of great personalities
2	History integrated with geography
3	Line of development in social history
4	Patch of history

Fig. 2.4 Integrated syllabus following Blackie's approach

Like John West he advocates the constant use of time charts.

The 1970s continued this uncommitted attitude of the 1960s with one or two exceptions in individuals writing of their own particular

19

approach. In the *Handbook for History Teachers* (1972 edition) Kay Davies sums up the dilemma of the period in her chapter on 'The syllabus in the primary school' when she speaks of 'the present uncertainty in this area of the curriculum'. Current practice is given of the infant school in which 'incidental talk' through stories, pictures, and visits outside school will make young children aware of the past. She then outlines the practice with junior children of topics and patches in history as the teacher chooses. Yet she emphasizes the need for 'depth and progress in learning' so that children are not just collectors of facts without learning how to use them. Thus Miss Davies is more concerned with standard of work and quality of thinking than actual content of syllabus. This is in keeping with the period in which the Historical Association published Jeanette Coltham's *The Development of Thinking and the Learning of History* (1971) and Coltham and Fines' *Education Objectives and the Study of History: A Suggested Framework* (1971) as well as the initiation of the *Schools Council Project: Place, Time and Society* in 1971. All these developments emphasize the need to teach skills and concepts rather than a particular content-based syllabus.

The last two books I am considering, both published in the early 1970s, are my last two individualistic approaches. They are interesting and inspiring to the experienced historian but possibly a little too free for the non-historian who is looking for security. Alan and Roland Earl in *How Shall I Teach History?* (1971) recommend variety: 'Variety of content and variety of treatment are the secret of success in teaching History'. They presume that the syllabus has been decided and proceed with considerable liveliness and humour to show how content can be taught to children between 7 and 13. Each chapter takes a different topic of history; medieval, Norman conquest, the Age of Discovery, ancient civilization, world history, local history and Elizabethan England on a 'patch'. These are obviously selected as satisfying areas of content for the age group but no mention is made of sequence or order for these worthwhile patches. It is presumed that the headteacher will have some golden plan at the back of her mind and the class teacher will work from that. The second book, *History with Juniors* (1973), is by Michael Pollard who has a definite view of what syllabus there should be. He believes that history should be taught backwards for juniors, starting from the present and not going further back than about 1800. Most of his content is English history and much of it local sources and field work. His use of folk music as a method of teaching industrial history is most useful. This book limits the teachers' content during the four junior years but its very limitations give security, and much excellent detailed work may be done in the four years. In his book the *rapport* between primary experts is shown by his references to John Fines and John West. Therefore, the 1970s have given teachers many excellent ideas and encouraged them not to isolate history in the curriculum but left wide open specific advice about a 'framework' for a syllabus.

References

1. A. J. Dickinson and P. J. Lee (ed.), *History Teaching and Historical Understanding*, Heinemann, London, 1978.
2. J. B. Coltham and J. Fines, *Educational Objectives for the Study of History: A Suggested Framework*, Historical Association, Teaching of History Series, No. 35, 1971.

3. Ideas for constructing a syllabus

3.1 Introduction

How can the writings of 1950 to 1980 help us today? It is a truism that what is taught in schools is influenced by the needs of society and that 'fashions' in education work round in full circle with the passage of time. But if teachers of today teach well they must teach what they and their children feel they need for living in their world. If the present indecision and large variations in content are not satisfying teachers and not enthusing children, then new approaches must be found. These books show that in spite of changing fashions there has always been some concern that the past should be taught to 7–11 children and that they should enjoy it. From the wealth of all this experience and knowledge and the particular inspiration to be derived from the four books already mentioned, teachers should be able to look at the alternative syllabuses given in this chapter more objectively and to use both past ideas and present suggestions to formulate a syllabus suitable for their own four-year course.

3.2 The beginnings of awareness of the past in the infant years

Junior teachers need to know what infants could do even if they rarely do; in small schools they may teach in vertical groups and need to know. Yet many primary teachers, both infant and junior, take it for granted that no one tells or writes down how the past should come into the 'integrated infant day'. In this section of the chapter I am going to suggest a two-year framework which I believe is flexible enough to be easily assimilated into the normal infant day.

In this scheme the first two terms are stories, at first each story complete in itself and in the second term grouped round one personality or event of the past to give a little more continuity. This would enable new children entering the school in September, at Christmas, and at Easter to start afresh. By the third term of the first year all children continuing into the second year are likely to have joined the class and therefore more purposeful work could be started on artefacts, at first selected by the teacher to illustrate a specific period or even widely

Age	Term 1	Term 2	Term 3
5–6	Myths through stories	Stories of the past grouped in topics—role-playing	Study of artefacts brought first by teacher then by class
6–7	Family history	Local topics of own village, town, area	Local visits

Fig. 3.1 Framework for a two-year syllabus for infants

different periods chronologically. Most museums are willing to lend certain treasures for a limited period (say a month). After that children know what you want and usually bring too much material for comfort. By the second year children are more likely to be starting to read and write, which broadens the methods through which they are taught, though at present there is more suitable material for them to look at than read. Finding out about the teacher and her family and then their own lives and families, and building up their own books becomes an enquiry-based exercise, more obviously 'true' than stories told by the teacher and artefacts brought from the museum or their own homes. The second term of this second year could take them from themselves and their own little world to their local environment (linking with 'the place' of the curriculum) be it village, suburb, or town. The local visits in the third term are closely linked to the work in the second term but carried out in the summer term for better weather conditions. Some liaison between the infant school and the teachers responsible for history in the junior school should be possible in the latter part of the summer term. So little work of this kind has yet been done in the infant years that it is not easy to give specific well-tested examples to illustrate this scheme. My own limited experience and ideas must replace the experience of others in what follows.

FROM MYTH TO ARTEFACT IN THE 5–6 AGE RANGE

In a recent publication[1] Kieran Egan has put forward the idea that between the ages of 4 and 9 or 5 and 10 children go through what he calls the 'mythic stage' of learning. Children's love of fairy stories involving the deep emotions of 'love, hate, joy, fear, good, bad' should be fostered, as this will engage their interest and attention most readily. Mythic stories involving stark opposites such as life/death, security/fear and courage/cowardice are clear as they have the black and white nature of the unreal rather than the grey haze of the real past. Egan believes that children must be fed by such mythic stories and will suffer if hurried on

23

too quickly to such matters as artefacts and family history which are real and therefore more complex.

If myths are to be told as stories, for example at the end of the afternoon in 'story-time', the question arises as to which myths, and how often they are to be told or read. In a term of approximately ten weeks any one good book of myths and legends may be divided up so that 20 stories are told (two a week) and if possible related to each other. Two books in my possession may act as examples. One is called *Classical Stories* told by Freda Saxey and published by Oxford University Press for very young children. Children of 7–8 years are likely to be able to read them for themselves but the teacher could tell or read them to 5- to 6-year-olds. The stories could even figure in family groups with the older children reading and then telling them to the younger ones. All six are adapted from Greek and Roman legends and involve the power of the Gods and the weakness and folly of humans. Stories such as King Midas growing ass's ears, Persephone being carried into the underworld by Pluto, and the saving of Rome from the Gauls by hissing geese introduce young children to people, action, strong emotions, and right and wrong. Each one could be read slowly in about 20 minutes with questions and discussion. Although this particular book tells six stories from Greek and Roman legend they are often requested again and again by children as the term advances. The book is also illustrated by black and white sketches.

My second book is *Myths and Legends* adapted by Anne T. White and published by Hamlyn (1964). This is delightfully illustrated by large, coloured pictures which can be seen by a class sitting on the floor gathered round the teacher—a considerable relief for the teacher compared with the task of making a copy or finding a picture for a story. The words of the stories are more sophisticated than Freda Saxey's but can be adapted, explained, or even overlooked since the actions of the stories and names (on the blackboard) are more important. Some of the stories are 'legends' in which there may be some truth. A useful introduction—'Gods and heroes'—helps the teacher. The book tells 18 stories but several are divided into parts and one story could be used for several story-times. For example, the story of Oedipus, the prince disowned by his father, King Laius of Thebes, has five parts which can be recapitulated to maintain the group of stories and show continuity. The story of Grendel from Denmark has 12 parts which could form a term's work treated as a television serial. The shorter stories form the first part of the book and the longer ones the latter part. As these stories come from many lands—Greece, Denmark, France— the children are also moving into lands other than Britain.

24

I have given examples of two books but most public libraries have suitable collections and some infant schools possess copies in their own libraries or book corner. Obviously, beautifully illustrated, large books are the most suitable, and children look forward to seeing a particular book in the teacher's hands. Many children look at the illustrations in their free time even if they cannot read the words. Two or three books including the same stories but having different illustrations make for useful comparisons even if the teacher uses only one for the stories. Two most useful books for teachers to use for reference are Elizabeth Cook's *The Ordinary and the Fabulous* first published by Cambridge University Press in 1969 and Ralph Lavender's *Myths, Legends and Lore* published by Basil Blackwell in 1975. The former is concerned with myths, legends, and fairy tales of many European countries for children between 8 and 14. Elizabeth Cook names the myths, suggests how they may be presented to children and then takes seven 'crucial scenes' in books and analyses them critically. Ralph Lavender's book is more of a bibliography of myths but his preface is concerned with 'why' and 'how' stories should be told. He gives additional information about films, filmstrips, music, and discs to accompany the stories. Both books are written by enthusiastic specialists very much concerned with the practicalities of the classroom and both authors provide detailed lists of myths suitable for different ages.

Listening to stories from myth and legend and discussing people, actions, and consequences is excellent preparation for the second term when legends and true stories of the past may be told and read more systematically. The teacher should decide which two periods of history are of greatest interest to her and tell five linked stories about each period. For example the conversion of England to Christianity could involve stories of St Augustine, St Columba, St Oswald and St Alban. Stories about King Alfred of Wessex and his heroic fight against the invading Danes could form another block. A satisfactory source of information are the Ladybird books published by Wills and Epworth. Each story may be used for simple role-playing with different groups of children used for different episodes. In these cases the story-time could come earlier in the day as children should not be tired when role-playing, otherwise they become silly and giggly.

In the third term, children are introduced to the fact that the past is not only learnt from stories told by the teacher, which have to be taken on trust, but from actual artefacts used in the past. After the earlier imaginative representation, children are introduced to commonsense, down-to-earth life by this change. Artefact work needs longer than story-telling and in many cases could use a whole afternoon very effectively. Some period from about 1800 onwards should be selected first and about six well-preserved articles should be chosen to illustrate different sides of social history: for instance a lady's hatpin of Edwardian days, a parasol, an Edwardian toy, an Edwardian schoolbook, a bowler hat, and a gentleman's tie-pin. These should be representative of as many family members as possible (father, mother, children, servants, etc.) and should be easy to compare with similar articles today, if they exist. By this means the 'then and now' approach of comparison, an historical skill, can be used naturally. Children should thoroughly investigate these articles which therefore should not be too fragile. The children should have 'hunches' as to their uses, in the words of Professor J. S. Bruner.

Another collection by the teacher could be concerned with the Second World War period of 1939–45 supplemented by artefacts lent by the children's grandparents. For this to be really effective the teacher should invite parents and grandparents to an evening coffee party to discuss the reasons for doing this work; in this way she can gain their support and loans of suitable articles from their homes so that a temporary classroom museum may be built up, cared for by the 6-year-olds as they would care for a nature table or a guinea-pig. It is usually better to have a locked display case so that these precious exhibits can be labelled by the children but handled only with the teacher present.

A third stage in the artefact work is a collection of old objects brought by the children, and compared with the first two collections for 'oldness'. By constant discussion, feeling the objects, and observation the children gradually become accustomed to comparisons of oldness. Some Museum Education Officers bring collections of objects to school to illustrate particular themes but this has to be for one afternoon only. This type of work is best limited to two different collections in one term, otherwise there is a lack of thorough investigation.

By the end of the first year in the infant school children will have started to be aware of people long ago and old objects belonging to a past they did not know. This naturally leads on to family history work in the second year.

FROM FAMILY HISTORY TO LOCAL VISITS IN THE 6–7 AGE RANGE
Contact with parents and grandparents during the third term of the first year should be revived by the work on family history in the first term of the second year. This is essential not only to provide the children with first-hand information about themselves and their families but also to find relevant artefacts connected with the family to establish a link with the previous year's work. In one 6-year-old class I taught, one of the

most shy little boys created a stir in the group when he brought to school a *Soldier's Bible* of the First World War which his grandfather had owned and which was inscribed with the grandfather's name and the date 1919. Perhaps a more important reason for talking to parents is to forestall any difficulties which may arise from strained relationships at home and knowledge purposely kept from children for their own benefit. This will be discussed in more detail in Chapter 5.

A study of family history may be undertaken for one afternoon a week for ten weeks, including 'story-time' at 3 p.m. It can be divided into four distinct areas as shown in Fig. 3.2.

Weeks		
1–2	Life-lines of teacher (or imaginary person) and children	
3–4	Family trees of teacher (or ?) and children	Story-time on families in the past and a visit and story from a grandparent
5–7	Family photographs, slides, films	
8–10	Family artefacts **Display of all material**	

Fig. 3.2 Ten-week study of family history

This is obviously work on the contemporary family of the twentieth century, spanning not more than 60 to 70 years. If found successful, and with more input from the teacher, it could be taken backwards to the Edwardian and Victorian family, and the excellent material of Sue Wagstaff could be used. (*People Around Us* published by A. & C. Black in 1978 Unit 1. *Families, Koli's Family, Two Victorian Families.*) More will be said about this series in Chapter 5.

Local topics in the second term should be attempted as a line of development, using a simple time-line as in family history. Specific topics within the village or town should be studied, first as it is now (links with 'place') and then taking two other periods for comparison, dependent upon the age of the town and the information at the teacher's disposal. If interest is shown in one period and can be developed there would be no need to cover more than two periods altogether. The scheme shown in Fig. 3.3 for a term's work may be helpful. This unit will depend upon the information available and the motivation of the teacher. Most libraries now contain pamphlets and books giving outline histories of villages and towns chronologically. Teachers can select and adapt topics from these. Many include helpful maps and pictures which can be simplified. The term 'local topics' is very flexible

Weeks		
1–3	Village/town now—in twentieth century, 1980	
4–6	Village/town in Victorian times—in nineteenth century—1837–1902	Story-time on local and national people/events—old person on recent past
7–9	Village/town in Tudor times 1485–1603; medieval times 800–1485	
10	**Display of work**	

Fig. 3.3 Local topics

and allows movement through two different periods (contemporary and one other). Resource material for this type of work will be discussed in more detail in Chapter 5.

The third term of the second year could be a continuation of the previous term with visits to places too far away for the winter months. Margaret West, Infant Adviser for Wolverhampton, has developed a field study centre for infants to visit for a few days with their teachers. More will be said about this later. An example of how to integrate terms two and three may be taken from the city of Southampton. In the second term of the second year Southampton could be studied in the seventeenth century from the very clear 1611 Speed map of the city. The excellent Tudor House Museum could be visited in the third term and Southampton 'below bar' and 'within-the-walls', including old and modern buildings, could be an extension of this work. Thus about three visits might be made including Mayflower Park, so named to celebrate the sailing of the *Mayflower* from Southampton in 1620—a topic which is, at least at the descriptive level, vivid and interesting to 6-year-olds.

This scheme for the infant years is intended to give the structure and sequence needed to see progression and variety of approach in relation to the past. It should not involve teachers in undue preparation; the only difficult part would be the second and third terms of the second year when local history has to be dug out from one or two local sources, the right book(s) found for preparation, and the information and pictures adapted to the needs of 6- to 7-year-olds. Otherwise material can be gathered from the children and their families or from easily obtainable reading books on conventional lines.

I am not suggesting any other schemes, as I shall for the 7–11 age range. This is partly because teaching the past to very young children is an adventure and very few experiments have been made. As a result few materials have been offered to teachers for the specific age range but the suggestions I have made can be taken up successfully by teachers with the minimum of preparation. They can also be spring-boards for work in language (oral or written), number, art work, R.E., literature, and drama. Therefore this particular scheme can easily be integrated into the normal infant routine and adapted as required, each term forming a unit on its own, joined only loosely to the rest of the scheme. The idea behind the scheme is to prepare very young children to have some interest in the past outside themselves, using as a starting point their natural interest in stories and objects, themselves and their families. In her book *Children's Minds* (Fontana, 1978) Margaret Donaldson shows the need for young children to 'decentre' in Piaget's sense by having vicarious experience beyond their own egocentric lives. This decentring helps to master all skills more quickly. Much of the scheme I have suggested may be considered as being part of this policy. In addition they come to their work in the junior school with some awareness of the past and how to think about it.

I hesitate to base any general scheme of work on BBC or ITV programmes, not because they are not excellent programmes in every way or are inappropriate in approach, but because the teacher can depend too much on the resources supplied by the BBC and ITV. On the other hand, some television programmes are excellent teaching media for young children who cannot yet read; they should be used as illustration and support wherever possible. More will be said about this in Chapter 5 on Resources.

3.3 Some history frameworks for the junior school

Turning now to junior schools, where interest is shown in history, their syllabuses tend to fall into two categories. One follows the national heritage from prehistoric times to the present, for which there is an ever-ready supply of suitable textbooks. This syllabus is usually based on loosely-knit headings of three or four topics for each year and therefore allows for good incidental teaching, use of television, filmstrips, literature, and the development of local themes where suitable. It has the advantage in a large school that all class teachers know what has been covered in the previous year (since the syllabus is usually written down). The other category found at present in junior schools is a scheme based substantially on local history, field work and an attempt to use source material from local records in the top class. This second type of scheme usually depends heavily on the knowledge and enthusiasm of a particular teacher and her contact with the local Teachers' Centre and/or the record office. Of these two, the first type of syllabus is more manageable by the non-specialist teacher, although it has its drawbacks. I am going to suggest five frameworks, all based on national history except the multi-cultural syllabus, and all chronological in approach. *The Heritage of Later English and World History 1800 to the Present Day* may seem to intrude upon the secondary school's favourite epoch. Yet I suggest this because so many comprehensive schools have developed integrated humanities work in the first two years and so many pupils drop history at 14 years of age. If they do continue, they may undertake a detailed twentieth century world syllabus for examination purposes, omitting much English history. Thus there seems to be little time for any chronological survey as these were known in the past. In fact 'History in danger', the cry of Mary Price in 1968,[2] has been only too true, with little done at all except in 'topic' or 'centre of interest' in most junior schools and integrated work in the early years of the secondary school.

THE HERITAGE OF ENGLISH HISTORY
(with local illustration and world background (Fig. 3.4))
In 1980, this syllabus was offered by one local education authority to teachers as a basis for their own more specific schemes which the chief inspector had requested from them. Many staff meetings were held in junior schools in that area to formulate a history syllabus and this particular outline is an excellent lead for the schools. Therefore it is not at all restrictive and even appears to be 'all things to all men'. Schools may select from a comprehensive list of topics, emphasizing some, omitting others and adding their own.

THE HERITAGE OF EARLY ENGLISH HISTORY UP TO 1800
(with local illustration and world background (Fig. 3.5))
This syllabus has more structure than the first since national history purposely comes before world/European history in the third term, and the second term follows on chronologically from the first term. The general approach is that of 'patch' rather than 'line of development' and a time chart would be necessary.

THE HERITAGE OF LATER ENGLISH AND WORLD HISTORY FROM 1800 TO THE PRESENT DAY
(with local illustration (Fig. 3.6))
I have included this syllabus to stimulate controversy. It goes against all the 'rules' about younger children liking the distant past as escapism and being able to understand the cavemen because they are unsophisticated and defenceless. It is concerned with a patch of colonial history in a day and age when the British Empire is virtually dead. It deals with war and

Age-level and epoch	Local	National	World	Development through time
Year One The Ancient World	Iron Age hill forts Roman villas Roman towns	Avebury/Stonehenge Boadicea Roman roads	Tutankhamen Greek gods/heroes Julius Caesar	Housing Clothes
Year Two The Middle Ages (c400–1450)	Medieval castles Churches/monasteries Medieval villages	Alfred Battle of Hastings Becket's murder	Vikings Crusades Joan of Arc	Fortifications Education
Year Three Early Modern World (c1450–1700)	Tudor towns Country houses Merchant venturers	Henry VIII Elizabethan Court Oliver Cromwell	Leonardo da Vinci Explorers Louis XIV	Ships Entertainment
Year Four Modern Times	Georgian Bath Roads/canals/railways 'The home front'	Nelson/Wellington Factory towns Winston Churchill	American West 1850–90 Russian Revolution Mao Tse-Tung	Inventions Sports

Fig. 3.4 The heritage of English history, with local illustration and world background

Notes on the Suggested Topics:
1. The topics are only *examples*; many others can be given.
2. The topic titles tend to fall into three categories—social life, important people, key events; they provide suggestions for starting points indicating areas of study which could be treated in a variety of ways.
3. The topics in the last column are suggestions for work in a 'line of development' to supplement the other work.

	Term one	*Term two*	*Term three*
Year one	Stone and Metal Ages (Iron Age fort) Roman Britain (roads, villas, towns)	Saxons and Vikings (Saxon Shore forts; Alfred in Wessex)	Roman Empire
Year two	Norman Conquest and life in Norman England (castles, churches, villages, monasteries)	Henry II, John and Richard I (Becket at Canterbury; John at Runnymede)	The Crusades (First Crusade and Children's Crusade) Joan of Arc
Year three	Edward I, Scotland and Wales (castles and Bannockburn)	The Early Tudors (Tudor mansions and manor houses)	Renaissance Italy Voyages of Discovery
Year four	Elizabethan and Jacobean times (The Court; poverty; towns)	Civil War and Oliver Cromwell Charles II (Civil War battlefields and sieges)	Georgian England (Bath)

Fig. 3.5 The heritage of early English history up to 1800, with local illustration and world background

	Term one	Term two	Term three
Year one	Life in Victorian times 1837–1901	Patch study of Victoriana (artefacts, houses, industrial archaeology, etc.)	The British Empire
Year two	Life in Edwardian times 1902–1910	Birth and development of USA 1776–1980 (as 'line of development')	
Year three	Life in the inter-war years 1918–1939	The Second World War and its effects on the United Kingdom; other important changes since the war ended 1939–1980	
Year four	USSR 1917–1980	China 1900–1980	The Third World 1955–1980

Fig. 3.6 The heritage of later English and world history from 1800 to the present day, with local illustration

CHRONOLOGICAL SEQUENCE

SOME EXAMPLES OF TOPICS

	Housing	Fortifications	Transport and discovery	Religion	Other topics (chosen by school)
Pre-history	Caves and huts	Iron-Age hill forts		Stonehenge	
Ancient world	Roman villas	Roman Camps	The Voyage of Ulysses	The Life of Christ	
Dark Ages	Saxon halls and villages	Offa's Dyke	The Viking ships and voyages	Mohammed/Islam conversion of Britain to Christianity	
Middle Ages	Timber-framed houses	Castles Walled towns	The Crusades	Cathedrals/Abbeys/ Parish churches	
Age of Discovery	Elizabethan half-timbered manor or town houses		Christopher Columbus	Luther/Calvin/Puritans	
Industrial Revolution	Late Georgian mill-owners' houses/ terrace and back-to-back houses		The triangle of trade/ or the steamship	The Wesley brothers	
Twentieth-century world	Advanced or alternative technology home	Trench warfare	Flight/space travel	Places of worship	

Fig. 3.7 The interrelation of chronological and topic approaches

so presumably panders to aggressive boys and their gory tastes. It involves considerable use of the atlas and some learning of foreign names (Mao Tse-Tung, Gandhi, Mugabe, etc.). Yet it is concerned with social life in Britain, how parents and grandparents lived, with the sources of history in the patch study (well supported by an excellent BBC programme 'How we used to live') and a much needed study of one of the world's leading powers—USA. Nazi Germany and the effects of the Second World War are crucial to an understanding of the television news and many other programmes, as are Russia, China, and the Third World. All this depends upon teacher interest and resources as well as time. Therefore, teachers obviously alter the framework, rearrange topics, add new ones, and omit much. Yet this syllabus seems to 'stand up' as historically respectable for those junior schools that feed secondary schools where not much history is taught as a separate subject. It can also claim the variety of approach so much needed in a four-year course.

THE INTERRELATION OF CHRONOLOGICAL AND TOPIC APPROACHES
This broader scheme was worked out by a group of primary and middle school teachers led by an experienced and enthusiastic college lecturer. They came to the conclusion that *seven* areas of the past had contributed in large measure to the development of modern British society which should be the course for 7–11 children. They are:

1. Prehistory
2. The ancient world
3. The Dark Ages 410–1066
4. The Middle Ages 1066–1485
5. The Age of Discovery
6. The Industrial Revolution
7. The modern world (twentieth century)

The scheme in Fig. 3.7 shows how these seven areas could be used in the four years of the junior school. It is firmly based on the teacher's knowledge of historical chronology but is flexible enough to include interrelated topics involving other disciplines such as literature in 'The voyage of Ulysses', R.E. in 'The life of Christ,' and science in 'Flight, space and travel'. Where possible, patches of local history may illustrate the general themes such as an Iron Age fort, a Roman villa, Stonehenge and castles. Any selection of these topics should be used with time-lines. The two essential features of this syllabus are the interrelationship between local, national, and world history, and the integrity of a scheme not necessarily following a chronological sequence.

35

HISTORY FOR A MULTI-CULTURAL SOCIETY

A final, fifth scheme, should be considered for areas of the country where there are ethnic minorities or majorities. It contains two alternative syllabuses, as shown in Fig. 3.8; one is for history as a separate subject and the other for history in an interdisciplinary context.

Year	1. History	2. Multi-disciplinary
1	*Family history* of last 50 years ⟶ autobiographical—environmental study of ethnic group	*Family history*
2	*Social environment*—last 150 years. Towns/villages from child's viewpoint, e.g., how taught; care when sick; punishment	*Traditional society*, e.g., medieval English community; an African community; an American Indian community
3	*Heroes and heroines*—round world explorers—warriors—chosen from a variety of countries	*Civilizations* (at their peak), e.g., Rome—West Africa—Mogul India. China
4	*Patch study*—of sixteenth– seventeenth centuries, e.g., Elizabethans, compare Aztecs; Mogul India; West Africa; Ming China	*Migration* Vikings; Spanish immigration to South America; Muslim movement in Africa; twentieth century population movements

Fig. 3.8   History for a multi-cultural society

This has the advantage of introducing children to the 'now' of their own lives and environment through family history and social environment. The hero of the past at one point in time, whole civilizations over centuries, a study in depth and the influence of people moving, add to their experience. Thus it covers all the fundamental ways of looking at the past, each way touching one child if not another.

Using the experience of other teachers and the five alternative syllabuses, a junior school teacher responsible for history in her school, in consultation with the headteacher and any interested adviser or HMI, should be able to construct a viable syllabus to be experimented with and altered after two or three years. The main consideration is to avoid introducing any new historical topics and/or periods which would require considerable preparation and the accumulation of new, expensive resources. It is therefore essential to hold detailed discussions prior to syllabus-planning and to take most views into consideration when a decision is finally taken. It is better, for example, to draft years one and two and leave the rest if lack of time prevents thorough discussion. It should be possible to seek the advice of the secondary school(s) which a particular junior school feeds in order to avoid repetition. Consulting parents and children is usually abortive as parents tend to want their children to 'enjoy' the diet which they think useful or which they had themselves, while children tend to evaluate a syllabus according to the teacher's popularity; then that teacher may leave the school! As emphasized earlier in this chapter, the main object of the exercise is to plan a syllabus rather than teach an unrelated sequence of topics with no principle of progression or, worse still, no plan at all.

3.4   Some integrated frameworks for the junior school

This type of syllabus in which history can, but might not, play a vital part is known by various names. It can be interrelated studies, topic, centre of interest or environmental studies. The essential argument for this approach is that the 'subject' divisions of the secondary, examination-orientated school, should not spoil the wholeness of approach which comes naturally to the 5–11 school. Since the Plowden Report of 1967, and indeed long before, much work has been done evolving schemes of this sort, and many able teachers have had the flair to implement them during the period of expanding resources. Mixed ability teaching, 'discovery learning', and individual assignments have all added to the need for this type of syllabus. So the affluent individualized instruction and topic work, inspiring at its best and pointless at its worst, began. Various factors are now militating against this approach. By 1980 there were fewer junior children, and therefore classes tended to be smaller; there were fewer teachers and less time for preparation and above all resources were becoming more and more limited.

There is no doubt that the integrated syllabus still has attractions and that many schools have carried out worthwhile work allowing the children to study the past in depth and relate it to other disciplines where natural in a 'patch' of history. Schemes which forced all manner of disciplines into the framework found some rather unhappy, obtrusive alliances, such as the past trying to take a part in a topic on 'Water', a favourite but not necessarily suitable theme. Honest teachers boldly omitted certain areas of the curriculum, and this is where history suffered. In the *Times Educational Supplement* for 26 April 1968 Michael Wynne of the Schools Broadcasting Council wrote:

> In primary schools the integrated curriculum is the new orthodoxy and 'history' is out; yet the pendulum may swing back a little in response to the child's needs to arrange his accumulated information about the past into a recognizable framework, and this framework may conveniently be labelled history.

More will be said in Chapter 5 about how the BBC responded to this new difficulty in providing programmes for junior schools.

A general view appears to be arising now that younger juniors (7–9) enjoy integrated work and that the last two years (9–11) should allow separate disciplines to appear in the syllabus in 'patches', or 'lines of development'. This has the incidental advantage of enabling the teacher to prepare more difficult work in the earlier years when children work more slowly and the amount of material for them to collect from diverse areas is not as great.

It is impossible to do justice to the many worthwhile integrated syllabuses worked out by colleges of education, advisers, Teachers Centres' wardens, and teachers during the period 1968 to 1978 but they seem to fall into certain well-defined categories. The most prolific are those concerned with geography, the locality, social studies, rural studies and environmental science, generally known as 'environmental studies'. Historians differ as to whether history is more closely associated with geography or with literature and the arts but this usually depends upon the particular teacher's interests and training. Another type is concerned with music, dance and drama, using the past as a backcloth. Third is the link with science, particularly inspired by the *Schools Council Science 5–13 Project* though it has been more explicitly discussed by its predecessor, *Nuffield Junior Science* (see pp. 46–48). Then there is the work mainly connected with art and those just called 'topic' or 'project' which involve many disciplines but are essentially based on an historical event, movement, or period of time. The *Schools Council Project: Place, Time and Society 8–13* could also offer 7–11 syllabuses, either as a separate subject or interrelated syllabus. Finally, a multi-racial syllabus works out a current social theme. Interesting and detailed as these schemes are, not one of them faces up to the four years in the junior school, at what point their contribution should come, and whether they should be part of a more conventional history scheme. Thus the teacher is left 'in the air', free to use or not to use, as for its part the Schools Council officially intended. This is the danger of the integrated curriculum. With no framework the inexperienced, uninspired, tired, or simply lazy teacher is allowed to omit any diet of the past during the examination-free period of four years. These categories of interrelated studies will now be considered in more detail.

ENVIRONMENTAL STUDIES

Most frequently, geography has dominated the environmental studies scheme in junior schools, possibly because of the greater interest of academic geographers in younger children and in field work, as well as their belief that 'place' could be taught effectively even to very young children. Michael Storm's *Playing with Plans* (Longmans, 1974) is an amusing and lively approach to the beginning of map work with infants. In the same way, two scientists and a geographer edited a text called *Teachers Handbook for Environmental Studies* (Blandford, 1968) specifically for 9–13 pupils and the only contribution by an historian, D. F. Vodden, is on 'Environmental studies in Surrey'. Linked thus to geography and social studies the type of history taught is entirely small-scale history, usually local history. This has tended to lead to a syllabus of history 'stories', often disjointed and at the whim of the teacher, during the first two years, and local history during the last two years of the integrated syllabus. This has excluded world history of any sort, supposedly left for the secondary school. Yet it has enabled the past to be studied in much greater depth using local archival sources and it has also encouraged teachers to undertake field work in history locally, and sometimes residential field work in another area. The work has been approached in topics, centres of interest or themes lasting about half a term and usually culminating in a display. It has depended upon team teaching and cooperation between at least two members of staff. This could become difficult if one member of staff left and the replacement did not prove as cooperative or able. In describing his work on Surrey, Mr Vodden shows how lack of local material led him to 'fill the gaps' in his chronological survey of the years 0 to 1500 by using standard class examples such as the Lascaux cave paintings, the Roman villa of Lullingstone and London medieval town life. The topic approach allows teachers wide choice from a number of disjointed titles, each able to last half a term, e.g., roads, doctors and health, houses and buildings, the Highway Code. This method could include an historical line of development, but that would depend upon how the topic was approached. For example, when studying the sea-shore the plan of a seaside town could be used showing buildings dating from the fifteenth century to the present day. This would be effective if the area was near enough for children to visit it and study the types of period houses.

Three other approaches to environmental studies should be mentioned. One already discussed (p. 18) comes from Moray House College, Edinburgh; it is really a history scheme with a strong local bias and some integration with geography. The second uses the 'neighbourhood' either as a topic in itself or to illustrate another course. This is particularly useful for schools in industrial areas which hold little historical interest before about 1880. In this way a syllabus may be constructed over one year, preferably in the 9–11 age range (see Fig. 3.9). As in other cases this scheme does not fit into a four-year syllabus and

39

	Half a term	Half a term
Term one	1. The District (a) Place-names for settlement (b) Place-names for character of settlement (c) Mapping of place-names will show settlement patterns over one area (d) Place-names may provide origins of local surnames	2. The Street (a) Street names provide clues to date of construction (b) They may provide evidence of former route (c) They may provide a clue to former buildings (d) They may refer to former industry (e) They may be reconstructed from Directories
Term two	3. The Buildings (a) Changed use of existing buildings may be noted (b) Study of existing buildings useful for architectural styles of period and before (c) Domestic architecture may be studied for changing building materials, styles, etc. (d) Shops and their signs (e) Pub signs—characters, events, loyalties	4. Street Furniture (a) Pillar boxes (b) Street lighting (c) Traffic signs (d) Fire control
Term three	5. Street Services Evidence of gas, water, electricity, sewage disposal, telephone, etc.	6. Local Parks (a) Previous nature of ground allocated for parks and gardens (b) Origin and former use of parks (c) History of existing park houses

Fig. 3.9 Using the neighbourhood: a syllabus for year 3 or year 4 (devised by F. Harris)

may be used at varying levels in all years 7–11. The third is the *Schools Council Environmental Studies 5–13 Project* (1969–72). This was principally based on geography and the team members found difficulty in providing historical material for their trial schools. This was made clear in their Working Paper No. 48 *Environmental Studies 5–13: the use of historical resources* (1973). It was concluded that an expert historian or archivist (often a trained historian) was needed to compile and interpret material in order to ensure that it was significant enough for children to spend time on it.

HISTORY, MUSIC, DANCE, AND DRAMA

The journey of man through time, which is the story about which history is written, has been closely linked with man's efforts to express himself through different media. This expression of man's thoughts and feelings has often most truly reflected the image of the past and has been a constant delight to the child, the adolescent, the mature man, and the old. So much of the true past is with us in art, architecture, music, dance, and drama which are such active subjects for children to pursue. Teachers concerned with history should emphasize that the past is the basic factor that these approaches have in common. From the syllabus point of view it means a topic approach as it would be almost impossible to construct a chronological syllabus on the creative arts that was suitable for the 7–11 age-range.

Although music and movement have become the sphere of the specialist in junior schools many class teachers can play the piano and most schools have recorder groups; some even have orchestras. All schools encourage children to sing, sometimes in elaborate presentations such as *Noyes' Fludde*, the opera by Benjamin Britten. Medieval history lends itself naturally to music, dance, and drama; this is the time when people make their own instruments and music in an unsophisticated and impromptu way. Oxford University Press has had the courage to publish a unit of work called *This Merry Company* by Alison and Michael Bagenal (1979) which gives supportive advice on medieval dances, three plays with musical accompaniment, and instructions on how to make three medieval musical instruments. In addition, suggestions are given for further work on two of the plays and a most useful bibliography and list of recordings is included. This information figures in the teacher's book but there is also a colourful book for children with instructions and music for the three plays, amusingly and truthfully illustrated from medieval manuscripts and carvings from misericords. A cassette may also be bought with the music for the three plays on one side, and medieval music for listening and improvising dancing on the other side. The whole project could last from half a term to one term or could be used incidentally, one play at a time, the instruments being made in craft work as time allowed. If the teacher follows the thorough and scholarly instructions no child could go untouched or unable to appreciate the medieval sense of fun and joy in music and movement in the period 1250–1400.

The first play is called *Chanticleer and Pertelote* and is taken from Geoffrey Chaucer's *Canterbury Tales* as the story told by the nun's priest. The scene of the play is a farmyard and humans (pilgrims), animals, and birds are characterized. The drama of the story is the capture of the proud Chanticleer (cock) by the fox and his release when the vain fox opens his mouth and allows Chanticleer to fly away. The pilgrims discuss the moral of a tale involving pride and vanity. The children, as pilgrims, would thus experience the equivalent of an R.E. lesson in a natural way. There are enough characters to occupy a class and the children can easily make up appropriate words as they go along. Music and dances accompany the play at appropriate stages. This style of discussion and impromptu words and movement will also be found in the work of Dorothy Heathcote, to be described later, though Mrs Heathcote is interrelating history and drama in a less structured way than the Bagenals. The teachers' book of *This Merry Company* also suggests appropriate and simple costumes.

The second play is *St. George and Bold Slasher; A Mummers' Play* written in blank verse which should be learnt by the characters. St George fights the Turkish Knight, Bold Slasher, presumably on religious and nationalistic grounds, and knights, a doctor, and others watch and encourage. St George wins and a morris dance is done by English and Turkish knights. Music and dances again come in at appropriate places. This play is more complicated than the first one as words have to be learnt, there is much more activity, and the introduction of Turks needs to be explained for those who have not studied the Crusades. St George always appeals to young children; in the words of Catherine Firth as long ago as 1929: 'A child would rather hear of St George and the Dragon than trace the line of the Roman Wall even though his own house lies on it.'

The third play, *To Market One Morning*, introduces a good way to learn about medieval village life. It could well be the finale to the term's work instead of a display. There are so many incidents in this play that the teacher could select which ones to act. The scene is a medieval market place and all the incidents take place in it including a short play and a wedding party that starts a dance for the whole company. Again, advice is given about costume, music, and dance.

Teachers will find the actual music for this project very simple but they will need to master the interaction of music, dances, and plays carefully, preferably working with a colleague in another class if books allow it. *Chanticleer and Pertelote* could be acted by 7-year-olds but the other two, particularly *To Market One Morning*, would be better approached with older juniors. The three plays together would be absolutely right for a school with vertical streaming as all ages could participate and older children could help younger ones. My delight in this project is not only its adaptation of scholarly work to 7- to 11-year-olds but its concise instructions to teachers who are not expected to be able to organize anything without careful preparation. Nor are the children expected to 'discover' medieval music, drama, and dance without teaching.

Alison Bagenal has also linked history, music, dance, and art in collaboration with the National Portrait Gallery in London. More will be said in Chapter 5 about museums and galleries as a resource for the history teacher. Writing in the *Times Educational Supplement* for 15 August 1980 Mrs Bagenal describes an Elizabethan Masque held on three successive days at the National Portrait Gallery for different groups of 9- to 15-year-old children. The day was well staffed as a group of musicians and a costume expert were added to the Gallery's education staff. The day started by the group of children being shown detailed slides of the famous Elizabethan picture of Sir Henry Unton and his life in tableaux around him. The main concentration was on the area showing Sir Henry and his family about to be entertained to a masque after a banquet (National Gallery). Then the children chose to be musicians, dancers, or craftsmen and dispersed into three groups to be taught their different functions. 'Craftsmen' used the children's studio in the gallery to prepare properties and costumes (masks, head-dresses, and decorations), 'musicians' and 'dancers' practised in the other galleries. Towards the end of the afternoon the masque took place helped by adult musicians. This was a memorable day for the participants who will not easily forget the Elizabethan picture, an original source, and particularly the detailed scene in it which they 'lived through'. From the point of view of the junior school, this highly integrated day using outstanding resources could not form a regular part of the syllabus and depended upon knowledge of the Elizabethan period having been taught in school beforehand. The 9- to 11-year-olds would obviously be helped by the 11- to 15-year-olds but the work could probably be tailored to 9- to 11-year-olds on their own.

If teachers find the expertise and organization of these projects rather awe-inspiring, they might find it easier to link history with drama. By drama I mean 'role-playing' and informal class miming of short scenes or incidents. It does not involve large full-scale productions on the school stage at the end of term for parents. Drama as a teaching medium only helps history if the individual class teacher provides an informal structure with plenty of discussion with the class, to stimulate disciplined imagination of the past through systematic use of questioning and empathy. Written plays should not be learnt nor plays not written by children. The work of Dorothy Heathcote of the University of Newcastle upon Tyne stands out as the right historical approach. In her work, children are made to feel and understand by discussion the people of the past even though their historical knowledge may not be great and their 'stage properties' simple.

An example of this remarkable teacher's work may be worth quoting. Mrs Heathcote ran a three-day in-service course in 1973 at the Gilmour Development Centre, Liverpool, called *Making History—An Approach through Drama*. She used a large class of ten-year-old children from a neighbouring school. The general theme was transport from the nineteenth century and then stretching back to the sixteenth century. The stimulus for the first day was a large coloured paper cut-out of a train on the Liverpool to Manchester Railway. This in itself was of local interest to Liverpool children, many of whom had studied the first, second and third class coaches of this railway in the Transport gallery of the City of Liverpool Museum. From this small knowledge the children eventually imagined that they were sitting in the train and several of them told the audience what roles they were playing. This made them think carefully about which people would be likely to travel on this train and in which coach they would sit. The nineteenth-century cotton magnate from Manchester coming to a meeting in Liverpool? The Manchester family of six children visiting their grandmother in Liverpool? Endless possibilities were discussed before the children had parts, big and small, to play.

The second morning their disciplined imaginations (*not* fantasy) were taxed a little more, starting from the picture of an eighteenth-century coach. In this case they imagined that they were a household of servants moving their landowner/employer from one residence to another. Mrs Heathcote used the blackboard to jot down all the articles they would have to remember to pack. This required detailed discussion as some children suggested modern articles, such as a television and film projector which had to be abandoned as anachronistic. Children's previous study of the past became very useful here as the majority opinion discarded obvious anachronisms and some even suggested obvious period pieces such as pendulum clocks and silver dishes. Eventually, after much bustle, they climbed into their coaches and wagons in an order of precedence, laden with articles, and reached the new house with great excitement.

The third morning posed the even more exciting problem of sailing to the New World in the *Mayflower*, starting from the picture of a seventeenth-century ship. This time some of the watching audience was used as crew while the children played the role of pilgrims. The difficult concept of 'pilgrim' as a certain sort of traveller, very different from travellers today, was discussed. Why were they leaving England? Where from? If they felt so strongly in 1620 about having freedom to worship how they liked, would they mind leaving their homes and many of their possessions? Did they take only essentials? What were the ships like to cross the stormy Atlantic? Do you think they were very brave? Would some be frightened, especially children, and need support and comfort? As the class boarded their ship and hoisted the flag there were mixed feelings and they faced many perils on the way. This led to much fervent and unabashed praying and the children were so relaxed by now that they broke into united singing of a hymn as part of their Sunday service. It will be noticed that the particular interest of this teaching was that Mrs Heathcote posed problems for the children to solve by thought and discussion rather than by seeking information from books. She was also 'teaching history backwards' in the chronological sense. Thus she gradually accustomed the class to 'difference' between 1973 and 1873, and more difference to 1783 and even more to 1620. In this way she used the 'similarity/difference' concept given prominence by the *Place Time and Society Project* in a way that runs contrary to the chronological syllabus and leaves its merits less self-evident than an author such as Unstead suggests. She also used the uniting element of 'travel' and yet the different vehicles of train, coach, and ship; this could have led to more discussion with more time. The class will probably never forget their individual feelings as they represented passengers on the train, servants in the coach, and pilgrims on the ship. It seems to me that this 'historical awareness' of 'difference' and 'change' is the most important part of 7–11 children's study.

Another less individualistic approach to the integration of drama and history has been developed by another expert in drama. Four topics may be used to illustrate this approach.

One is a broad historical topic such as 'schooling'. Different elements which illustrate varying stages in the development of elementary schools should be selected. They should be linked together by a commentary written by the children. (This departs from Dorothy Heathcote's approach of oral rather than written work.) For example reading, physical education, needlework or history could be taken and the

45

children could mime different types of lessons from 1870 to 1980 with a written commentary. Children always enjoy portraying children in school in harsher periods.

Another topic might be the Industrial Revolution; for example, the weaving of cotton cloth at different periods. Children enjoy becoming machines and they can learn a lot about the way weaving and spinning machines work by trying to portray one in movement with their own bodies. Each depiction should show changes in the cotton industry; the price of cotton falls and father comes home with too little money to buy food and clothing. Someone is sacked because the new looms need fewer operatives—a too pertinent theme if the very children dramatizing have fathers or mothers made redundant for quite different economic reasons. The family has to decide whether to move into the town where there might be a possibility of new jobs, just as nowadays they might consider moving to the south-east.

A very important historical event could form a third option; for example, the moment the wind changed to allow William of Normandy to cross to England in 1066 (or the Allied armies to move in the opposite direction in 1944). The details of looking after the horses; filling the long boats with food, arms, and horses; a man leaving his family to accompany William reluctantly; and the overworked armourer complaining about the lack of consideration of his superiors; all could culminate in this moment of time.

Popular uprisings, clear moments of drama within recorded history itself, might form a fourth alternative. Within English history it might be Wat Tyler's 1381 revolt, Ket's rebellion of 1549, the Midland rising against enclosure in 1617, the Jacobite rebellions of 1715 and 1745, the Tolpuddle Martyrs of 1834, or the General Strike of 1926. Here the class should concentrate on a few contrasted families, find out what pressures were on them and role-play the moment of decision when the rising was started. These themes of historical movements and particular events all show how individuals were involved and how they felt. They also show how conflict influences the course of history and is captured in drama.

Whichever approach is adopted, Heathcote or otherwise, drama adds to the dimensions of thought and feeling for the individual in the past.

HISTORY AND SCIENCE

Emphasis on integration and on science in the junior school in the 1960s led to attempts to involve history and science. Two attempts will be described here, both of them being projects sponsored by large grants of money.

The Nuffield Junior Science Project published its findings in a pamphlet called *Science and History* (Collins, 1967). From this pamphlet the able teacher can be helped to link the disciplines of science and history through 'discovery learning'. Two approaches are suggested. One is a series of stories told by the teacher of famous scientists who made discoveries such as Pasteur, Ron and Grassi (malaria), David Bruce (sleeping sickness), Ronx and Behring (diphtheria), Walter Reed (yellow fever), and Humphrey Davy (safety lamp). These would be simple stories with no experiments. The second approach would involve the children in more activity and actual experimentation. The period most easily used is early man and his need for food, shelter, clothing, illustration in his cave (paintings), and weapons. The diagram named *Stories about Cavemen* (see Fig. 3.10) may help to amplify this for a 7- to

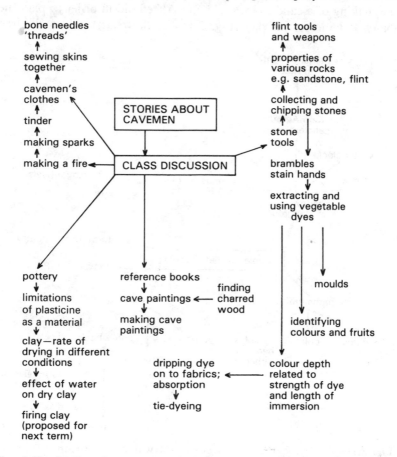

Fig. 3.10 Stories about cavemen (from *Science and History*, Teacher's Background Booklet, Nuffield Junior Science, Collins, 1967)

47

8-year-old class. Other topics to be tackled in this way are the voyages of discovery, involving ships, chronometer, and new foods; and transport, starting from moving stones to Stonehenge and at Stonehenge, in order to build the temple to the Sun God.

The second project is *Science 5–13*, sponsored by the Schools Council, the Nuffield Foundation and the Scottish Education Department. In 1969 it published two pamphlets on *Time* through Macdonald, publishers. One is subtitled a 'background book' and the other 'a unit for teachers'. Children would work on units of time (day, week, year, etc.), time measurement (clocks), standard time, places and time (Greenwich and ships), biological clocks, and people and time (e.g., Galileo). An interesting topic developed from a display of old clocks which involved the making of a candle clock as King Alfred did in order to plan the many activities of his day (Fig. 3.11 for flowchart). Older children

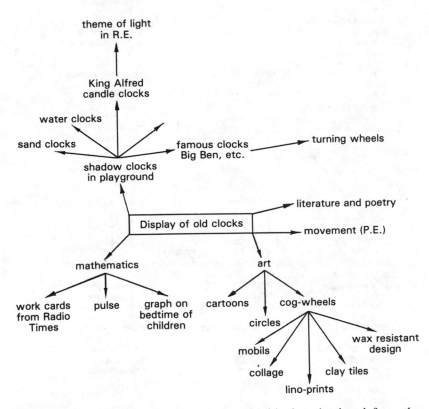

Fig. 3.11 A variety of activities connected with time developed from the starting point of a display of old clocks (from *Science 5–13*, Schools Council Project pamphlet on 'Time', Macdonald, 1969)

interested in the measurement of time by famous men of the past could study Isaac Newton, Galileo, Christian Huygens, Robert Hooke, Thomas Tompion, and John Harrison. This would also involve practical work connected with time. Since history teachers find difficulty in teaching children an understanding of historical time and therefore feel insecure in their teaching of the past, this approach of time as used every day might be another way of looking at the problem. Once the concept of 'time' has been grasped, sequence, change, dates, centuries, 'periods' of history, and time charts will fall into place in the child's mind.

The Nuffield Junior Science Project and *Science 5–13* view the syllabus as a series of topics, complete in themselves and unrelated to each other except through science. However, the integration of science and history appears to be rather a strained relationship and could only be worked by an able, experienced, and highly-motivated teacher.

HISTORY AND ART

Sybil Marshall, an experienced primary teacher who became an English specialist, believes in the integrated approach to the curriculum, with history very often as the basic component. She thinks that: 'Historical events are like pearls on a string of time' and that 'History comes into its own in the integrated thematic approach'.[3] As the headmistress of a small village school at Kingston, Cambridgeshire, her main interest was in art and this combination of interest in the past and creativity produced some outstanding work described in *An Experiment in Education* (Cambridge University Press, 1970). A model brought to life an early lake village, and a term's work on Roman Britain led to a cooperative painted frieze showing a Roman procession. Old objects lent by villagers were examined, sketched, painted, and modelled. The church and the churchyard were used in the same way, stone rubbings of gravestones being made and the old writing deciphered. At one stage all the children in this all-age village school made a *Book of Kingston* telling the story of their village, using illustration freely. They also made a history of their village green culminating in a frieze of a procession of villagers. Since drawing, painting, and creative work are the natural medium of primary children and the past presents objects, buildings, and scenes needing representation, history and art are more natural bed-fellows than history and science. Art thus becomes a necessary form of record for the past.

INTEGRATED TOPICS BASED ON HISTORY

In the four integrated frameworks so far suggested, history is the

49

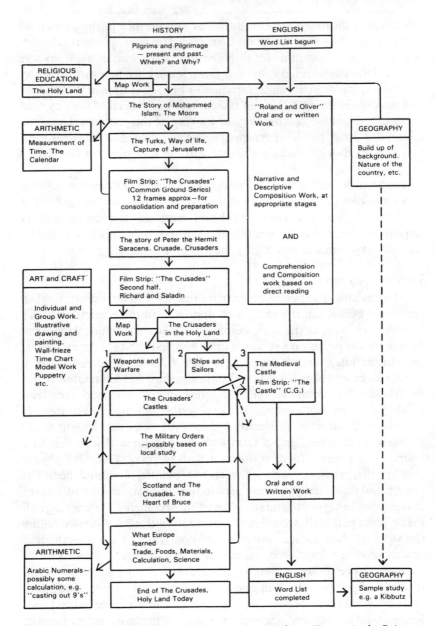

Fig. 3.12 Programme for a patch on the Crusades (from *History in the Primary School: A Scheme of Work*, Moray House College of Education, 1965)

handmaiden of other disciplines. In some topics, however, history uses other disciplines as supportive material. Two good examples of this approach are: 'The Crusades' suggested by Moray House College of Education and 'Life at the time of Napoleon 1806' evolved at an in-service course held in Liverpool in 1969.[4]

In 'The Crusades' (Fig. 3.12) such units as 'Weapons and warfare', 'Ships and sailors' and 'The medieval castle' could be treated in more detail. This particular topic is more relevant to history and English; geography, art and craft and R.E. would not be extensively involved. 'Life at the time of Napoleon 1806', also based on history, is suitable for a 9- to 10-year-old class. It should be integrated with mathematics, geography, science, language, music, R.E,, art and craft, and economics. The theme running throughout is a comparison between the life of an English girl/boy in 1806 and a French girl/boy at the peak of Napoleon's power and therefore a period of great danger to England. A similar comparison between young people of both countries in 1940 would lead to interesting discussions, as 1940 was the year of the fall of France to Hitler, the isolation of Britain and the Battle of Britain. The aim of the work is to study a patch of history dependent upon a particular year (1806), and to invoke other disciplines where appropriate. The patch would last for one term, one afternoon a week. The work could be introduced by an active stimulus, such as a novel, film, poem, song, story, or picture. Teacher and class should discuss this introduction and see where it leads, using the diagram (Fig. 3.13). Half the class could take on the French role and half the English, and each group could imagine they were journeying from a town in England/France to the coast to watch the soldiers massing for the wars. *En route* they see how people lived and report back their findings at various stages of the journey. Comparisons could be made between the groups at each stopping point. Alternatively, the 13 topics under the heading 'Social conditions' could be divided into four groups, some studying the French children and some the English children in each group. Visual presentation should be an on-going activity and other classes should be invited to view the progress and the culmination of the project. Other disciplines (as suggested on the diagram) could integrate with this work to a greater or lesser extent. Help is given in Fig. 3.14 with sources and resources.

In a recent article entitled 'The drawbacks of projects', John Eggleston says 'A feature of many projects is not so much their spontaneity, but their open organization. Often the detailed structuring of the activity is left to the child or group of children.'[5] The two projects outlined in this section, on the other hand, are exceptions to this rule as they are highly structured and demand detailed preparation from

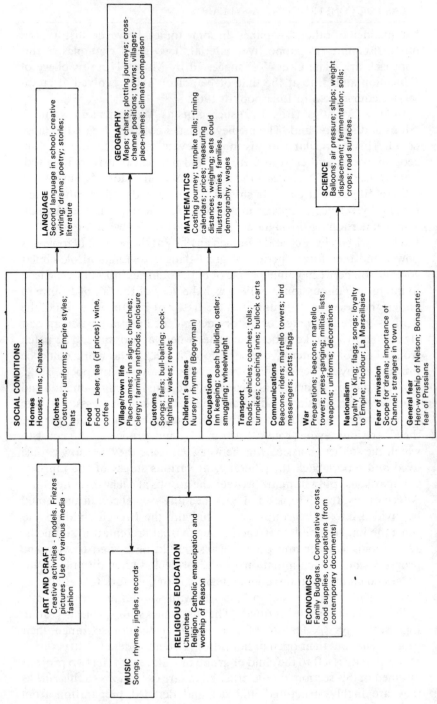

Fig. 3.13 Life at the time of Napoleon 1806: a comparison between an English and French boy or girl

SOCIAL CONDITIONS

Homes
Houses; Inns; Chateaux

Clothes
Costume; uniforms; Empire styles; hats

Food
Food — beer, tea (cf prices); wine, coffee

Village/town life
Place-names; inn signs; churches; clergy; farming methods; enclosure

Customs
Songs; fairs; bull-baiting; cock-fighting; wakes; revels

Children's Games
Nursery rhymes (Bogeyman)

Occupations
Inn keeping; coach building, ostler; smuggling; wheelwright

Transport
Roads; vehicles; coaches; tolls; turnpikes; coaching inns; bullock carts

Communications
Beacons; riders; martello towers; bird messengers; posts; flags

War
Preparations; beacons; martello towers; press-ganging; militia; lists; weapons; uniforms; decorations

Nationalism
Loyalty to King; flags; songs; loyalty to Empire; tricolour; La Marseillaise

Fear of invasion
Scope for drama; importance of Channel; strangers in town

General fear
Hero-worship of Nelson; Bonaparte; fear of Prussians

LANGUAGE
Second language in school; creative writing; drama; poetry; stories; literature

GEOGRAPHY
Maps; charts; plotting journeys; cross-channel positions; towns; villages; place-names; climate comparison

MATHEMATICS
Costing journey; turnpike tolls; timing calendars; prices; measuring distances; weighing; sets could illustrate armies, families, demography, wages

SCIENCE
Balloons; air pressure; ships; weight displacement; fermentation; soils; crops; road surfaces.

ART AND CRAFT
Creative activities - models. Friezes - pictures. Use of various media - fashion

MUSIC
Songs, rhymes, jingles, records

RELIGIOUS EDUCATION
Churches
Religion, Catholic emancipation and worship of Reason

ECONOMICS
Family Budgets. Comparative costs, food supplies, occupations (from contemporary documents)

Sources of information	Materials suitable for classroom presentation
1. Visits	1. Booklets
2. TV, Films, Radio	2. Friezes, collage
3. Filmstrips	3. Diarama
4. Archives and study kits, transcripts required	4. Tape-recordings
5. Maps	5. Slides with commentaries
6. Cartoon pictures (Art prints)	6. Drama
7. Books (e.g. Quennell)—Reference/Historical Stories	7. Films
8. Post cards	8. Artistic presentations—paintings/pictures
9. Newspapers	9. Models
10. Recordings (Music Readings)	10. Costumes, uniforms, dolls, puppets
11. Museums/Churches	11. Poems, creative writing
12. Firms	12. Musical activities, songs, jingles
13. Stories, rhymes e.g. Opie *Language and Life of Schoolchildren*	13. Ballads, records linked to slides
14. Personal Contacts—Relatives	14. Newspapers
15. French materials	15. Children's news sheets
16. Historical Societies	16. Maps—routes—France/England—Channel
17. UNESCO Bias in History	17. Registers
18. Diaries—contemporary	18. Militia lists
19. Calendars	19. Posters
20. Memorials and Statues	20. Flags/Heraldry
	21. Coins
	22. Displays—Interest Tables e.g. French/English food

Fig. 3.14 Life at the time of Napoleon : sources and resources

teachers before they start. Yet when any interrelated work is undertaken either the balance between subjects is maintained in a rather contrived fashion, with history claiming its proportionate share in the four-year (or two-year) programme as a whole, or history takes its chance of being the central subject, depending on who decides on the syllabus. Thus a syllabus based on topic work of some kinds could have little historical continuity or purpose, or even historical content, while elsewhere it might be history undisguised and perhaps unjustifiably overstressed.

The Schools Council has never actually supported a project on history in the junior or infant school, but many ideas that could be helpful to teachers in junior schools have been developed under the aegis of the Council's programme for the 'middle years of schooling', 8–13. Working Paper No. 39, on *Social Studies 8–13* (Schools Council, 1971) included some interesting ideas on syllabus construction, notably the suggestion that children over 11 years should follow a chronologically sequential syllabus, that is, one with history as its basic dimension, but that those under 11 could follow a topic approach without this structure. That Working Paper was followed by *Place, Time and Society 8–13*, a project covering all kinds of middle school and also upper junior and lower secondary schools as well as the social subjects separately or in combination. This project's ideas were worked out in a flexible way in different types of school, and were very much concerned, as all middle-years teaching should be, with what went before in the children's experience, and what came afterwards.

The main purpose of the project was to have been the production of teaching materials, and a number of teaching units were in fact published. As it developed further, however, the principal emphasis within the project came to be laid on the need to think out thoroughly and constructively the approach and content appropriate for the social subjects in the middle years. Thus aims, broad objectives, and principles of selection were given prominence. Special attention was paid to the development of critical thinking skills and of empathy, and to the evaluation of evidence and, perhaps more controversially, to the selection and organization of content by means of seven key concepts: four 'substantive' (communication, power, values and beliefs, conflict/consensus) and three 'methodological' (similarity/difference, continuity/change, causes and consequences). These, rather than attempt to provide a basic factual framework of English history or of world geography, were to govern the actual nature of syllabuses. Considerations of this kind are now much more widely accepted than they were a decade ago. Meanwhile, the project itself has continued to make a wider impact, both directly and through the work of teachers, advisers, writers of children's texts, and others who have adapted and extended the initial ideas or have worked along similar lines. As in the case of the earlier work, some of these more recent developments have taken place in schools where history is taught as a separate subject and some in schools where it is combined with others.

At no stage has *Place, Time and Society 8–13* ventured to prescribe actual syllabuses for junior schools in general. This is because it has always been a tenet of the project that each situation is unique, with particular children, teacher, school, and environment; that no single pattern can or should be appropriate in the social subjects for all situations; and that in any case nobody should presume to lay down a pattern for others. However, there is a case for suggesting examples for juniors, as the project did for the middle years in its basic publication *Place, Time and Society 8–13: Curriculum Planning in History, Geography and Social Science* (Collins/ESL Bristol, 1976). Figures 3.15, 3.16, 3.17, and 3.18 embody two related examples of junior school syllabuses based on the project's ideas, one for a single-subject curriculum and one for use where subjects are found in combination. Instead of providing two separate sets of charts, these are combined into one for each age level; the words in *italics* apply more specifically to the combined-subjects situation. This not only saves space but also shows that the basic considerations in syllabus making do not really differ radically between the two types of organization. Both, however, represent a marked departure from traditional content-based syllabuses on the one hand and from unplanned, repetitive topic work on the other. Instead, they envisage the sort of purposive development looked for in the social subjects by the HMI who issued *Primary Education in England* (HMSO, 1978).

The content of these syllabuses does not differ markedly from some o the other, older patterns. Those who built such syllabuses may well have worked intuitively on very similar principles. What distinguishes the mode of procedure used in these examples, and in others similarly constructed, is that they are systematically thought out, working from left to right across the chart but with the actual historical material depending on some awareness on the teacher's part of the general layout of history and of some specific episodes and developments within that general layout.

For this reason it would be foolish to pretend that any or every teacher could put them fully into operation without acquiring some further historical knowledge. To make full use of these examples it would be necessary to have some acquaintance with prehistory, the history of writing and of transport, and local history, as well as of some of the best-

Suggested frameworks for syllabus content and approach

Characteristics of children 7–8	Objectives and key concepts	History (assuming about one hour per week)	*Interrelated social subjects (assuming about two hours per week)
(a) Capacity to understand broad differences in time: then/now and before/after differences (b) Some grasp of simple human motivation (c) **Rudimentary capacity to work together** *(d) Capacity to understand broad differences in place (here/there) and in society (us/them)	*Main objectives* (a) To convey a grasp of the whole of a story and of its significance (b) To introduce some idea of sequence and of **place-order** (c) To develop a sense of the significance of evidence (d) To develop interests and expressive communication *Key concepts* (to be used in selection and organization of content) *Substantive* Communication *Methodological* Similarity/ difference	*Signs, messages and stories* First term: *How language began* How animals talk; talking to our pets. Different ways of talking with and without words. (Relation to previous work e.g., Joan Tough's *Communication Skills* projects). Signs, tracking and trails; classroom tracking games. Beginnings of alphabets and writing; inventing a sign language Second term: *Stories and Story-Tellers* Great stories chosen from different historical periods (Hebrew, Greek, Arabian, Norse, etc.). How do we know these stories? Why have they lasted? Arrangement of stories in their order in time; enactment through mime, drama and expressive movement Third term: *Messages from the Past* Use of objects, photos, etc., from home, school museum, neighbourhood; other experiences e.g. of festivals and rituals. What we know, believe and imagine about them; their message for us—is there one? How could we find out more about them? Presentation of display	*Signs, messages and stories* First term: (part of general language development across the curriculum) How animals talk; talking to our pets. Different ways of telling and of understanding stories; mime and nonverbal communication; sign language. Comparison of individual accounts of an incident experienced by all the class; the need for a true record. The beginnings of writing and of alphabets; inventing and testing a sign language Second term: *Stories and Story-Tellers* Great stories chosen (according to availability) from different cultures; arrangement of stories in their order in time and also by places on the world map. Consideration of why these stories are famous, why they have lasted, and how we know them; enactment through mime, drama and expressive movement Third term: *Messages* Selection of objects and photos etc. from home, school, museum, neighbourhood; other experiences e.g. of festivals and rituals. What we know, believe and imagine about them; why they are important. How could we find out more about them? Examples of messages that children in other countries receive from past and present (e.g. through TV). Visual and oral record of the work—our own 'message'

Fig. 3.15 Schools Council *Place, Time and Society 8–13 I*: syllabus 7–8

* considerations relevant to interrelated syllabus

Characteristics of children 8–9	Objectives and key concepts	History (assuming about one hour per week)	*Interrelated social subjects (assuming about two hours per week)

Suggested frameworks for syllabus content and approach

Add to the previous list:

(a) Greater capacity to read productively

(b) Greater precision in arranging and expressing information

(c) Greater ability to organize group work and to take initiatives in relation to school work

*(d) Sufficient understanding of symbolic representation to be able to use globe, atlas and maps

---

Main objectives

Add to the previous list:

(a) To introduce simple instances of historical inference

(b) To develop the idea of a social group as both means and object of study

*(c) To develop, at the descriptive level, some idea of the relationships between places and people

Key concepts

Add to the previous list:

Substantive
Power
Values, Beliefs

Methodological
Continuity/Change

The first kinds of men

First term: (a) *We were hunters*
(b) *We were farmers*

Prehistoric communities, illustrated by drama and modelling but also stressing the use of reasoning and the weighing of evidence. Ideas about the lives of early hunters, herders and farmers

Second term: *We were inventors*

A continuation of the previous term's approach but also a start with group work. Origins of significant inventions: wheels, ploughs, sails, glass: then bronze and iron: many potential links with science at a rudimentary level

Third term: *We were traders*

Inventions lead to trade. In order to develop thinking skills a little further, a game or simple simulation could be introduced, based on the elements of prehistoric and early historic trade. Local and regional instances (e.g. Cornish tin) could be included. The year could end with a dramatization of a Bronze Age village

---

Simple societies

First term: *Hunters and farmers*

Prehistoric and contemporary communities, illustrated by drama and modelling but also stressing, progressively, the use of reasoning, the weighing of evidence and the importance of location. Use where possible visual material from today

Second term: *Inventors*

A continuation of the previous term's approach but also a start with group work. Attention could be focused on a selection of early inventions (wheel, plough, sail, glass) and some recent ones (jet engines, plastics) and how their introduction affected people's lives. This in turn could lead to a consideration of the social conditions which can encourage inventions

Third term: *Traders*

The term's work could be based on an imaginary island 'discovered' and mapped by the class. This island has particular resources, including human resources. Simple ideas about scarcity, barter, money and monopoly could be introduced and a game constructed and played: this could also be valuable in social development. The year could end with a 'visit' to a famous trading island e.g. Zanzibar

Fig. 3.16 Schools Council *Place, Time and Society 8–13 II*: syllabus 8–9

* considerations relevant to interrelated syllabus

Suggested frameworks for syllabus content and approach

Characteristics of children 9–10	Objectives and key concepts	History (assuming about one hour per week)	*Interrelated social subjects (assuming about two hours per week)
Add to the previous lists: (a) Considerable expansion of capacity for carrying an enterprise through to completion (b) Demonstrate capacity to understand something of historical continuity (c) Noticeable improvement in fine hand–eye coordination and generally in manipulative skills	*Main objectives Add to the previous lists:* (a) To encourage the use of simple tools and equipment (b) To introduce the conventional time-scale (centuries, etc.) and the major time-divisions of Western history: prehistory, ancient, mediaeval and modern *(c) To develop more systematic use of maps as aids to familiarity with the layout of the continents and oceans *Key concepts Add to the previous lists: Methodological Causes and consequences (simply)	*Man the Traveller* First term: *Roads and travellers* Beginnings of roads; prehistoric trackways and their traces; Bible roads; Roman roads; old roads and new roads in our area. Use of models and a time frieze; imaginative written or dramatic accounts Second term: *Sailing the seas* How ships first ventured on the high seas; sailing our own sea (the Mediterranean); sailing the oceans (who first knew how to cross the Atlantic and the Pacific?); Arabs and Europeans; from sail to steam and oil. Another time frieze to set alongside the first; and another set of art work Third term: *Road, rail, and air* A selection of key episodes in the development of modern transport as a series of responses to particular situations and challenges; steam locomotion; internal combustion engines; early aircraft; some recent developments. A third-time frieze on a different scale, to emphasize the relative 'density' of recent history	*Travel and communication* First term: *Roads and road users* How could we build a road? How modern roads are built and maintained. Vehicles that use roads today; their respective ages as shown on a time frieze. Importance of roads to the people who use them. Different kinds of roads. Map of an imaginary journey on a great highway, e.g. Trans-Canada Second term: *Ships and sailors* How ships first ventured on the high seas; exploring the oceans; ships in trade and in war. Types of ships in use today; importance of each to different kinds of people; sailors and their ships. Mapping the route of a particular vessel e.g. a super-tanker. A second time frieze to show the respective ages of different types of ship in use today Third term: *Railways and airways* Group work on simulations of the planning and construction of railways; the role of inventors, engineers and financiers; the making of a report on a local railway and its importance today. A briefer look at early aircraft; the importance of air travel now; simulation on the construction of a new airport. *Alternatively:* planning of a world journey, using official timetables etc. of rail and scheduled air services, with individuals each writing a log of a part of the 'journey'

Fig. 3.17 Schools Council *Place, Time and Society 8–13 III:* syllabus 9–10

* considerations relevant to interrelated syllabus

Suggested frameworks for syllabus content and approach

Characteristics of children 10–11	Objectives and key concepts	History (assuming about one hour per week)	*Interrelated social subjects (assuming about two hours per week)
Add to the previous lists: (a) Growing capacity for critical thinking skills: 'perhaps' and 'probably' (b) Growing capacity for empathy (c) Beginnings of a capacity to study more than one aspect of history at one time *(d) Beginnings of a capacity to appreciate the contributions of different subjects to the study of problems	*Main objectives* *Add* to the previous lists: (a) To introduce 'creative uncertainty', though in relation to concrete situations (b) To develop the capacity to 'live into' unfamiliar lives (c) To develop the understanding of fine differences and small-scale changes. *(d) To develop more systematically ideas on the importance of place and of beliefs in human affairs *Key concepts* *Add* to previous: *Substantive* Conflict/consensus	*Our town/village yesterday and today* First term: *Making a history map* Large map made by whole class. Discussion of 'sorting out' in time; what evidence to rely on and how far; choice of symbols. Combination of map and time-chart (*Possible additional objective*: to develop familiarity with periods in English history: Tudors etc.) Second term: *Our town/village in grandfather's time* Systematic use of family history, local press and archive material: group and individual work. Extension of use of symbols; consideration of varieties of possible explanation of changes; final exhibition 'then/now', bringing out uncertainties Third term: *Our town/village in our lifetime: ten years of change* Use of time-line to relate self, family, locality and the wider world. Choice of one particular aspect of local change past, present and future as subject for final exhibition/pageant, designed so as to show the difficulties and uncertainties involved in explanation and prediction	*Our town village* First term: *Making a local map* Making of 'personal' maps by individual children; comparison and analysis of these (with some sensitivity); separation of historical from other data; comparison with earlier maps and modern printed maps; choice of symbols. Combination of map, time chart, graphs etc. (*Possible additional objective*: to develop familiarity with periods in English history) Second term: *Our town/village and others* Correspondence with a 'twinned' school elsewhere, overseas if possible; reliability of correspondence as evidence; what do we and they omit? Study of fine differences; tentative explanations (homes, schools, transport, work, beliefs) Choice of material to be sent to the 'twin' to summarize our town/village; what kinds of generalization are legitimate? Third term: *Our town/village in our lifetime: ten years of change* Use of time-line to relate self, family, locality and the wider world. Use of detailed maps of change; use of public statistics to show social changes. Choice of one particular aspect of local change, drawing on all the social subjects, for final exhibition/pageant, bringing out the difficulties and uncertainties involved in explanation and prediction

* considerations relevant to interrelated syllabus

Fig. 3.18 Schools Council *Place, Time and Society 8–13 IV*: syllabus 10–11

known and most durable myths and legends of the past, drawn from different cultures. Chapter 5 in this book, 'Sources and resources', gives some guidance in this respect; but all such preparation does make demands on time that are far from negligible or superfluous and it is very important for a non-specialist teacher to know quick and reliable ways of finding information. It should be part of the function of an LEA, and of a school too, to enable teachers to seek—and give—advice on aspects of the curriculum, especially those such as history and geography and some elements within science, where factual information and accuracy is essential.

In any event it must be remembered that syllabuses of this kind are *frameworks*, not obligatory prescriptions of content that must be covered. To ignore this would be to return to a content-based syllabus in another guise, one so demanding that it would require a budding junior 'Brain of Britain' to contend with it. In any actual situation, a teacher would select from a suggested term's work the nature and extent of content that appeared appropriate for that class's needs. Much would have to be omitted. Much of any syllabus is always omitted. It is an important advance when the omissions are purposefully planned in advance instead of arising through inadvertence.

These four schemes can, of course, also be criticized on other grounds. They are controversial; all history is controversial. But they are intended to build upon children's experience without being unduly parochial, or biased against (or in favour of) any one nation, group, creed, or class. They are also frankly based upon the assumption that children's culture and their range of interests must be valued and respected, wherever they live and whoever they are, but that this culture and these interests are in themselves inadequate to form a basis for education as members of a wider community without some kind of planned intervention and extension. Such a stance may not please those who are totally committed to a child-centred approach, or a community-centred approach, or a multi-ethnic, or any other approach depending on a single purpose. Yet it is intended to promote, strenuously, by practicable means, many of the ends which each of these has in mind. As for those who consider that it is too ambitious or simply too expensive for young children, perhaps they should ask themselves what kinds of enterprise or social commitment children will develop during their most open and eager years if their basic skills are not combined with social understanding. To judge such syllabuses from the 'finish' of what is displayed when the work is done would be to judge the process by the product, whereas it is the residue of attitudes, interests, and continuing motivation and skills that really indicates the abiding influence of these syllabuses and others like them, in the hands of wise and perceptive teachers.

Invasion, Migration, and Immigration was originally intended for the first two years of the secondary school and was implemented in a Manchester school in 1973 by Mr R. Hertzog (Fig. 3.19). At the time it was thought possible for the syllabus to be adapted to the 9–11 age range in the primary school: 'But recent discussions among Manchester teachers have indicated that the syllabus would also be of value at the top end of the primary school, so that such work could be undertaken before the pupils' prejudices had become fixed.'[6] The theme 'Invasion, migration and immigration' relates to Britain throughout history more or less chronologically and considered in topics. Teachers might find difficulty in collecting suitable information for certain topics but High Commissions and other agencies would probably be helpful. Correlation with other disciplines is essential. R.E. is evidently involved through the consideration of beliefs and practices that might be thought over-ambitious for 9- to 11-year-olds. But it must be remembered that for many, their daily experience includes contact with other belief systems and that where it does not, a school should not simply accept this cultural isolation without even considering the need to widen that experience. However, this is a policy question that does, and should, apply to the whole curriculum. It should not operate as a constraint on history alone. Music of past and present immigrants could be used, starting from the seafaring songs of Vikings. Dance is an obvious necessity as are home economics, P.E. and drama. Geography is an essential with such wide-ranging homes of immigrants and social science should also be introduced. This scheme should be compared with the previous scheme, 'History for a multi-cultural society' (p. 36, Fig. 3.8). It would be possible to omit some of the peoples included in the fourth year immigration syllabus if time and the lack of knowledge of the teacher prevented its implementation.

Conclusion

No syllabus for the 7–11 age range is appropriate without due recognition of the development of children and their interests and abilities at different stages. Kieran Egan in his book *Educational Development*, which I have already mentioned, when discussing children aged 5–7, views the 8–14 years as those influenced by romance. Following, but reinterpreting, Whitehead, and even Hegel, he calls it the Romantic Stage. Any syllabus, therefore, should emphasize 'the most

	Term one	Term two	Term three
Year three: Invasion and migration	Invasions of Britain 55 BC to AD 1066 Romans Saxons Vikings Normans	Migration of Scots and Irish in the eighteenth and nineteenth centuries	Immigration of Jews 1066–1200 1650 1880s 1930s
Year four: Immigration	from 1939 Poles Lithuanians Estonians Czechs Hungarians Ukrainians	Pakistanis Indians Italians Africans	from about 1950 West Indians Cypriots Maltese Arabs

Fig. 3.19 A multi-racial syllabus in years 3 and 4. Britain and other races : invasion, migration and immigration

Method of study

Each set of people should be studied under a specific series of headings in order to ease the making of comparisons and generalizations by the children and the teacher, *based on their findings*, at the end of the study.

Examples of topic headings

1. What reason(s) did they have for coming or moving?
2. How were they received by the indigenous population?
3. What opposition was there to them once they had established themselves?
4. What have they contributed to the British Isles?
5. In what ways are their customs and traditions different from those of the indigenous population?—dress, language, eating habits, etc.
6. What types of living conditions have they established or had to face?—villa, ghetto, etc.
7. What happened to each group over a period of time?—overthrown or assimilated? how and why?

exotic and bizarre socictics', very different from their own—'the more alien the world with which students [i.e., children] can be connected, the more relevant is knowledge about it to their educational development'.[7] This use of the very different is not only interesting but *necessary* to the 8- to 11-year-olds for them to advance to the next stage of learning. It should also allow, I believe, for studies in depth, since 8- to 11-year-old children have the ability to master and memorize considerable detail if adequately structured. This would not mean that all patches should be studied in equal depth.

Although children of the 7–8 age range also enjoy stories of 'the exotic and bizarre' and children of 8–11 are more competent to undertake and enjoy local field work, this reminder is salutary in making sure that we do not lose sight of dramatic personalities and events in the 8–11 syllabus. I believe that Kieran Egan's view of history at the romantic stage is true of all study of the past in the junior school. 'History is best understood at this stage as a kind of mosaic of bright elements— anecdotes, facts, dramatic events—which are composed into a small story, which in turn is a segment of a larger story.'[8] It is to be hoped that selection of one of the many syllabuses suggested in this chapter will enable teachers to help 7- to 11-year-old children to experience a small story, which is a segment of world history, a larger story.

References

1. K. Egan, *Educational Development*, Oxford University Press, New York, 1979.
2. M. Price, 'History in danger', *History* vol. 1, no. 3, p. 343, 1968.
3. S. Marshall, 'Threading pearls on a string of time', *Times Educational Supplement*, 27 February 1970.
4. J. Fines, 'Aspects of other disciplines useful to the history teacher', *History in Schools 8–14*, University of Liverpool Institute of Education, 1969.
5. J. Eggleston, 'The drawbacks of projects', *Times Educational Supplement*, 12 September 1980.
6. R. Hertzog, 'Multi-racial history', *Times Educational Supplement*, 3 November 1972.
7. K. Egan, op. cit., p. 47.
8. ibid., p. 45.

4. The classroom operation

4.1 Introduction

At the beginning of the last chapter I emphasized why I regard methods of teaching and the resources of the classroom as more important than the content of the syllabus. Each discipline has its established methods and in following these, the teacher will find teaching easier and more effective. 'Methods' of teaching have been equated with the 'tips for teachers' of older training days, yet *how* teachers structure and plan their work and provide activities for children must always be crucially important. How teachers conduct 'the classroom operation' is closely linked to what resources they have at their disposal. In writing this chapter I shall assume that teachers have very few resources at their disposal and shall suggest ways of overcoming this.

The natural methods of the historian as outlined in Chapter 1 should always be borne in mind. Story-telling at any level of teaching history is one of these methods. More story-telling is done at certain ages, but explanation of events and people is always needed by the good teacher. As a story is usually told from beginning to end there is a strong time and sequence element and a teacher must tell the story in the right order to make sense. Second, the historian is closely concerned with people and events, especially in the 5–11 age range; historical movements and ideas are not suitable at this stage. A third intrinsic method is to ask questions about evidence; how do we know that this or that happened? Teachers should always be asking children questions even if they have not taught them the facts, and showing them books about history as the way to find out. Fourth, teachers should also bear in mind that change and difference are fundamental to the subject and, therefore, comparisons between the 'then' and 'now' and different people and periods should constantly enter teaching methods.

These four essentials seem to be mainly concerned with oral work, discussion, question and answer. Teachers should beware of being 'the fountain of knowledge' and dominating the learning situation, which can easily be done in history. They must purposively think out activities for their children, particularly in this age range, remembering that 5- to 8-year-olds find reading and writing a slow method. Most preparation time for this age range will go into preparing suitable activities rather than collecting and remembering information. Although I shall provide suitable bibliographies at the end of the book and to read the most appropriate book is half the battle in preparation, teachers can make a good lesson out of a less good book if their methods are well thought out. It is natural for some methods to appeal to some teachers and it is tempting to keep to a method 'which works', but variety of approach is the secret of success and teachers should be daring enough to experiment with new approaches gradually as confidence builds up.

In this chapter, different methods will be discussed and at the same time experience from past teachers and different approaches for varying ages will be considered. The approach advocated in this chapter is summarized by Fig. 4.1 in which the centre circle is concerned with basic methods indispensable to teaching the past and the outer circle shows more ambitious and experimental ways of teaching. Both circles are grouped into four interdependent concepts of how the work is treated by the teacher, how children are organized, what the outcome of the work is, and what sources may be used. Time charts finally link 'outcome' and 'sources' since they form the result of work and also the basis or source of other work (in another year of the school). Drama and role-playing have already been discussed in Chapter 3. Story, illustrations, and time charts form part of this chapter. In this way Chapters 3, 4, and 5 are closely linked and are the heart of the book.

4.2 The story lesson

Two well-known methods of teaching the past are telling a story, and a lesson starting with a story and leading to related children's activity. Both are now considered 'old-fashioned', mainly because they give sole initiative to the teacher and involve her in a considerable amount of oral work. In actual fact, both methods are more difficult than they appear at first sight, but they still remain the essence of history teaching. They are difficult because they require detailed preparation and reading, they necessitate good discipline and above all a high standard of presentation in order to hold the attention of children of any age. But there are certain pieces of advice that are very helpful to teachers. It is better to start learning story-telling by reading a short, suitable story and then progressing to telling it, first with your book open and finally without it, but always helped by as large an illustration as possible.

Story-telling is not only a successful method but has been discovered more recently by one historian and teacher to correspond to an essential stage in a child's development which, if missed, will jettison his future

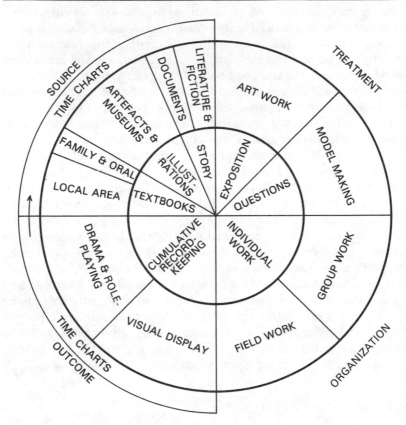

Fig. 4.1 The classroom operation

educational development. For example, Kieran Egan in his *Educational Development* (Oxford University Press, 1979), writes of 'the power of stories in the mental life of young children'. In his amplification of this theme, 'the necessity of the story form', his main contention is that the real past is too indecisive and grey for young children, but that the story form is satisfying because a story, according to Aristotle, 'has a beginning which sets up expectations, a middle that complicates them, and an end that satisfies them'.[1] In other words, the historian's problem to be solved by seeking out relevant sources and reading different viewpoints, becomes to the young child the description of a person relating to an event (the problem), made more interesting by crises and complications (added problems), and resolved by a usually satisfactory end (problem solved). Therefore 'an end' is essential in a story and what happens afterwards does not matter.

This idea, developed for the 'mythic' stage of education, was practised by an outstanding story-teller, Freda Saxey, for many years. To her the principles of story-telling were clear. The teacher starts by reading and re-reading her story from its original sources (many such sources are translated if originally written in other languages), trying to visualize the people and actions as vividly as possible. The second stage is to plan it into four to six parts 'like the act of a play and find a title for each part'. The teacher should jot down at the foot of her working page phrases and ideas from the sources which will appeal to children of the age group concerned. Third, the teacher should go over each titled part and put specific words (if possible exact ones) into the words of the characters. R. J. Unstead suggests Becket's reply to the knights looking for him in Canterbury Cathedral—'Lo, I am here, no traitor but a priest of God'— if a story was being told of Archbishop Becket's murder. Last, Freda Saxey advises teachers to try to *see* the action of the story happening, as this will help memory and add to the vitality of the telling. Obviously, a visual illustration is very helpful. More will be said about pictures later in this chapter. Freda Saxey does not think of story-telling as 'talk without chalk' but as a shared experience of teacher and class. If the advice is to be followed, stories of people, actions, and crises are the best. At whatever age stories are told, and they are basic throughout the primary age range, discussion should be planned and leading questions asked in the second part of the story session. In this way 'good and bad' and 'right and wrong', 'selfish and unselfish' may naturally form part of the curriculum. Shirley Makin, a pupil of Freda Saxey, writes about telling a story to blind and partially-sighted children on pages 69–72.

Another teacher with a flair for story-telling is John Fines. His advice on how to teach about castles to 6-year-olds over a period of six weeks hinges on the 'half story'.[2] This means telling a story up to an exciting point from which the story could go in several directions. This stimulates children to use their thinking and imagination to complete the story, and leads to much discussion as to how the story should end. In one example, John Fines imagined that he was Sir Ralph, a medieval baron owning a castle. Sir Ralph was short of money, was expecting a visit from the king and had many other problems; he went to bed one night with these problems unsolved and the children were left to solve them. Although Dr Fines had the help of six student teachers and was teaching a class of bright 6-year-olds, his methods could be adapted to the normal class situation. It would only be possible for the class to work in groups, tackling Sir Ralph's problems, if the work was attempted with 7–9 year olds. The half-story could lead to model-making of a castle(s), a coach trip to Porchester Castle (ruined) and preparations to furnish the castle for the royal visit. The teacher, taking on the role of Sir Ralph, could still act as the promoter of discussion to solve the problems and the final episode could be a role playing of the royal visit. Thus the six sessions start with story and lead to drama in Dorothy Heathcote's style of living the parts. For this type of work to be effective the teacher should know many details about castles and life in castles and the children should be able to refer to reading books on castles, of which there are plenty. The advantage of this half-story technique over the previous method is that the children have to solve the complications of Egan's 'middle' of the story in order to reach 'the end'. This necessitates thought, discussion, and knowledge. At the end, they will remember the difficulties a Norman baron had in entertaining the King.

Although the two teachers mentioned so far happen to be particularly skilled as story-tellers and good historians as well, most primary teachers would agree that every teacher should be able to tell a story reasonably well. In *Why Teach History?* (University of London Press, 1974) Pamela Mays recognizes that not all teachers are gifted as story-tellers and wisely suggests that stories can be *read* by the teacher if suitable books are used. She names a very simplified series called *Awake to History* (Pergamon, 1964), Ladybird books (Wills and Epworth) and Eileen and Rhoda Power's *Boys and Girls of History* and *More Boys and Girls of History*. Her good reason for this is that children will gain a more varied vocabulary if the teacher reads from different books rather than always putting stories into her own language. Therefore teachers fearful of embarking on the task of learning how to tell stories should gain confidence legitimately by reading them. This will also depend upon the nature of a particular class and their place in the 5–11 age range, younger children preferring 'telling' and older 'reading'.

The Historical Association published a very valuable small pamphlet entitled *Story-Telling: Notes for Teachers of History in the Junior School* (T.H. No. 13) but unfortunately this is now out of print. Five different specialists considered areas of the past in detail, giving sources and assessing the value of their particular area. The five areas were:

1. Stories of Alfred the Great.
2. Stories of the Norman Conquest.
3. The Canterbury Pilgrims and Thomas á Becket.
4. Discovery of the Mississippi valley.
5. Roman Britain: an archaeological approach.

The five authors consider their topic in relation to the whole age range of 7–11 and suggest ways in which their particular stories may be used. For example, D. M. Dannett makes it quite clear that her stories of

Roman Britain are best treated as introductory material for a museum visit and possibly an archaeological dig and therefore are more suitable for the last year of the junior school. The second part of the pamphlet is a list of-suitable stories with books in which they may be found and illustrative material to be used with them. However, the bibliography is out of date and needs revision as many more suitable books are now on the market and teachers will find them readily in public libraries.

Thus story plays a fundamental part in any teaching of the past particularly in the 5–8 age range when reading and writing is so much slower for children. In the first two terms of the 5–7 syllabus (Chapter 3, pp. 22–29) it is the basic teaching method, and stories should be grouped round important figures or events. It is a good introduction to any work done even from 8 to 11 but need not be used as frequently in the last two years of the junior school. One way of getting older juniors to read history in their own reading time is to set aside one part of a term, with preparation, for groups of children, after discussion, to read or tell their favourite story of the past. This would involve the class in reading, group discussion of stories, decision as to which one to use, and selection of a pupil capable and willing to read to the class. If the class had six groups it could lead to a competition, in the presence of the headteacher, as to which was the best story and why. Story can also be a base for role-playing and dramatization. Children should be reminded that every story must have a beginning, a middle, and an end. If they have been told stories well by the teacher from 5 years upwards they would be in no doubt how to judge a good story of the past.

How I tell the story of 'The Assassin' to a visually handicapped class of 8- to 11-year-olds.

INTRODUCTION

The children range in age from 8 years 11 months to 11 years 6 months and form a very receptive class in a school for the visually handicapped. Three of the children have some residual vision, the other five are almost or totally blind. Some of the children have additional problems, one has difficulty in walking, one can eat only liquidized foods and one is emotionally disturbed. Two of the children are above and two or three are below average intelligence. Two are girls, six are boys.

The Assassin is a story about the attempted murder of Prince Edward (later King Edward I, 1272–1307) by a Moslem messenger in the Holy Land during one of the crusades. At the time Edward, accompanied by his wife, Eleanor, was resting after a battle.

THE FIRST LESSON

Introduction

The meanings of a few of the words to be used in the story were discussed, e.g., assassin, Crusade, Moslem, Christian, knight.

69

I had made myself very familiar with the text of the story so that when I needed to adapt to the feel of the class and be more forceful I was able to tell parts of the story rather than read them. However, I did read most of the story because I did not want to lose any of Dr Mowl's* choice adjectives, fine phrases, or patterns of repetition. She wrote this story in such an excellent manner always using direct speech, that even when the story was being read, it sounded as if it was being told. The children were asked not just to listen to the story but to imagine that they were living in those times and conditions, and were the people in the story. They were asked to think about what they would hear, smell, feel, or see if they were able to.

The story
They listened to the story very receptively and obviously enjoyed it and found it interesting.

The discussion
They asked many questions, e.g., Was it a true story? Which King Edward did he become? Which King Henry was his father? When was the Crusade? How could Eleanor be Queen; Prince Philip is not King?

The children were asked what they could imagine most vividly. The two girls both chose to describe gentle parts of the story. One described the chess pieces beautifully and the other the scenes where Edward told Eleanor the reason for him placing a cross on the shoulder of his cloak and the people attempting to persuade her not to go on the Crusade. The boy with emotional difficulties said 'Eleanor saving his life'; when asked how, he resorted to his favourite answer 'I don't know'. After discussion he said 'nursing and looking after him'. One boy whose speech is a little incoherent when helped by the other children settled for 'When he was given the paper by the little brown man'. He was referring to the letter. The brightest of the boys said confidently 'The keystone falling down and smashing the chair'. Another boy referred to Edward killing the Assassin and the guard picking up the stool to strike the dead man. This was immediately corrected to 'the minstrel' by the other children. The oldest boy said 'Riding a horse getting hotter, paler, and dying'. The most boisterous of the boys said 'When the assassin took the dagger out of his belt and stuck it in Edward's arm'.

I asked them a few general questions, e.g., What do the words 'fair', 'brave', 'loyal', and 'sweet' mean? What are the differences between a soldier, a knight, and a general? Do you think that Edward was right to say that it wasn't knightly to strike a dead man? Should people hurt each other because they are not members of the same religion? Did Eleanor do the right thing to accompany her husband? Did Edward do the right thing to go on the Crusade and free the Christian knights? How was the climate different from England? What was different in those days from today?

THE SECOND LESSON (Two lesson periods on the timetable)

The children were asked which parts of the story they remembered and if they remembered any of the words or phrases used in the story.

* Dr Mowl = Freda Saxey, p. 67.

I found that they had remembered most of the actions that had taken place in the story but found it difficult to recall phrases apart from 'the little brown man' and 'three hundred English knights'. Unfortunately there had been over a week's interval between the two lessons. I decided to re-tell the story quickly as I felt they needed to be reminded about some of the detailed descriptions and phrases before they could dramatize it, write about it, or illustrate it. Each child was then asked to tell me about their favourite part of the story.

Dramatization

The two physically handicapped children had to go to another class so I was left with only six children to do the acting. I asked the most intelligent of the remaining group what scene she would like to act and what part she would like to play in it. She said she would like to play the part of Eleanor in 'the poison dagger' scene. We then discussed who we should need for the other parts in that scene and who would like to play them. Finally three boys agreed to be the minstrel, the assassin, and Edward. They then discussed what 'props' they would need. They used the divan, which they sit on for story-lessons, for the bed, an anorak for the cloak and they were going to use a pencil for the dagger but decided a ruler was better. The minstrel and Edward were rather diffident about speaking their parts so the Assassin rose from his position as a dead man to tell them what to say—which caused great amusement! The two children who did not take part in the acting of this scene were then asked to choose a scene to act and the parts that they would like to play in it. They chose the chess scene, the girl choosing the part of Eleanor and the boy the part of Edward's chess companion. Two other children were chosen to act in the scene, one to be Edward and one to drop the keystone. The 'props' they chose consisted of a table, two chairs, a sorting board turned upside down for the chess board and pieces of a plastic construction toy for the chess pieces and finally, having rejected a chair, they decided to use a football for the keystone. Great amusement was caused when the friend did not jump or move when the keystone was dropped!

The written work (in braille)

Most of the children re-told a section of the story; the assassination scene was the most popular. Two children re-told the conversation between Edward and Eleanor after the keystone had fallen. One child wrote about the climate in the country of the Crusade. Two of the children managed to repeat several of the phrases and adjectives used in the story and others an odd one.

The illustrations

The three children who have some residual vision did illustrations. They chose scenes rather than isolated figures. One was the bed scene done by a child who is obsessed by time so he insisted on putting a clock in the picture. This led to a discussion on how people told the time in those days. Another child chose the scene where Edward and Eleanor returned to Windsor Castle as King and Queen with crowns on their heads. The third child chose the scene where the keystone fell. These illustrations were all done in wax crayons.

The models
The class made two models, one of Edward and one of Eleanor. The cardboard centres from toilet rolls were used for the foundations. They chose red velvet for Edward's cloak and the selvedge of the material for the cross which was pinned on with a safety pin. Blue taffeta and white lace were used for Eleanor's dress. The materials were attached by rubber bands and staples and parts were just tucked inside the rolls. The faces were drawn with felt pens on white adhesive labels by the children who could see. Their crowns were made from tinfoil and attached with staples. One child made models out of plasticine.

CONCLUSION

The story provided stimulus for lively discussion and imaginative experience. It gave impetus to the children's creative individual and group work. They listened purposefully and their vocabulary was enriched as a result of hearing words and phrases skilfully used. They remembered in detail incidents, words, and phrases. They thought about and discussed emotions, feelings, and ethical values. An interest was aroused in what life was like 700 years ago. They enjoyed the story and asked if they could hear more historical stories.

Shirley Makin
The Royal School for the Blind
Liverpool

4.3   Interpreting illustrations

A second basic method used by most primary teachers is the use of illustrations in the classroom. It may seem a truism to emphasize the value of visual evidence, especially to younger children, but in recent years teachers of all ages of pupils have found that 'seeing is believing' and that many pupils can understand and remember better from a visual approach. Therefore this method is not to be considered childish or unimportant. Although books on teaching history to primary children seldom make a specific effort to show teachers how to do this they all presume that illustrations are vital. Fred Clarke said: 'Pictures will always have a very high value to imaginative reconstruction' though he did not favour model-making in history, seeing that as really handwork or art and craft. Catherine Firth, about the same time, had a whole chapter on 'Pictures and their uses',[3] decrying *Little Arthur's History of England* for including only six pictures. She called the use of pictures 'A precious means for the learning of history'. She had to rely on postcards from London museums and the Quennell's *History of Everyday Things in England* series (Batsford), but today teachers have much more help than this.

In this part of the chapter I am concerned with how the teacher uses illustrations rather than how children make them. The latter will be considered later when expressive work is discussed in more detail. In his book *Let's Use the Locality* (Mills and Boon, 1971) Henry Pluckrose, a prolific writer for young children and a practising teacher, combines history, art, display, and environmental study for the 5–11 age range in a most fascinating and valuable way. He has also written *Let's Make Pictures* and *Let's Work Large*. Henry Pluckrose shows that illustration is essential to all methods of teaching about the past from story to time charts, in the summary of different approaches.

'Illustration' covers a wide field and it is impossible to give much detail here where we are concerned with uses. The most useful are those made by the teacher either before the session or during it on blackboard or paper. The building up of a picture, in the style of Rolf Harris or Tony Hart, has obvious advantages. But this is a gift and most of us have to rely on commercially published pictures. Macmillan's large 'class pictures' of English history, though highly coloured and therefore not always accurate for real life, are at least a starting point. So are the illustrations from the long-running *Pictorial Education* (see pp. 106, 144). These old faithfuls are often still to be found in schools where newer illustrative material is hard to come by. A new series of textbooks *The Story of Britain* by Philip Sauvain is being published by Macmillan on the same lines as the class pictures though there are coloured photographs interspersed with the imaginative, highly coloured pictures. A second type of illustration is a black-and-white line drawing copied from a contemporary picture and simplified. In many respects these are more correct historically though the lack of colour makes them lose some appeal to infants and younger juniors. A third category are contemporary pictures, either medieval manuscript illustrations, actual contemporary sketches or maps. The teacher has to be very careful to select clear and fairly large examples and earlier maps, such as John Speed's seventeenth century ones, which are really simple plans. A delightful book for 7- to 11-year-olds is *The Map that Came to Life* by H. J. Deverson (Oxford University Press, 1967) which is a story about a walk taken by two children using part of an Ordnance Survey map shown in the book. On each page a full-colour picture illustrates a detail (amplified) on the OS map which is very well explained. A fifth type of illustration is a genuine painting done by an old master such as the Sir Henry Unton picture in the National Portrait Gallery already mentioned (p. 43), the famous *Thomas More Family Group*, the new *Coronation Portrait of Queen Elizabeth I* or the well-known picture of *The Field of the Cloth of Gold* when Henry VIII met Francis I of France. An embroidery such as the *Bayeux Tapestry*, depicting the Norman Conquest, falls into the same category.[4] Lastly, there are illustrations in

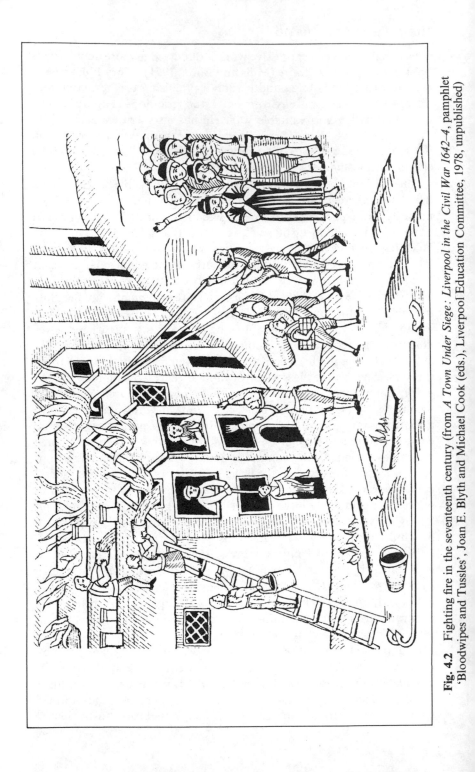

Fig. 4.2 Fighting fire in the seventeenth century (from *A Town Under Siege: Liverpool in the Civil War 1642–4*, pamphlet 'Bloodwipes and Tussles', Joan E. Blyth and Michael Cook (eds.), Liverpool Education Committee, 1978, unpublished)

most textbooks and reading books, some of which require careful selection. The publication of resource packs, archive teaching units, and 'Jackdaws' over the last 15 years may be used with careful selection of the fairly large pictures used as support to the archival material. All these types of illustrations provide starting points for discussion with the teacher or by the children in groups. The visual approach is more likely to elicit response, comment, and questions from most children than the spoken word.

Using two specific pictures and one map I hope to show how a lesson may be taught mainly from illustrative material, probably more effectively than using the spoken word. My first picture is a contemporary early Tudor one of *Lord Cobham and his family at table*, used as a Frontispiece to this book and on the back cover of a reading book by Susan Yaxley—*Tudor Home Life* (W. R. Chambers, 1980). This could be taught to 6- to 7-year-olds either as part of a patch on the Tudors or as part of a line of development on 'children'. The picture could be a 'starter' for a session on meals in a noble household at the time. There are comparisons with today crying out to be made; a family of six children, a nurse, grown-up clothes for the children, their ages (2, 1, 6, twins, written above five of the children), the great amount of fresh fruit eaten, animals including a monkey and birds actually on the table, pewter plates, and parents in the background showing the growing importance of children in the family. This picture is so rich in contemporary detail that only a poor teacher or a very unresponsive class would not learn from it; in fact the picture actually teaches the lesson.

My second picture for 6- to 7-year-olds is a sketch made from a contemporary line drawing in *A Town Under Siege: Liverpool in the Civil War 1642–4* (Fig. 4.2). It shows townsmen fighting a fire with leather buckets and the scene could easily be drawn and coloured by children in their own inimitable way. On the other hand the teacher could sketch in the main outline of the sloping street and house roofs and duplicate copies for children to complete. Children will quickly see the simplistic ways that people of the seventeenth century had for fighting fires in their wooden houses; water in leather buckets, long hooks to pull off the flaming wood to stop it causing more fire, taking goods out of the house, and praying to God both inside and outside the house. A child can also be seen being let down on a rope from a window. Certain references from *Liverpool Town Books* enforcing law and order may easily be understood by very young children as relating to the illustration:

1619   We present Richard Lune's wife for carrying fire in the open streets uncovered.

1636   We do order that the now Bailiffe of this Town shall provide and have in readiness for the Town's use a dozen leather buckets for such use as the Town shall have occasion or need of.

1641   Item. We do order that there shall be no fire carried through the streets either in the night or day.

A story could be started from these extracts and the picture, based on Richard Lune's wife unwisely carrying fire in the street to warm an ill neighbour and a fire starting. The children could suggest how the story might be developed (the middle) and completed (the end) and pictures could be drawn and coloured for notebooks. Thus again, one contemporary illustration and a few extracts provide the lesson, and could lead to other stories of town life in the seventeenth century.

My third illustration, also for 6- to 7-year-olds, is *John Speed's 1611 map of Southampton* (Fig. 4.3).[5] This has the great advantage of delightful little models of the castle, bargate, All Hallows Church, Holy Rood Church, the Customs House, as well as ships on the sea, the medieval wall, the 'Butts' for archery and small figures playing ball in the fields. The area within the medieval wall is still clear today and can be walked round and many of the streets today have the same names. This map gives endless scope for discussion, drawing, mapping routes, and even field work for very young children. Most of the maps drawn by John Speed contain the main town in one corner in more detail. Local Record Offices usually sell them. They are wonderful illustrations for intensive work in detail and for display. It is possible to 'read' modern pictures in reading books, if they are big enough, but the contemporary illustrations yield much more detail for discussion and children between 5 and 11 are very observant of detail which they find intriguing.

4.4   Exposition and questions

Constant use of story-telling in the early years of the 5–9 age range gives the teacher of junior classes the confidence to start a session by a short stimulus talk involving question and answer as well as description and illustration from blackboard, chart, or pictorial illustration. The teacher can also start from a poem, source reading, or short tape recording. Although the teacher takes the initiative in this type of lesson she should be training her class to participate in oral discussion. In a recent paper, P. J. Rogers and R. H. Adams looked in some detail at 'Discovery

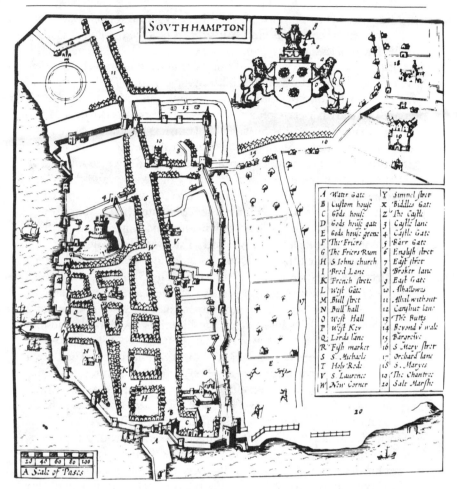

Fig. 4.3 John Speed's 1611 map of Southampton (by permission of
Southampton City Council)

learning' from their own work with 9- to 10-year-olds on castles.[6] More
will be said about this in the section on group work, closely allied to
'discovery methods', but the general criticism of this method was that
discovery learning, if too global and diffuse, was too difficult for
children to do well. The sentence 'The teacher is not just *in* authority but
an authority' is closely linked to the oral method of teaching. Although
most history is not taught by specialists in the primary school, one
teacher, as suggested in the 1978 Primary School Report, should be
encouraged to become a history specialist in order to at any rate advise

her colleagues. Thus the class teacher already *in* authority in her own classroom, may become *an* authority to some extent in the syllabus taught. The oral lesson is one sure way of indicating that the teacher is *an* authority. This does not mean that she must know all about the work or have read all the books which the children have read collectively, but she must be thought to know more than any one child and should not be prepared to start her class on any period of the past regardless of her own knowledge. The oral approach also transfers the enthusiasm of the teacher to the class more quickly than any other method.

It is obvious that many questions are asked and answered informally in group work but these are not planned by the teacher and they often seem to be questions of fact or finding out about source material. Recent work in the primary school on language, conducted by Dr John Tough in Schools Council projects, has shown the importance to very young children of the teacher 'talking' and 'listening' to children.[7] This develops towards the top of the junior school into planned discussions with purposive questions of different sorts. The *Schools Council 8–13 Project (Place, Time and Society)* has experimented to some extent on two types of questioning, 'closed' and 'open', as a means of encouraging critical thinking skills. 'Closed' questions are those expecting a factual, right/wrong answer.[8] These are the questions usually associated with history teaching, too many of which lead to rote-learning. They are a good way to start a session as they are easy for all to answer, revise what has been done earlier, and help a class to settle down and concentrate. They may also be used effectively in ten-point oral tests checking on names, dates, and main events, as well as words difficult to spell.

'Open' questions usually expect longer, less cut-and-dried answers, requiring thought rather than memory. They do not expect the right answer (as there may not be one) but to anticipate other questions from the teacher as follow up, to clarify the question further. Thus they play an essential part in the cumulative, planned piece of teaching. They also are a teaching method which helps children to use historical material relevantly since a face-to-face questioner usually obtains a relevant answer to a question. 'Open' questions have three objectives: to encourage children to use evidence to draw conclusions; to encourage them to be aware that all evidence is not trustworthy; and to encourage them to use thought and common sense in their reasoning. Thus 'open' questions follow the base of fact and knowledge laid by 'closed' questions and are long-standing in result. 'Open' questions may be used regularly from about 9 years old to build up an attitude that history is not all fact. To undertake this type of work a teacher should know her class well and so have enough control to get other children to listen to the questions and answers of their peers. A teacher must make sure that as many children as possible are questioned individually and that other children *listen* to each other's answers and enter into discussion with their peers through the teacher. The chart shown in Fig. 4.4 gives the specific example of Henry VIII to show how 'closed' and 'open' questions can lead to critical thinking. It is obvious from this chart that the answer to these questions cannot be 'discovered' without teaching and that the 'open' questions depend upon the answers to the 'closed' questions being correct. As soon as questioning becomes at all complicated the teacher is well advised to prepare three or four leading 'open' questions to be asked during the oral lesson. This means that she must be prepared to evolve another 'open' question related to the answer to her first at the time, to carry the thinking of the class further. She must also be prepared to bring the discussion back to the oral lesson in order to complete the first part of the story approach, i.e., the beginning and the middle. Questioning is an essential part of the oral lesson and has to be learnt by the teacher.

The obvious request from the non-specialist teacher is for good,

Closed questions		Open questions		Critical thinking
Asking for memorizing of names, dates, events	Encouraging children to sequence and break down the past into understandable parts	Encouraging children to use evidence to draw conclusions	Encouraging children to be aware that all evidence is not trustworthy	Encouraging children to use thought and common sense in their reasoning
Examples What were the names of the six wives of Henry VIII? On what occasion did he meet the King of France to show off his wealth and power? In what year was Thomas More executed?	*Examples* Put the wives of Henry VIII in their order of marriage to Henry. Can you think of one reason why each wife was discarded?	*Examples* Did Henry VIII want a son badly? How do you know? What makes you think he was very sad even when a son was born to him?	*Examples* Did the evidence of Thomas Cromwell's visits to monasteries show them to be inefficient and therefore necessary to 'dissolve'? Did Cromwell visit the monasteries intending to close them before compiling his evidence?	*Examples* Can you think of any reasons why Thomas Cromwell agreed with Henry VIII about the monasteries? Why did Henry VIII execute Cromwell in the end?

Fig. 4.4 Encouraging critical thinking through questions in later junior years (topic: Henry VIII)

concise, and easily obtainable reading material to help to prepare even a short introductory oral lesson. Rather than search out the many excellent reading books now on the market I suggest two particularly succinct books specially written for this purpose. One is *Teachers' Handbook: History*, edited by John Fines (Blond, 1969). After a general introduction this book is divided into five sections, written by different specialists, all of which are concerned with historical material, different approaches, illustrations, and references to source material, films, filmstrips, and BBC programmes. The five topics are comprehensive in range: prehistory, the Roman period, the Middle Ages, early modern times and contemporary history. There is enough in each section to construct a series of good lessons without any further reading.

Year by year advice on further reading and source material may be built up. The section on the Middle Ages is conveniently divided into subsections such as heraldry, children and childhood, town-building and urban life. The book is not written to provide material for a specific age range but most of the material is suitable, with some selection, for the 8–11 age range.

My second book is one already mentioned in the previous chapter— Alan and Roland Earl's *How Shall I Teach History?* (Blackwell, 1971). This less detailed book may be useful to the teachers of 5–8 children as well as 8–11 children. It covers most of the ground of the other— medieval history to the Norman Conquest (a patch), the Age of Discovery, ancient civilizations, world history and local history and Elizabethan England (a patch)—but is more humorous and less academic in style, as well as being much cheaper in price. It includes some references to further study and gives the excellent advice which all teachers of history should heed—'Be ruthless in selection'. The two books complement each other and together form an excellent basis for oral teaching. In the following account John Pelling uses the oral method as his chief teaching medium.

How I teach the Saxons to first year juniors

Seven-year-olds want things they can touch, and plenty to do. What can I offer them, in Bassingbourn, from which, by touching or doing, they can learn about Saxons?

It is a large Cambridgeshire village which, with the adjacent military depot, maintains a two-fold entry primary school. Only a few parents now work locally, except at harvest times; several travel the 40 miles to London. Outside is farmland, inside suburbia, with some poverty and some disturbance.

The environment is always our starting point. A walk through the High Street allows us to 'peel off' buildings of the past three centuries.

Nevertheless we note their role in the village economy—granary, bakehouse, car assembly plant, gasworks. From the few older buildings we get some idea of the historic 'core' of the community. We can look at a timber-framed house, and one with timber-cladding. Neither is remotely connected in time with the Saxons, but both offer tangible evidence of how the Saxons *could* have built. We can make models based on them, and see how the construction 'works'.

To come closer to the Saxon era we look out of the window. On a misty morning Royston Heath, south of us, is barely visible but there are alders, hazels, and willows surrounding a spring in the middle distance. Just off the school premises a brook flows through woods. In such conditions, I can tell the children, men have walked the Icknield Way over the Heath since long before anyone had thought to live here. Why would they come to Bassingbourn? What would they find? We can look at where the wild boar may have run or where the fish still swim. If all this land was marshy, how did men travel? How did they make their way through the woods?

At this point we are able to compile a picture of the area in the days of its first settlement. A Roman road (Ermine Street) ran north through it; the Icknield Way and its summer alternative, Ashwell Street, crossed it from east to west. From Ermine Street into the village runs the Causeway, still raised above the level of the fields. The children will readily draw quite accurate maps of the district. From observation they can also make good drawings of the landscape in its 'wild' state. They superimpose on these figures cut from the worksheets of *Alfred the Great.** The house models, now related to the worksheet examples, give a third dimension.

Only the Saxon background elements of the *Alfred* unit are used at this stage. The narrative material and the Viking aspect will only appear if appropriate. Social life takes priority. We look for and discuss the various tasks being performed in the illustrations: how the boar hunt scene has its culmination in the feast; how the bread for the feast is prepared in the village scene; how the farmers work; how their farming calendar relates to ours; how the clothes are made.

Drama is a natural development from here. Costumes and props need to be made. Stories from saga and legend add spice. Poems and riddles can be learned. Why learned? The earlier Saxons wrote only inscriptions. The children can write too, using runes of Saxon script as a novel way to record old-fashioned facts from the blackboard. For us, these must include Ekwall's definition of Bassingbourn as 'the stream of Bassa's people'.† Other areas may not have the same points of contact with the Saxons; but then neither does Bassingbourn, if you do not look. Many places have Saxon name elements; there are 407 churches with Saxon features noted in Taylor;‡ there are the forts of the Saxon shore, and always the days of the week. In any case, it is not necessary to teach the Saxons to first-year juniors: in other places it may be more appropriate to teach some other period. The good thing about the current freedom is that, provided we teach something systematically and make children aware of possibilities, the particular subject matter at any time is for us to determine.

Notes
* Pelling, *Alfred the Great*, Cambridge University Press, 1977. (The 'hunt' scene mentioned is in fact the worksheet on men's costume.)
† Ekwall, *The Concise Oxford Dictionary of English Place Names*, Oxford University Press, 1960.
‡ Taylor & Taylor, *Anglo Saxon Architecture*, Oxford University Press, 1965.

John Pelling
Bassingbourn County Primary School, Royston
Hertfordshire

4.5   The essential product: cumulative record making

So far we have looked at three 'musts' in the classroom operation for the teachers of history in the primary school: the story, interpreting illustrations, and oral work. Before more varied methods are discussed a fourth essential is written work of some sort. People sometimes ask what there is to show for the history that children have studied, what 'the product' should be. Much of what they write is necessarily transient, part of a particular display. What really matters in the long run is what they retain and make part of themselves. This is 'the essential product'. For this purpose a special kind of written work is particularly useful: cumulative record making. Since most people, including children, find talking easier than writing and young children have to *learn* how to write, there has been a tendency to overlook the need for young children to write about the past. Informal methods of teaching have encouraged this, as well as the drudgery of marking or even looking at work repeated 30 times. Yet if over the six years of primary education we are hoping to provide some framework related to time, children must have some record to aid memory, to relate to their time charts, and to see for themselves where this or that year's work 'comes' in chronology. Thus, work is built upon as the pupil goes through the school. Therefore, I am naming this part of the chapter 'cumulative record making' which is also related to assessment (Chapter 6).

Very little attention has been paid to this side of history teaching on the assumption that a child who can write English can also write history. Although this is true from the point of view of language (spelling, punctuation, handwriting), a start should be made in the primary school on the unique features of writing about the past. The particular pitfalls when writing about the past are the temptation to copy whole sentences and paragraphs from books (often regardless of their meaning), to write at far too great length in the belief that knowledge is what the teacher wants, and finally the habit of writing on scraps of paper. It is only too usual for these scraps of paper to be read once, fastened to a display and then discarded because there is nowhere to keep them. More will be said later about the last pitfall, which is most easily overcome by making history workbooks. The other two difficulties can be avoided to a large extent before children reach the secondary school by careful training as to how to write about the past. As in other methods of teaching, variety in record keeping is the key to success.

The only primary teacher who has written about record keeping is R. J. Unstead in a section of his book called 'Written work'.[9] He rightly emphasizes the importance of display of work, particularly by 5- to 8-year-old children, and believes that this is one way of avoiding copying from books, as the children check on each other with warning from the teacher. The teacher also must read the books that her children read and look at work to check on copying. It is usually easy to find this out, as children do not usually write as adults however able they are. In Appendix 1 to Unstead's book he gives a very useful list of suggestions for written work in history (pp. 81–85).

How to get primary children to write easily and well, except by luck, does not seem to have been tackled. I believe that there can and should be a building up of technique from the infant stage to top juniors. Starting from story-telling in the first two terms of the first infant years, children may build up *Books of the Past*; these are large books of different coloured paper stapled together to avoid disintegration and decorated on the front by the child concerned. Each story should be illustrated by a drawing or crayonning, a title put by the teacher at first, until the child has learnt to write, and the papers pasted into the book in order of the telling of the stories. The same could apply to the artefacts studied, though representation of real objects is more difficult. The family history studied might include a child's life-line and brief family tree, both of which could form part of the book. Local history could be represented by simple plans, perhaps completed from the teacher's outline, and the visits might be recorded by a brief account (at age 7) completed from the teacher's account with key words (on the blackboard) omitted. When teaching 6-year-olds I was surprised to find how keen they were to complete an account of a visit we had to the museum. To them this was the favourite piece of recording though it possibly smacked of old-fashioned junior practice. Looking through their *Books of the Past*, taking pride in them, and showing them to parents proves an enjoyable way of putting the term's or year's work together. I have found 6-year-olds anxious to 'remember' what has been studied and pleased to have some record to jog their memories. These books would show in retrospect not only what history had been 'done' but also how the child had developed his powers.

Many infants reach the stage of writing one sentence about their pictures and this may be built on in the 7–9 age range. Children of 7–8 years should be encouraged to write at least one sentence under their pictures (models) and then to develop from one to two and more so that by the end of the second year in the junior school most can rise to a short paragraph about one person, event, or building studied. By 8–9 it might be possible to build up a simple horizontal time-line of about six events in sequence as in Fig. 4.5.

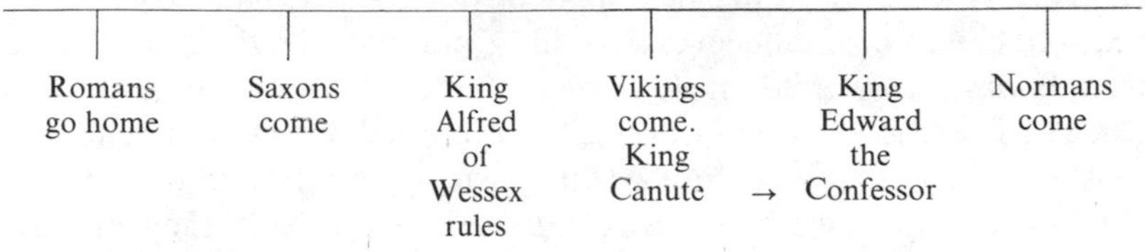

| Romans go home | Saxons come | King Alfred of Wessex rules | Vikings come. King Canute → | King Edward the Confessor | Normans come |

Fig. 4.5 Horizontal time-line

This purposely takes no notice of *length* of time between events and is only concerned with order or *sequence of events* (i.e., what comes before what, in time). The book may also contain an answered worksheet and a cartoon strip with 'balloons' depicting the voices of historical characters. If a topic or patch approach has been adopted for a period of half a term a scrapbook of photographs, postcards, and newspaper cuttings might be made with sentences about them. This would replace the book for one part of the year.

The years 9–11 should again build upon the record making of the younger juniors. The one-paragraph accounts should be developed into three- or four-paragraph accounts and later imaginative accounts of the same length. The final stage of top juniors should be to get beyond the *account* of fact to a beginning in writing relevant work on a more specific, less open-ended title. Examples of such titles are:

How a Victorian school was different from ours.
How did the Romans improve Britain?
Make a list of some reasons why Francis Drake deserves his fame.
Write a letter from one of the Pilgrim Fathers to a brother who stayed at home.[10]

For children to undertake any of these last tasks, the teacher should build up on the blackboard the main topic of each paragraph and advise children to write only about that topic in one of the three to four paragraphs. Thus, in the Victorian school answer, comparison paragraphs might be:

BLACKBOARD

How a Victorian school was different from ours
Paragraph 1. The school buildings ('then' and 'now')
Paragraph 2. Teachers and punishment ('then' and 'now')
Paragraph 3. Lessons ('then' and 'now')
Paragraph 4. Games ('then' and 'now')

For the work on the Romans, paragraph headings might be:

BLACKBOARD

How did the Romans improve Britain?
Paragraph 1. Roads
Paragraph 2. Fortresses and Hadrian's Wall
Paragraph 3. Villas

More complicated maps and diagrams can be expected in the fourth year and it is a good time for children to keep a list of important dates from their year's work on a vertical time-line at the end of their book. As in the third year, contributions are made to group work in one form or another, either written, artwork or modelling. This planned method of slowly developing a page of paragraphed writing will also help all other written work.

So far I have been concerned with the content of children's books. In his most useful booklet *Activity Methods in History* (Nelson, 1967) John Fairley gives two types of worksheets which children can make for themselves. One is a loose-leaf book with decorated cover and the other a zigzag concertina type which folds up and is tied by tape fastened at one end. He gives instructions on how to make both types of books. The advantage of the loose-leaf workbook is that pages may be added and taken out. It is much more suitable for older than younger juniors.

Children should be encouraged to take pride in the neatness and appearance of their history workbooks and to keep them from year to year for teachers for reference, and to develop in their next class. From the point of view of marking this could replace written work in English or other subjects at certain times.

4.6 The organization of individual and group work

Referring back to the classroom operation chart (see p. 66), we now advance from the inner circle of basic essentials for teaching the past to more specific methods, probably used less frequently but needing in some cases more preparation. Although these methods are teacher-controlled in organization they do not depend so much on the teacher for classroom functioning. The methods to be considered in this and following sections of the chapter are: individual and group work, field work, art work and model-making, and the regular use of time-lines and charts.

It is unwise to give the impression that individual and group work are distinct methods. Group work often includes children working on their own chosen piece of work contributing to the group, and if a group is as big as eight children, smaller sub-groups will be formed according to friendship patterns. Most writers take it for granted that group work is done only with older juniors, presuming that children below 9 will be unable to cooperate enough to accomplish a task. With training in this more open-ended form of learning along the lines I shall suggest from John Fairley's experience (*Patch History and Creativity*, Longmans, 1970), I believe that it is possible to start this type of work, developed from individual work, at the age of 8. An absolute necessity is plenty of resources in the classroom: books, pictures, paper, coloured pencils, documents, artefacts, photographs, art and handwork materials. More help will be given with this in Chapter 5 on 'Resources'. John Fairley says in his excellent book:

> It is an assumption that the individual will occupy different work situations at different times. Thus, according to the nature of the task, so will he find himself involved as a member of a class, or of a group, or simply as an individual employed in some unique pursuit.[11]

Let us first consider generalizations about individual and group work but looking in detail at more specific examples that have been tried and found satisfactory. Infants spend so much of their time doing individual work at their own speed that it is unnecessary to emphasize its importance in the 5–7 age range. It would seem wise to try some group work (four children in the group at the most) with the rising sevens as preparation for future cooperation with their peers. Therefore individual work is the staple diet of all 5–11 children though it should be intermixed with group work and other forms of organization from the 8-year-old stage onwards. After the exposition of the oral lesson most of the session is spent in children's individual activity. During this time they are preparing their records based on the stimulus of the oral lesson. So they will be reading books, looking at pictures and time charts, touching artefacts, and reading source material, drawing or preparing for a short test at the end of the session. This individual work provides an opportunity for the teacher to help individual children either by going round the classroom or having them at her desk or table. If many children are having difficulty with word meanings or a document the whole class may be stopped and more oral work undertaken, possibly using the blackboard, before individual work is resumed. Children who have completed their work can have it checked and then return to another area of the curriculum. This is the period for writing sentences underneath drawings, and paragraphs, building up a piece of work as suggested in the previous section. Benefit is gained by all if a quiet atmosphere is maintained as far as possible to allow concentration and the use of initiative by individual children.

Group work is usually more suitable for 8- to 11-year-olds. The size of group varies according to natural divisions of the topic, resources available, and the friendships and interests of different children. Obviously, trouble-makers will have to be separated and groups rearranged if necessary. Groups usually choose their own leader who helps the teacher to organize the group and to find suitable material for the work. I have found that one afternoon a week for six weeks is usually about the right length of time for one topic. The culmination of the group work is often a big display with or without some dramatic or expressive presentation, each group having a section of the classroom. This leads to considerable healthy competition. From the historical point of view this provides ideal opportunity for a 'patch' study in depth.

In addition to these general views about individual and group work it is helpful to refer to two writers who are particularly concerned with this method. Alan Jamieson in *Practical History Teaching* (Evans, 1971) has a chapter called 'Projects in the classroom' (pp. 8–16). By project he means a period of history, often interrelated with other disciplines, studied in depth and for longer than a normal lesson would allow. It is sometimes called a topic, centre of interest and may be tackled through individual or group work, the latter being most usual in the 9–11 age range. He praises this method as allowing children of different abilities to work at their own speed. The most useful part of this chapter is the section on 'Materials for use in projects' in which Alan Jamieson subdivides material into visual material, picture books, postcards, wallcharts, and printed books. Much of this material may now be augmented but some may by now be out of print. More will be said about this in the next chapter.

John Fairley in *Patch History and Creativity*[11] (pp. 91–160) puts forward a three-staged approach to accustom children gradually to greater freedom in organizing their own learning. He writes about them for the 9–11 age range but on consideration I believe that they are suitable for 8- to 11-year-olds, given suitable resources. Figure 4.6 is a summary of Fairley's three-stage approach with his suggested content.

Stage 1 8–9	Ancient Rome	Life at home School and work Leisure		Teacher controls with an oral lesson before each topic and then individual work on assignment cards by class after each introduction
Stage 2 9–10	The Norman Conquest	Bayeux tapestry and Battle of Hastings. Buildings Dress and pastimes Village life	 (1) (2) (3)	Teacher controls Bayeux Tapestry and Battle of Hastings as core study; all do individual work on this Three groups choose *one* topic for group work
Stage 3 10–11	The Voyages of Captain Cook	The Anglo-French struggle for Canada. Voyages of Captain Cook My town in 1780 Transport changes 1700–1800	(1) (2) (3) (4)	No teacher exposition Groups choose *one* of four topics and start work at once

Fig. 4.6 Summary of patch study examples by John Fairley (from *Patch History and Creativity*, J. Fairley, Longman)

In this way children are gradually weaned from too much dependence on the teacher and are allowed more choice as they reach their final year. Helpful detailed information is given in Fairley's book, including making models and pictures.

Three other uses of group work have figured in my experiments with older juniors. The first is on the lines of Fairley's patches, as it expects teacher and class to find suitable material. The other two are based on *Liverpool History Packs* (archive teaching units) made for top juniors and lower secondary children. The advantage of ready-made packs supported by a handbook for teachers is that the basic material is already prepared and, although more reading books are needed, much work can be done just from the packs. For a class of about 30 children six packs are needed and one for the teacher for preparation.

The work on 'Voyages of discovery' was undertaken in a city primary school with a top class of very mixed ability (about 40 children). The headmaster was interested in history and had stocked up suitable books on the subject in spite of limited accommodation. The organization was simple and rather loose-knit but gained the desired results. It lasted half a term for one afternoon a week. I introduced the topic at some length in the first session both from the content point of view and from the point of view of how we were going to organize it. Friendship groups were formed and each group concentrated on one of the following topics: Drake, Hawkins, Raleigh, Gilbert, Frobisher, Columbus and Magellan, Diaz, and Prince Henry the Navigator. As the class was very mixed in ability, resources were not prolific, and space was at a premium with few level surfaces on which to work, I kept the numbers of groups small enough for me to be able to help each group every session in order to suggest 'ways forward' when the group came up against problems of books, materials, etc. The concentration on well-known (obvious) personalities also had its purpose as more material could be found in public libraries on them and some children had encyclopaedias at home. Towards the end of the afternoon each group prepared a short account of the work done that afternoon and the group leader read or 'said' it to the class. I found this an efficacious way of checking up that all children had been trying to do something! Towards the end of the half term I made plans with group leaders for a display of the work. The children became very enthusiastic about this as the headmaster allowed us to use the school hall and keep the display up for three days to enable parents, most of whom lived in the area, to visit in the evenings. Each group contributed to the large relief model of the world showing the routes of our adventurers; this became the central feature of the display as all viewers had to look at the model first before reading other parts of the display concerned with the different explorers. Each group made one model (in addition to their contribution to the relief map) and also a group booklet to which each member contributed. The enthusiasm of the parents living around the school was our reward.

The second experiment was undertaken with the help of a published archive teaching unit in a stiff envelope. This was more highly planned as the unit gave the structure and much of the material. The result was work of a higher standard in the same time. The teacher can concentrate on finding resources in addition to the unit as the work proceeds, instead of having to assemble them in the first place. I used *A Tudor House: Speke Hall and the Norris Family 1500–1700* (ed. M. Cook and J. E. Blyth for Liverpool Education Committee 1971) with third and fourth years at different times in a suburban school in good buildings and with a tradition of solid history teaching. A pamphlet *How to Use the Teaching Unit* discusses how illustrations, documents, and booklets may be used by children both individually and in groups. The content of the unit falls naturally into six groups; the Norris family, the building of Speke Hall, secret hiding places, Royalists in the Civil War, fashion, and furniture. In order to give children a broader view of the work I gave a short oral

89

lesson with aids and board-work (e.g., the wall picture of a simplified bird's eye view of Speke Hall) at the beginning of *every* session. All children had to record the main points of this in their own words (from a skeleton plan on the blackboard) before they proceeded with their specialized work in groups. All groups had display space on wall and table near them for temporary display to assess progress. This silent recording replaced the reporting back in the previous experiment. Therefore, each pupil had a folder of the main history of Speke Hall at the beginning and more detailed work on their own topic in the second half of the folder. The work was further improved by a visit to Speke Hall about half way through the work and the use of documentary material for many pupils. More will be said about the use of source material in the next chapter. A classroom display completed the work.

Before the publication of history packs for sale, John West, then a General Adviser with Liverpool Education Authority, was the power behind the Liverpool Teachers' Archives Study Group which compiled a large box of documentary and other material on the *Liverpool–Prescot–Warrington Turnpike Road 1725–1871*. This was the basis of my third experiment with top juniors. The box is kept in the Teachers' Centre and lent to Liverpool schools for half a term. This box contained enough material for 30 pupils to have their own copy of most items to use in individual or group work. It also contained several copies of reading books, slides of the road today, a filmstrip, and maps of the road. The documents were divided into five categories: maps; how the road was administered; tolls; travellers and traffic; and finally road-making and repair. I organized the work in a similar way to the Tudor House project but a coach trip from Liverpool to Warrington replaced the visit to Speke Hall. On the trip we stopped at important points on the road related to our work, such as a coaching inn and a toll house, the original buildings still standing. In the same way I gave five lessons on the five topics at the beginning of most sessions, and folders were kept in the same way, covering general and particular information. On this occasion our display in the classroom was enlivened by the showing of a short film made during the seven weeks, as well as art work of quality relating to the topic. The film was also shown to parents at a Parents' Evening and is an encouraging record of work and a display long since destroyed.

All the types of work detailed in this section involve children in activity of their own, demand much more reading to be done by children and allow individual initiative to be shown, while also exposing those who might be tempted to take it easy. The variety of tasks set is so great that most children want to participate fully and group work ensures the checking of work by peers in this age range when 'fair play' and 'justice' are of paramount importance. Thus individual and group work are a form of 'discovery learning', yet emphasizing the teacher's vital role.

In recent years, doubts have been cast on the value of this type of work, In a thought-provoking paper, Rogers and Adams[6] question the value of the 'patch' approach which often forms the content of group work. They wonder whether the 'patch' explains *change* in the same way as does a 'line of development' or the teacher-controlled lesson. They criticize the *Then and There* series of books published by Longmans as accepting that one method—'patch' approach—is sufficient. This series certainly caters for the patch approach, though surely one title, *A Hundred Years of Medical Care*, must involve change. Nevertheless, Rogers and Adams sound a warning to be careful when teaching 'patches' to emphasize change within the topic. This is ensured if there is plenty of discussion between groups and within groups. Certainly many changes took place on a turnpike road between 1725 and 1871 and in building and living in a Tudor house between 1500 and 1700. There is no doubt that if the teacher is going to carry out group work effectively as a learning experience much preparation is needed and it is indeed a 'classroom operation' of the highest order. Beryl Fox writes the following account of how she undertakes group work.

How I teach the Elizabethan Age to 9- to 10-year-olds

The school is divided vertically into three houses, named after famous men with local associations—Dickens, Hawkins, and Pitt. My class are in 'Hawkins' house which coincides conveniently with the prescribed period for third year history. This approach could be used with many other more significant historical persons appropriate elsewhere. Although Hawkins is not the best known of Elizabethan seamen, his enduring work was done for the navy in Chatham and has relevance for the children. He is not an obvious 'hero' but this provokes discussion and avoids the pitfalls of over-favourably biased biography, while not whitewashing a villain.

The work is carried out for half a term, one hour a week. We begin with informal contributions from the children based on local reference, folk-memory/knowledge, accidental information from books and the media. Amount and value varies from class to class. Sorting, correcting, and supplementing is necessary before proceeding. As soon as it is established that Hawkins was a sailor, most children from the Medway area presume (rightly) that he was in some way connected with the Naval Dockyard in Chatham. (At this point there is some digression on the rise and fall of the Dockyard which was the *raison d'etre* of the town and of immediate concern to families of pupils.) We then look at what the Tudor naval situation was and what the Treasurer to the Navy actually did. I usually read part of a *Life of Hawkins* here (if not, as a revision summary at the end). Previous class—or personal—projects on transport and/or ships can be utilized to enliven discussion about the importance of a fleet to an island nation, and the need for and effects of Hawkins' reforms in design and management of ships. Rivalry with Spain is then isolated for further detail.

As we are supposed to be using an integrated social studies approach this subject lends itself to geographical interest and skills. We use atlases and map illustration to introduce and explain New World trade and piracy and international hostility in Europe and Central America in the sixteenth century. I have found that simple sketch maps built up in stages on the board and reproduced by children are more comprehensible than complicated printed maps. The essentials of, for example, the Atlantic slave-trade triangle are lost in agonizing over millimetres of error on a traced coastline. 'Treasure' has undoubted appeal for 9- to 10-year-olds and this part of the subject has much scope for creative work in art and writing.

From the flamboyant adventures of the sea-dogs we turn to the darker side of unprovoked attack, treachery, greed, and dissembling on both sides. John Hawkins' participation in the slave trade comes as a shock to children who have been brought up on obvious labelling of 'goodies' and 'baddies' on television. Results of the plunder and legitimate trade on wealth and standards of living of the Court and others are 'recapped', as a lead in for group work on aspects of Elizabethan social life, using reference books (from school and public libraries as well as their own and mine).

Genuine contemporary illustrations and documents are enjoyed and used more beneficially than idealized, pretty 'Merrie England' style children's books. I encourage even the least academic to describe what they see in their own words rather than to copy technical terms which mean little at the time of encounter and nothing later, e.g., 'The Queen's dress stuck out because she had a sort of cage on under it' conveys the appearance and probable discomfort which 'farthingale' does not. Each group of five or six children works on several subjects to gain a picture of life in a prosperous later Tudor English household. From time to time, individuals read out a passage or a group pools its findings for the rest. Guidance in use of index, suitable illustration, and cross-referencing from the teacher, attempts to give some form to the end product.

By now, we can formulate some ideas of what Hawkins, his cousin Drake, and Queen Elizabeth wore, ate, travelled in, lived or stayed in, and used in daily life. Class oral lessons are resumed for build-up to the climax in the narrative of the Great Armada. Significance of its failure for national independence is emphasized, rather than Protestant v Roman Catholic. Epilogue is the last years of Hawkins and Queen Elizabeth (they were near-contemporaries) to his death at sea in 1595.

ASSESSMENT

Revise his improvements in naval conditions—pay, seamen's hospital (opportunity to define non-medical institutions of the past), founding of the Chatham Chest (which the children assure me is a pub which explains Hawkins' popularity with sailors, but which was, in fact, a fund for dependants of seamen). This is also the time for contrasting life of the poor people with merchants and courtiers.

DEBATE

Discussing, sometimes in dramatized form, his claim to be a hero—national and/or local—reveals how far the children have absorbed not only information but the concept that people's attitudes were different in the past.

Beryl Fox
Balfour County Primary School, Rochester

4.7 The organization of field work

History teachers realized rather late the critical importance of field work to the learning of their discipline and therefore even now few schools, either primary or secondary, insist upon this way of teaching as essential. Geographers and scientists have long made practical experiment a built-in obligation in the curriculum of all young people. Yet this way of teaching and learning is a natural way of looking at, and finding out about, sources of the past, and is as important as written records. One has only to read Herodotus, Thucydides, Gibbon, Macaulay, and Trevelyan as well as contemporary writers such as A. L. Rowse, Asa Briggs, and E. P. Thompson to know that 'seeing is believing' and that no professional historian can afford to overlook the 'history around us'. Nor can teachers, particularly of younger children, ignore this dimension of their work. Here is the built-in 'activity' we make such an effort to create in the classroom. In addition, field work is the natural 'visual aid' of any local history content in the syllabus—the evidence of what is learnt in the classroom. It broadens the outlook socially for children normally kept within the walls of the classroom and school to go on a visit, and it is also a gift to those who want to integrate disciplines, particularly history, geography, and sociology. It is essential for those favouring a skills/concepts basis for their work, since no other way of teaching enables many important skills of the historian to be taught and used. Observing, discussing, recording in a variety of ways, using indexes and parts of reference books, team work with others, and finally synthesizing work by display as final record, all these skills are used to the full in field work. Incidentally, it is also valuable in that it demonstrates, directly, that the record of the past is imperfect. Some parts have survived intact; some have been partly destroyed; some have vanished completely. So we can never be quite sure how things were, still less how people were.

When considering the most helpful literature on this topic three types of books may be found besides several articles in *Teaching History*.[12]

93

The first category are books specifically written on field work (as distinct from local history), one particularly for primary schools. This last one is *Let's Use the Locality* by Henry Pluckrose (Mills and Boon, 1971). This is a combination of 'method' and 'information' book and is rightly subtitled '*A Handbook for Teachers*'. It treats 13 types of place in which field work may be done and ends with a county gazetteer over all England for purposes of a school journey. Henry Pluckrose helpfully goes into the mechanics of organization (clip boards, pencil sharpeners, sugar paper, and crayons), of actual visits, and the important follow-up in school with some excellent advice on display, as one might expect from an expert in the teaching of the visual arts. He believes in large drawings by children rather than the completion of worksheets, though the carefully-planned record of a visit to a church in another book by him (see Fig. 4.7) shows that his older juniors are capable of putting their observations into writing and thought. He gives an example of a large-scale map of a village including children's drawings (Fig. 4.8). The lively presentation of this book with its photographs, line drawings, and sketches is a stimulus to even faint-hearted colleagues to try their hand 'in the field'. The second book of this very practical nature, written specifically for field work, though also for the 11–13 range, is *History Field-Work* by F. J. Johnson and K. J. Ikin (Macmillan, 1974). This book takes all the likely kinds of buildings and sites to be explored, gives clear information and tasks for field work in note form with many practical line-drawings and plans for the teacher to work from. It emphasizes the great value of teacher preparation in a practical, concise manner.

The second category of books are those with single chapters on field work or those concerned with local history basically or with secondary as well as primary children. Alan Jamieson has one chapter in his *Practical History Teaching* (Evans, 1971, pp. 67–79); he advises teachers to look at a building both inside and outside and to talk to a whole group of children from a vantage point of a building and then divide them into groups to complete different tasks on the building from prepared worksheets. Tom Corfe has edited *History Field Work* (Blond, 1970); in the section on 'Preparing for field work' John Fines advises teachers to visit the site and seek out information from record offices and museums before preparing sketch-maps, plans, and worksheets for the children. He goes on to warn teachers to tell children enough but not too much. For example, he took very young children to visit Silchester Roman museum as Roman soldiers having to leave Britain in a hurry and being asked by their commander to assess what to take with them; thus the children divided into groups and selected valuable or essential items

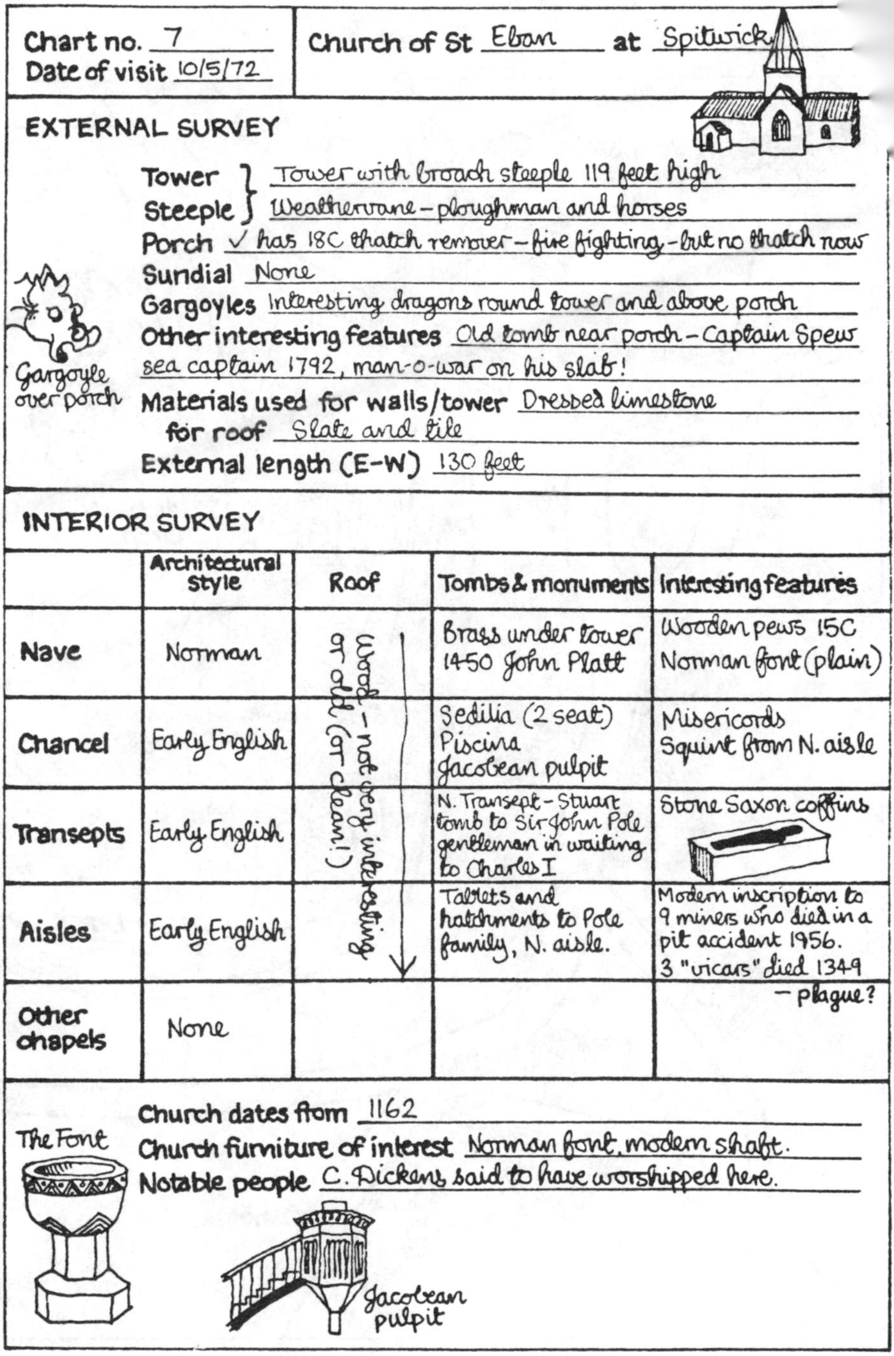

| Chart no. 7 | Church of St Eban at Spitwick |
| Date of visit 10/5/72 | |

EXTERNAL SURVEY

Tower } Tower with broach steeple 119 feet high
Steeple } Weathervane – ploughman and horses
Porch ✓ has 18C thatch remover – fire fighting – but no thatch now
Sundial None
Gargoyles Interesting dragons round tower and above porch
Other interesting features Old tomb near porch – Captain Spew
sea captain 1792, man-o-war on his slab!
Materials used for walls/tower Dressed limestone
for roof Slate and tile
External length (E-W) 130 feet

Gargoyle over porch

INTERIOR SURVEY

	Architectural Style	Roof	Tombs & monuments	Interesting features
Nave	Norman	Wood – not very interesting or old (or clean!)	Brass under tower 1450 John Platt	Wooden pews 15C Norman font (plain)
Chancel	Early English		Sedilia (2 seat) Piscina Jacobean pulpit	Misericords Squint from N. aisle
Transepts	Early English		N. Transept – Stuart tomb to Sir John Pole gentleman in waiting to Charles I	Stone Saxon coffins
Aisles	Early English		Tablets and hatchments to Pole family, N. aisle.	Modern inscription to 9 miners who died in a pit accident 1956. 3 "vicars" died 1349 – plague?
Other chapels	None			

The Font
Church dates from 1162
Church furniture of interest Norman font, modern shaft.
Notable people C. Dickens said to have worshipped here.

Jacobean pulpit

Fig. 4.7 A chart for field work on churches (from *On Location: Churches*, H. Pluckrose, Mills and Boon, 1973)

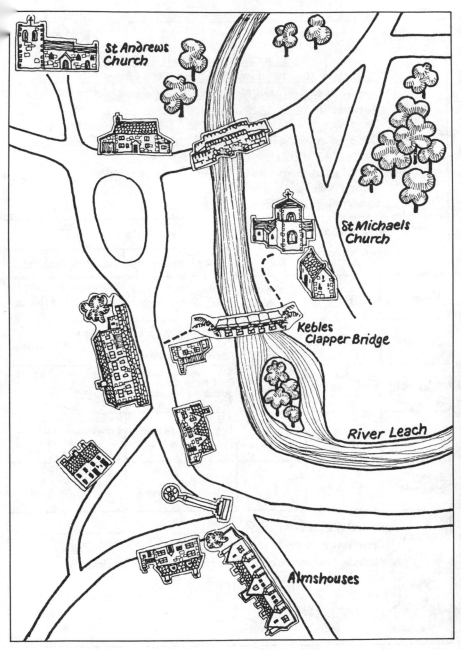

Fig. 4.8 Map of a village (from *Let's Use the Locality*, H. Pluckrose, Mills and Boon, 1971)

from different parts of the museum. A valuable idea in 'follow-up' with young children is given by John Salt and R. R. Cumming in their simple outline map of an area to which symbols cut from coloured paper could be fixed.[13] The third book including some reference to primary schools is by Robert Douch: *Local History and the Teacher* (Routledge and Kegan Paul, 1967). This gives useful case studies from junior schools mainly with children of the 10–11 age range in the Hampshire area. All examples show links between written and field work sources and most involve other disciplines intensively over six to eight weeks. The most interesting example involved all classes in a junior school for a whole summer term and was called 'The changing face of Crawley'; each age group of the school investigated one area of the town according to their abilities and most of the work was done from observation, as little is written and Crawley was then a 'new town'.

The last type of literature is a full and scholarly reference book by W. B. Stephens *Teaching Local History* (Manchester University Press, 1977) written from great knowledge and experience with exhaustive references and bibliography. One chapter is concerned with field work and presumes that serious attention has been given to the teaching of local history. From the point of view of the 5–11 age range W. B. Stephens distinguishes between 'immediate' and 'intermediate' follow-up; the first is essential with younger children while the memory is fresh and the experience immediate and will probably take the form of discussion and immediate completion of quick records. The second will result from more reading and writing and will probably take the form of an end-of-term display or exhibition. It is certainly true from my experience that a field visit with 6-year-olds in the morning must be followed up by immediate recall through discussion in the afternoon of the same day; it also allows children to let off steam. W. B. Stephens believes that field work in history is important even if field work is also done in geography because, although both disciplines may be concerned with the same 'now', the 'then' of history involves 'at what point in the past'. The 'now' of history is compared with very many 'thens'.

Taking into consideration the experience of these writers and the needs of the three age ranges already discussed, teachers should work out three methods needed to accomplish successful field work. These are: preparation, field work visits, and follow-up activities. Preparation is very important because weak organization could lead to serious practical consequences with children of primary school age. These preparations include adequate staffing, insurance, informing parents of the visit, safe transport, and safety while walking round buildings and even walking on the streets. Knowledge of the facilities and pitfalls of an area is essential and teachers should work out in detail time schedules, places for rest and refreshment, and toilet facilities. Other preparation obviously means reading the appropriate sources, preparing information and a follow-up programme. All authors reiterate the need for thorough preparation. 'It cannot be emphasised too much that the value to be derived from field-work visits is in proportion to the amount of preparation done before hand by both teacher and student.'[14] In his account at the end of this section Frank Harris emphasizes the need for a teacher to visit the site before she takes the children (pp. 102–104).

On the actual field day it is a good thing to divide the time into information given by the teacher (usually more tailored to the class than can be done by the curator), use of prepared maps and hand-outs for the children to follow, work in pairs or small groups on specific topics, and final putting together of findings before returning. If children are under 9 years the visit should be well enough staffed for groups to work with individual teachers. It is impossible for children to work on more than one topic in detail (e.g., chairs or beds in one country house, or one room of a house) even though they learn more about the whole topic on their return to school. Too much information or finding out can spoil a visit and lead to superficial, unsatisfying work. The teacher should hold the visit together by referring to each group's work. Some teachers believe in structured worksheets and definite tasks to be performed on site, others prefer discussion and imaginative drawings and sketches. All work necessitates clip boards, waterproof covers, pencils, crayons, and large sheets of 'detail' paper if rubbings in brass or stone are to be done. It is usually wise to provide a sketch-map of the route and its interesting buildings. Recording on the site is different from more detailed recording back at school but all field work should be followed up in some way. Infants are usually satisfied by discussion and simple recording in their notebook or for a display. Top juniors are capable of using the visit of half a day or a week's school journey as a big stimulus for work on source material, visits to the record office, compilation of individual and group books, and the making of models and reading of reference material. Junior schools still involved with the 11 + examination can use the whole of the summer term after the examination for a week's school journey and detailed follow-up. Time allowed for such work as a whole naturally varies in the three age ranges. Infants find more than two weeks too much, whereas top juniors could easily spend half a term in useful activity. These weeks should fit naturally into the syllabus and therefore be planned as an exercise to be repeated by teachers. The work involved in preparation is too great for teachers to change the venue of the visit more frequently than every three years,

98

unless they are already familiar with the locality of the school and very well read in the history of the area.

Although it is impossible to suggest precise field work experiences for 5- to 11-year-olds in all areas of the country, certain themes are suitable at certain stages of development in order to show that a progression can be built up. General help may be given on many well-known themes and teachers should branch out from these outlines to illustrate the themes from their own localities. Obviously top juniors could undertake all the field work done by the 5- to 9-year-olds but if the work is properly planned they should already have done it and it is important not to repeat visits already made earlier in their school career.

During the infant years field work is usually restricted to half-days or days in the more immediate neighbourhood, though a visit to a small parish church or a walk round part of a medieval wall of a town is not precluded. Three types of visits are appropriate to this age range: the environment of the school, a local museum, and a study of statues of famous people in the home town. A school founded in the nineteenth century is a gift for this work as children can get used to looking at the school building as a whole on known territory, then branch out to the local environment of the school and compare the 'then' of the school and the 'now' of the more recent buildings surrounding it. When taking such young children to a museum it is best to concentrate on rooms whose contents are well arranged and will appeal to them. Children should be given about four to six items to find in their particular room and be able to describe them from careful observation. Statues of famous people should be viewed from both near and far and photogaphs of them studied in school. Vantage points in tall buildings near the statues should be found for viewing. This work can lead to many queries as to why the statues are erected in their town. It takes considerable skill to take infants on field work lasting more than a day but Wolverhampton Local Education Authority has had the courage to set up a field centre for short courses for infants lasting from one day to several days. Margaret West, Infant Adviser for Wolverhampton, initiated this work and describes 'Kingswood', the field centre, on pages 101–102.

If possible, younger juniors should continue from this work in the infant school by studying the parish church as a complete building and then progress where possible to a walk round a town wall, from which much may be seen of the buildings in a town. Understanding ruined buildings is a more difficult concept than complete ones and children will need help with plans to study a Roman villa or a castle. Most books on field work devote much space to showing how castles may be used. Study of a castle from motte and bailey to Norman keep castles, and finally to

Edwardian Welsh castles, is a progression in itself and younger juniors are better concentrating on the first two and leaving the more complicated edifices to the later junior years. Alan Jamieson gives a detailed scheme for studying a castle in his *Practical History Teaching* (Evans,1971, pp. 71–3). An interesting experiment was conducted by P. J. Rogers and R. H. Adams[6] with a mixed-ability class of third year juniors to get them to make a scale model of a castle using two visits and considerable preparation and follow-up. This use of field work to make an accurate model of a castle required expertise in teaching and the use of sophisticated skills. Rogers and Adams concluded that 'discovery learning' was not appropriate in this work as the children needed a great deal of direct teaching and direct practice with skills. Their use of a castle in field work was a very different way of approaching it from the 'guided tour' type of exercise which could be used with younger juniors.

The village is another favourite study for the 7–9 age range and this may form a 'patch' of study of a village at a certain historical period or a 'line of development' approach showing how the village developed from prehistoric times to the present day. Edward Osmond's delightful book *A Valley Grows Up* (Oxford University Press, 1953) is an outstanding example of this type of work. Both Henry Pluckrose and Johnson and Ikin give constructive help on how to prepare for a village study.

Older juniors will find three topics a useful culmination to their field work. Starting with the monastery they may use imaginative reconstruction to live the life of a monk in the twelfth century, to make a model of the building, and to learn about the medieval church. It is usually preferable to choose a 'substantial ruin' such as Rievaulx Abbey in North Yorkshire rather than a building with only low walls left. From the monastery, the town, if it is reasonably small, could be studied either as a 'patch' or a 'line of development'. For example, Ludlow in Shropshire is a small town replete with different types of historical buildings; a magnificent castle (the original venue for acting Milton's *Comus*), an impressive almost cathedral-like church, several streets of half-timbered buildings (including the famous Feathers Hotel) and Stokesay Castle (a fortified manor-house) within easy coach distance. In fact, Ludlow could well occupy top juniors with a week's field work, which would bring it into the purview of children from elsewhere, perhaps from Birmingham. If a school is in the city, an area of the city is the only possible approach for a short period and much useful work can be done on the neighbourhood as described in Chapter 3 from the work done by Frank Harris in Liverpool (pp. 39–40). The final topic may well be a country house, which can be very confusing and tiring unless a limited amount of work is done and the class is strictly divided into groups, each group finding out about one room. It is better to return a second time to a country house rather than undertake too much of it on the first occasion. On the second visit the children could make a quick tour of the whole house, after the unifying work in the classroom between the two visits.

Although I have suggested some of the very usual topics in order of difficulty from age 6 to 11, all topics can be handled by good teachers in some way for all age groups. As it is essential to fit the field work into the syllabus it may be necessary to adapt these suggestions. It is usually better to undertake field work in good weather, during the summer term. But in all cases topics should form an integral part of the syllabus, be prepared thoroughly, and used for several years.

Kingswood   An imaginative approach to history

Important as it is to predetermine the main functions of an education authority's resources, it is often even more necessary for opportunities to be built into the curriculum which enable children to explore and develop their own skills and interests. Our experience in Wolverhampton is a vivid illustration of this. In 1977 we opened what we envisaged to be a field study centre for infant and nursery children. An adaptation of a disused camp building with the addition of a nursery unit, it provides residential accommodation for 20 children and day visit facilities for 40. Some 14000 children aged between 3 and 7 have used the centre with excellent results during the past three years. Much credit must reflect upon the planned approach to each visit, a responsibility shared by the staff of the school and the permanent centre staff who combine respect for, and recognition of, the learning opportunities which the centre and its surrounding countryside provide. Additional facilities such as a mini-bus make it possible to follow through the children's discoveries and experiences without a dulling time lag.

Recently a small group of children visiting the centre entered into discussion with each other as to the King to whom the place-name referred. At the time they were crossing the common, and Amanda, one of the older children in the group, volunteered the information that she had at home a book about Staffordshire in which there was a story of a King named Charles who had hidden in an oak tree. Could this be the place they wondered. The teacher was drawn into the conversation at this point and the children's interest further aroused by the new knowledge that the King had certainly been very near this place after his escape from the Battle of Worcester and that the position of the oak tree was known to be at Boscobel where he had eventually found shelter. Could they go to Boscobel and see, they asked excitedly. The teacher agreed, recognizing the need to catch the opportunity at interest peak and exploit it to the full. In a short time the children were actually at Boscobel looking at the oak tree and reliving history together, through story and imagination.

Although the name of the centre has been left in its most general form we recognize that 'language centre' would be an appropriate

101

subtitle. We have always emphasized the need for all new experiences to be described accurately with the use of the correct words. For example, 'farrier' has become part of many Wolverhampton children's vocabulary as a result of a visit to Kingswood and a demonstration of his skill. A most appropriate follow-up to this experience was the discovery in a nearby field of an old long-forgotten horseshoe which consolidated the learning situation and gave rise to much interesting creative work. The country skill of alert observation which is fostered and encouraged at Kingswood has led to a collection of objects found on the site and the nucleus of a museum being formed.

Imagination has been seen to play a large part in laying the foundations for an interest in the past, and handling objects from that time of 'long ago' brings forth discussion and leads to conclusions which often show that we underestimate the young child's ability, and fail to offer sufficient opportunities for extension. This has been found to be true across the full range of ability. Objects as diverse as a large key, a squirrel trap, nails, and an old spade, have each in their turn given rise to excitement and speculation as to identity and use. Perhaps equally revealing are the occasions when the teacher has been reminded of the generation gap as, for example, when a child bringing back to the centre his newly-discovered 'treasure', an old bucket, disclaimed on its usage because it was made of metal and not, as the child expected, plastic.

The very nature of the countryside surrounding the centre leads to imaginative play and we are only now beginning to develop the use of drama and the acting out of ideas stimulated by a setting unfamiliar to urban children. The uneven nature of the common gave rise to one such opportunity. A group of boys thought that it would be a good place for a battle because the trees would afford fine hiding places and they wondered if a battle had in fact ever taken place. The noise overhead of an RAF jet flying low startled the children at this point and, reminded them of hearing of air battles in the more recent past, and of the need of protection from such attack. It was interesting that immediately the mounds in the ground became a subject for conjecture, some knowledge of trench warfare and of air raid shelters became apparent as the children dug deeply into each other's minds for possible explanations.

We are continually finding that the opportunities of learning alongside children at Kingswood are legion, and we recognize the value to teachers as well as to pupils. Away from the more formal school environment we are finding a richness in young children's minds of which we have been all too often unaware and not least among our discoveries is the certainty that an interest in the past should not only not be ignored but should be positively fostered.

Margaret West
Infant Adviser for Wolverhampton LEA

How I undertake field work with junior school children

All of the texts recommended by Joan Blyth in her chapter on field work stress the value of a preliminary visit on the part of the teacher. I would go further than this and argue that a class should *never* be taken on a visit unless the teacher has had the opportunity to go over the ground previously. Decisions will have to be taken about which parts of the site will be visited by the whole class, perhaps with a guide or with the teacher acting as guide, and which parts will be explored by the children working individually or in groups, perhaps with the assistance of worksheets. In this respect safety as much as historical relevance may be the determining factor. In between the extremes of 'turning the children loose' and organizing a crocodile for a guided tour, are a number of possibilities. Part of the class may be positioned for sketching while the next are taken away to measure, count, record, etc. Children may be sent off individually with a time limit, ten minutes, a quarter of an hour, to complete a task, rejoining the main group at a signal and so on.

Only by inspecting the site in advance can the teacher decide where and when certain activities will take place. In an urban study of nineteenth-century Liverpool undertaken by 28 10-year-olds the class was kept together 'in twos' through the busier streets, with stops at key points for specific references to be made by the teacher and for particular observations to be recorded. In Chatham Street the children were released to work individually on manhole cover rubbings, sketching Georgian fan-lights, recording the variety of uses of wrought iron in balconies, railings, boot-scrapers, etc. Chatham Street was chosen first because of the wealth of relevant historical evidence, but also because at the time of the project it was turned temporarily into a cul-de-sac while work proceeded on a nearby car park. Thus, ease of supervision was assured and the danger from passing traffic eliminated; but it was prior inspection that had revealed the possibility of working in this way.

The teacher organizing a field trip is always faced by the dilemma of whether to point out, or to let the children find out, the evidence. Clearly 'planned discovery' (with the teacher planning the situation so that the child has the opportunity to discover) is the better way. However, given the expense of the journey, in time and money, most teachers will have at least a short list of things that they will want all the children to experience and will not hesitate to draw their pupils' attention to them if need be. It would, for example, be a great shame to bring junior school children away from the aqueduct at Pontcysyllte on the Llangollen canal without making sure that each of them experienced the thrill of placing their fingers in the grooves in the iron railings made at each end of the aqueduct by the ropes of the donkeys as they drew the barges across a couple of hundred feet above the river Dee.

Quite apart from the problem of *how* to do field work, the primary school teacher has to face up to the problem of *when* to do it. Given, for example, one day's visit to a distant site, should this be taken at the start of the project so that sketches, plans, notes, diagrams, etc. may be brought into the classroom for further development? Or should the visit be kept to the end to round off a project? The best solution is probably two visits, but in practical terms this may be out of the question. One visit, carefully placed midway or two-thirds of the way through the course will have the advantage of preparing the children, and for junior children often the thrill of recognizing, general features is rewarding—'Look, there's the motte—its just like one we learned about!' A visit so placed will have the advantage also of leaving time to study peculiar details about the site which has been visited, in the classroom later. The more the teacher puts into field work in the form of preparation, the more the children will get out of it, and the reward, as far as the child is concerned, might well be the birth of a life-long interest.

Frank Harris
City of Liverpool College of Higher Education

4.8   Art work, model-making and visual displays

We have already seen that one of the basic ways of teaching history is explanation and questioning. More ambitious and experimental ways of teaching may be developed from this: art work and model-making is one of these. It is especially applicable to primary teachers who usually have been well-trained at college in these practical and interesting techniques. The monthly magazine *Art and Craft in Education* (Evans) is a stimulus to good practice. Children who find book learning difficult and oral work embarrassing can often learn through drawing and model-making which necessitates record keeping and assessment in this sphere as well as in the more traditional ways. The primary teacher is in a much stronger position than the secondary teacher since she has her ready-made 'history room' in the classroom. Yet this type of work is only relevant to the past if the drawings, models, etc., are a ready illustration of the history syllabus and are also as authentic as possible. Therefore, all practical work should be prepared with reference to historical sources and plenty of discussion should surround children's preparation of materials, execution, and follow-up. Evidence of children's real understanding of their practical work in relation to their history scheme is shown by the captions, accounts, and setting out of their display. Therefore visual display is an essential method of the good teacher.

Many books known to art and craft specialists will be useful for teachers. Most local education authorities have at least one specialist art and craft adviser who will be very willing to help teachers. Also most LEAs run at least one short course a year on art and craft for primary teachers; unfortunately this is not yet regularly done for those interested in teaching history. Some of these books may be needlessly complicated and strike fear into the non-specialist. Therefore I am recommending two particularly useful short books entirely devoted to history and practical work. With either of these as one's 'Bible', history will be very well taught through practical work. One is by John Fairley—*Activity*

Methods in History (Nelson, 1967—Teaching Aids Series No. 15) and the other is by Tony Hart—*Fun with Historical Projects* (Kaye and Ward, 1971). John Fairley, a historian rather than an artist, gives a comprehensive review of most methods involving practical work, ranging from visits to museums to dramatization. Every double-page spread has relevant sketches showing how the model should be made. Tony Hart, of television fame, concentrates more on houses and how people lived and gives detailed advice about four particular topics: early British settlement, a Roman villa, a feudal village, and a Norman castle. As an artist he has provided his own large drawings and sketches which are delightful artistic exercises as well as being practically helpful. The second book is less comprehensive than the first and possibly of most use to the teacher of 5–8 children rather than older juniors.

Two more books have sections concerned with practical work. One is *Let's Use the Locality* by Henry Pluckrose (see pp. 94 and 96); appendices 3 and 4 give 'working drawings' which teachers and children can follow and a list of suppliers of art and craft materials.[15] As Mr Pluckrose is an art and craft specialist, ambitious materials such as leather, clay, brass pins, and the use of an electric cutting tool are suggested. R. J. Unstead has a section in his book[9] on 'Model making'. Photographs show the different stages of construction. For example, a medieval house is shown in three sections of shoe boxes; balsa wood and foam rubber are used for thatch. Simple and complicated models are given, suitable for individual or group work. Many books are helpful in providing pictures to use for reference but probably the most comprehensive is *A History of Everyday Things in England* by M. and C. H. B. Quennell (Batsford, 1954–68).

Another pair of books, less specifically helpful for art work and model-making, though certain parts are worth noting, is F. E. Parker's *History and Handwork for Young Children* (George Philip & Son, 1925) and E. and E. K. Milliken *Handwork Methods in the Teaching of History* (Wheaton, 1949). They give examples for younger and older juniors and rely on more common materials such as paper and cardboard. But the authors are dedicated to these methods of teaching history and go into minute detail about how to set about this work in a professional way. The Millikens provide a useful chart at the back of their book showing specific individual and collective models to be used for different periods of English history. Alan Jamieson in *Practical History Teaching* (Evans, 1971) and Pamela Mays in *Why Teach History?* (University of London Press, 1974) are naturally more up to date in suggestion of materials than Miss Parker or the Millikens. Alan Jamieson runs over many types of 'active history' such as mosaics, friezes, stained glass windows, collages, as well as models. He suggests reference to the monthly magazine *Pictorial Education* (Evans) which usually has one item on history models, and how to construct them from the paper of the actual magazine. This magazine also provides a syllabus and information to accompany the models, free of charge. (More reference is made to *Pictorial Education* in Chapter 5, p. 144.) Pamela Mays pays particular attention to the making of dolls representing people of the past. These are made from bottles, wire, pipe-cleaners, papier mâché, and rolled paper. She also describes how to make different masks which the children can wear to represent different historical characters. All these experts have their special interests and teachers must decide which suits them, their children and circumstances best. They all help children, especially the less academic, to feel for people in the past.

It is obvious that the enthusiasts who write about art work and model-making have been able to work in adequate surroundings physically. As already mentioned, primary teachers have the in-built advantage of their own classroom, occasionally with a store-room attached, and they can plan how to use their room's table and display facilities to suit their way of teaching. Thus it is essential to have more actual space than the space allotted for desks/tables and chairs, blackboard, etc. Certain parts of the classroom should be reserved for history, probably one table and part of the display boarding as well as a good share of reference books in the class library. In the store-room (if any) there should be different colours and types of paper, from plain white drawing paper to coloured sugar paper. Also card, cardboard and corrugated cardboard, boxes, balsa wood, polystyrene, end-toilet rolls, and matchboxes should be stored. A large box could be kept for children bringing 'throw-out' materials ready for practical work. In addition, plastic ceiling tiles and the packing from electric equipment are useful. As well as these items pencils, crayons, felt pens, paint brushes, glue, and paint are essential preparation for modelling. The ingenuity and resourcefulness of juniors, particularly older juniors, should not be underestimated and one should never be pessimistic about the reality of the final product if careful use is made of pictures in reference books. Shirley Makin shows how even visually handicapped children can make figures to represent 'Edward' and 'Eleanor' in her account of telling a story (pp. 69–72).

Pictures, models, and friezes are three usual types of practical work in history. The first two are suitable for all age ranges between 5 and 11 but particularly for the 5- to 8-year-olds. From the reception class, children draw and crayon readily. In spite of their inclination to draw very small flowers/figures/articles/animals on a large page, children should be encouraged to use wax crayons to draw bold pictures filling the page, following the advice of Henry Pluckrose in *Let's Work Large*. Pictures should always be given a title by the teacher and as soon as possible by the child in a word or a sentence. From the point of view of the past children must know what they are trying to represent, even if their effort is not at all representative! Later on painting, collage work (glueing material to a background), cloth pictures, and embroidery are appropriate. Younger children usually prefer to make their own individual matchbox model, but as experience grows and they become more capable of cooperative work, collective models can be made (e.g., a medieval walled town). For example a 'line of development' built up in a topic such as 'the village through the ages' or 'the development of housing' may be undertaken by different groups of children providing the different stages of development. An all-age primary school in Liverpool built most of its history/handwork on models of buildings, landscape, figures, and animals described in local sources for the town. The additional advantage in this small school was vertical grouping so that the older juniors worked with infants to create sea front scenes of Liverpool in the seventeenth century and Everton Lane in 1790.[16]

Besides the free-standing model, made either individually or collectively, other types of model easily made are the relief model, the diorama, and the tableau. They are explained by John Fairley on page 117 in *Patch History and Creativity*.[11] The relief model usually depicts an outdoor scene or a map needing two-dimensional treatment. A strong wooden or cardboard base is needed and a paper scene up the wall at the back depicting the distant landscape. John Fairley's example is the Norman invasion fleet approaching the English coast. He also suggests using shoe boxes for small dioramas depicting a single event such as William I's coronation in Westminster Abbey. This is usually the work of one or two children and can be easily moved about, suffering little damage in the classroom. The Millikens speak of dioramas being useful for display of individual figures as well as a particular event. They suggest either shoe boxes or a shelf of a glass-fronted bookcase. Such dioramas at their best may be seen at the Geffrye Museum, Shoreditch, and the Science Museum, South Kensington. Tableaux are a cross between the free-standing model (large or small) and the enclosed diorama. They are easy to use if there is display boarding on the wall and tables pushed up to them. As they can be extensive, a group of children can be involved, some drawing and painting the back-cloth and others making the models of buildings and people for the table. R. J. Unstead provides a sketch of a tableau depicting a Tudor town scene with the cathedral on the back-cloth, street, part of the town wall, and a 'Globe' type theatre.[9] He suggests attaching the background picture to stiff card or wood so that the whole tableau can be moved.

A form of craft work almost always undertaken by a large group of children, but more often by the whole class, is a picture sequence frieze. This requires adequate length of display board round the room or at least at the back of the classroom. This type of work is a great help to the building up of a time sense since the pictures must be arranged in the correct historical sequence. The obvious frieze sequence is the Bayeux Tapestry, an eleventh-century embroidery showing William of Normandy's preparations for invading England, his crossing the Channel, the Battle of Hastings, and William's final coronation as King of England. Although the whole tapestry cannot be depicted, key scenes may be selected; on pages 113–14 of his book[11] John Fairley suggests eight scenes from Harold's oath of allegiance to William in Normandy to William's victory at Hastings and the death of Harold.

It is impossible to mention all ways of using art and model-making in the teaching of history, but more individualistic approaches than the one discussed are: the making of mosaics from potato, wood, or lino cut (Tony Hart, *Fun with Historical Projects*, p. 35), making stained-glass windows from polythene bags (John Fairley,[11] p. 18), making medieval musical instruments (Alison and Michael Bagenal, *This Merry Company*, Oxford University Press, 1979, and *Teacher's Book*, pp. 25–32) and the whole industry of brass-rubbing and stone-rubbing. More is said about brass-rubbing in Chapter 5 (pp. 196–197). Stone-rubbing in graveyards is less expensive though it requires permission; Liverpool juniors are 'developing skills of research and recording'[18] while rubbing the grave of a member of the Norris family who died in 1726 (Fig. 4.9). Kenneth Lindley's book *Graves and Graveyards* (Local Search Series, Routledge and Kegan Paul, 1972) is invaluable for teachers.

If children do not keep notebooks or files, display of work is the best form of recording and allows children to learn from each other. It would be nice to think of a history display for each term in which the past is taught and children should be encouraged to help with its mounting from as early an age as possible. So much depends upon the temperament and training of individual teachers, but one would hope for an artistic presentation, each item relating to the others and not too complicated, with clear captions telling the story of the past. The whole display should be at the correct level for the smallest children to look at and read. At least one session should be spent discussing it and getting individual children to talk about their contribution. If possible other classes should be introduced to the work so that all may benefit. Some teachers prefer to have an 'on-going' history table in the same way as the nature table, but this is more difficult to maintain intact without a display case. No display should be kept up for more than two weeks at

Fig. 4.9 Developing skills of research and recording (by permission of Liverpool Corporation)

the most. A most helpful booklet, written by an art specialist, Ruth Phelps, *Display in the Classroom* (Blackwell, 1969), gives more detailed help which applies as much to history displays as to many others.

This section of Chapter 4 has been concerned with how children can learn about the past from art work and model-making. Earlier parts of the book have discussed how this type of material can be used for teaching purposes. Work of this kind should be done in the primary years both as an individual task, a group effort, and as a class project. It has natural display potential which is a normal culmination for any topic in the primary school. Two considerations should always be borne in mind. One is that variety in the use of these different practical methods of work should always be retained. Yet one teacher should not take on too many different approaches, so never becoming reasonably successful in any one or two. The other is that practical work should always be an illustration, as in the case of field work, of some part of the normal syllabus.

Claire Parker's description of an Elizabethan project illustrates a variety of teaching methods: model-making, field work, oral work as well as role-playing.

How I teach an Elizabethan project—Hinchingbrooke House to 9–11-year-olds

This work, based on the 'box of delights' provided by Mr Bagenal, our adviser, was done towards the end of the school year and the children were ready and able to approach a project in a mature and lively manner. I introduced them to the topic at the end of the previous term and sent home a brief plan of the proposed work for the benefit of the parents. I have found that in this way the parents often help their child to look forward to the term in a practical way by pointing out related TV films, books, and postcards etc.

During the holidays I prepared work cards in conjunction with those sheets provided by Mr Bagenal. These were mainly to be used as a formal hand-out type of card for those times when a child needs extra written work to enjoy or needs the security of a set framework within which to work. Also during the holidays I ordered the books most suitable from the school's library service and supplemented them with the best selection of pictures and postcard presentations available. These I arranged or mounted in readiness for the class's arrival on the first day of the term. My own personal preparation of the subject involved as much reading as possible of the more palatable biographies of Elizabethan personalities, novels based on the period, research into the history of the period, and the buildings of the time to be found in my own school district. This early work was by far the most valuable preparation and 'keyed' me up to the subject in such a way as to enable me to be brimming over with infectious enthusiasm for the project.

Our first afternoon spent on the project began with a dramatic description by me of the return home of Sir Henry Cromwell to Hinching-brooke near Huntingdon. With the aid of some taped Elizabethan 'mood' music and the showing of pictures related to the theme, I endowed Sir Henry with the type of character I thought would most appeal to a large proportion of the boys in the class. This was the beginning of the role-choosing that I was so anxious to initiate. Within a very short time a large part of the class was keen to claim a role that suited their personality. Even within this one afternoon we covered most of the possible role-playing that could be used during the term, although I was very aware that I was rushing rather quickly into quite a few fields at once.

The net result of that first afternoon was a basic grasp of the following points:

1. Houses, transport, clothing, food etc. were very different and life was much narrower in all directions.
2. People could be put into four main groups:
   (a) the courtly set including famous personalities in the fields of government, the arts and explorers, as well as the queen herself;
   (b) the landowners of the countryside and their families who had power and money;
   (c) the domestic servant classes;
   (d) the outdoor and agricultural servants and those who lived a vagabond and roving existence.
3. The Cromwell family really existed and lived in our own district.
4. That research could fall into two categories—the particular: i.e. factual stories, and the general: i.e. ways of life, music, cooking, and gardening, etc.

The next lesson was taken up with making files to put their work in and drawing up a flowchart to their own specifications. This latter they had already had experience of and it helped them to see an overall picture of the work to come.

From this point on the work veered between the effort to experiment with the activities that would have been normal at that time, e.g., clothes making and cooking, writing and learning by heart of poems, music making, pretend falconry, and much enacting of daily life scenes at court, in the home, on the road, in the countryside, etc.—and the careful recording and research that would make up the basis of a written presentation.

A large-scale model of Hinchingbrooke House and its grounds was made, many self-portraits of the children in their roles were painted or collaged, costumes were made ready for presentation acting, music prepared, and dances learned ready for a performance.

Our final production, involving a visit by the parents, was much enjoyed by the children who had by this time become so involved in their role-play that they even spoke in their own style during such lessons as mathematics and P.E. In the production they enacted the visit of Queen Elizabeth to Hinchingbrooke House, her welcome there,

111

the entertainment for her as provided by the locals, family, and members of the court itself, speech-making, dancing, music, and the proffering of real food made by the children from recipes of the period.

I think that the role-playing afforded the children the best chance to become totally absorbed in the project and while drawing many children out of themselves in the play-acting they were able to take refuge from the very beginning in choosing very much *their* type of personality. For instance the one or two retiring little girls who would have blanched at the thought of acting, quite happily set about being mouse-like maidservants who scuttled with real authority about the room doing their menial jobs with great confidence. At the other end of the scale the two children—boy and girl—who had the greatest confidence and greater imaginations were able to extend themselves enormously within the roles of Queen and courtier, going to the lengths of using rather period style speech and grandiose gestures while conversing about facts of the time in a fairly erudite fashion.

Other events within the scheme were a visit to the Fitzwilliam Museum, Cambridge, which was greatly enjoyed, an inclusion of the music studied into a concert of other music, and a parents' afternoon when the children entertained those parents who could not come previously. This time we made a link up with a Yorkshire school who had studied the same project.

Claire Parker
Milton Road Junior School, Cambridge

4.9 Time charts

In this chapter the classroom operation has been looked upon from the point of view of the basic elements and the more ambitious and experimental ways of teaching history. So we reach the most important and most difficult part of teaching history—a sense of time—which practically may be linked to time charts. Sequence charts of pictures for younger children are ideal as a starting-point. Time charts are a source of learning for children, since the time chart used in the 7- to 8-year-old class may be further developed in the other three junior years, and also an outcome of their work in a particular year and eventually in the four years.

Time charts not only relate closely to the classroom operation but also to the syllabus, since most of the schemes suggested in Chapter 3 necessitate constant reference to time in order to be understood. Thus it is possible to think of time charts as providing a unifying factor in teaching the past in the junior school and the framework suggested by the 1978 primary school report. The problem of whether time should control the syllabus or vice versa will be discussed later in connection with Michael Pollard's views.

Time is of the essence of the past and many teachers and psychologists have viewed this difficult concept as a sufficient reason for not attempting to teach history, except as story, until at least the later junior years. It would be burdensome to describe the mountain of research done on this topic yet three names stand out as sufficient to summarize the pessimism prevalent until quite recently. Jean Piaget, the famous Swiss psychologist, though not directly concerned with teaching about the past, has strongly influenced all teachers of younger children by his belief that children go through stages in mental development roughly at certain ages. The stage needed to understand time is well into the secondary school! E. C. Oakden and Mary Sturt as long ago as 1922[18] found that the naming of a given year (at the time) was difficult up to the age of 7 or 8 and that only half a sample of 9-year-olds knew their own year of birth. Yet they were not entirely pessimistic since the concept of time apparently begins to develop at the age of 4 and teaching can improve this concept from that age. They concluded by praising the use of time charts in teaching:

> Time-charts could be much more extensively used than they are at present. The concrete and pictorial representation of a conventional and abstract thing is thus given to the child. In no school where the tests (i.e. their research tests) were carried out was a time-chart used.[19]

A third important contribution to the debate is made by Gustav Jahoda who, over 40 years later in 1963, believed that it was not until the age of 11 that children understood the implications of historical dates; age 11 is a 'turning point' in this concept development. Yet he also is not entirely pessimistic; 'Gradually around the age of five an ordering of past events into earlier or later begins to emerge.' He thinks that the difficulty of time charts might be overcome by planning them to work backwards in time starting from the child's present.[20] Thus psychologists have been very tentative about the ability of primary school children to understand time. But they are more hopeful than the Gittins Report on the Primary School (1967) which believed that even 11-year-old children could only understand time as far back as their grandparents and that time-lines were useless until children were 13 years of age.

This pessimism and caution of research psychologists has been borne out only to some extent by practising teachers. There is a steadily growing number of teachers who are willing to use time charts in an effort to teach the concept of time gradually during the 5–11 years of schooling. Mary Barnes in her book *Studies in Historical Method* published in 1904 came to the conclusion that children could not understand time because they were not taught properly:

> I think then, that, in teaching History a child should always have by him a chart of centuries, as one has a map of the world, so that the children may place their heroes in time, as they do in space.

She records how one 9-year-old girl in an American school said to her mother:

> I shall always try to keep my History book, because it has something very precious in it. It has a long line running through two or three pages all marked off in pieces, and each piece is a hundred years, and it tells you just where people are.[21]

Allowing for the Edwardian turn of phrase this child obviously understood the past better when using a time-line; it was her anchor and security in the mass of events and people.

The only full-scale treatment of time charts yet published is Helen Madeley's *Time Charts* (Historical Association pamphlet No. 50, 1921, reprinted five times up to 1954—now out of print). Although Helen Madeley is mainly concerned with the use of time charts of various types for children aged 10–14, much of her experience is useful to teachers of younger children. She suggests the folding time chart (or card) of pictures of historical events and people put in the right chronological sequence; this 'panorama chart for young children' may be opened at one picture or any number to its full extent and it can stand up on a table. She also emphasizes the need for simplicity and few entries on the time chart, and compares the necessity for the chart in time with the map in space.

Sir Fred Clarke believed that young children could learn the concepts of change, duration, and sequence of events but not dates which could just become 'telephone numbers' if learnt by rote. He also cautioned against children assuming that a later date betokened advances in man's way of life. C. F. Strong is more cautious than many writers before him when he says: 'As to the sense of time, this should not be touched at all', at least until the later junior years when clock time is learnt and then charts should only be related to the child's family. By 1956 R. J. Unstead is not so positive; teachers should certainly use them themselves in their preparation and make them for children to use. He thinks that few juniors like making charts themselves (the skeleton plan) but like using them and adding their own pictures to them in the appropriate places. Probably influenced by Plowden, John Blackie is honest when he says: 'There is no general agreement about what should be done'. Like Strong and Pollard he wants to use a time chart only when related to the child's life and going back about 150 years. As in Strong's book his time charts are varied ones from top to bottom of the page.

More will be said later about construction of time charts. Michael Pollard agrees with short time charts, starting with the present and going back for not more than 200 years. There should also be constant cross-referencing by the teacher to relate projects, stories, and all parts of the past to the time chart. Michael Pollard writes: 'Presenting a child with a time-chart is like presenting a traveller in an unknown country with a map from which the scale and key are missing.'[22] A child must be taught how to use a time chart as he must be taught how to use a map.

Yet these somewhat doubtful words of encouragement are not echoed by those experienced with the 5–7 age range. Three pieces of research work offer more hope. Professor Ruth Beard believes that Piaget and Sturt are too pessimistic; she found that infants could say the date of the year and know the names of the days on which they had arranged to attend parties and go out to play.[23] The authors of a book about language and young children—*Understanding Children Talking*—give a delightful example of 3-year-old Stephen saying to his mother 'I used to be a little boy years ago'.[24] I am sure that Stephen could easily use time charts with success by the time he reached his eighth birthday! F. Dobson found that children aged 5–9 years had more advanced concepts of 'time' than 'movement' and 'speed' and believes that purposive training with clocks and time charts can accelerate learning.[25]

Time-lines and charts are best made by the teacher and duplicated for each pupil or made by older juniors. The commercially-produced time charts are usually overcrowded and confusing. A new set of folding time charts (for individual use) or wallcharts (for display) have just been published by Oxford University Press (1980). They are *The Unfolding Past* by Patrick Gordon and could be useful to top juniors for reference. Six books or charts are in the series. They may be used as pictorial display and analysed *after* work has been taught on home-made charts. Two recent series of books (discussed in Chapter 5) use pictorial charts for reference purposes. Figure 4.10 comes from the last page of a pamphlet by Peter Reynolds in which time is viewed as a winding road from the horizon to the present day. In *Norman and Medieval Britain* by Ray Mitchell and Geoffrey Middleton (*History in Focus* Series No. 3. Longman, 1980), time is shown as a long book mark, part depicting the period covered in this particular book (i.e., 1066–1485). These examples of recently-published time charts show a reversion to more traditional practice. The particular appeal of time charts is personal and ideally teachers should evolve their own.

Pamela Mays illustrates a time clock in her book (Fig. 4.11) from which I have drawn a time clock of a monk's day (Fig. 4.12), using information in various textbooks. In this, 'work of the day' is the time

Fig. 4.10 Time as the winding road (from *Cassivellaunus, the Celtic King* (Teacher's Notes) by Peter Reynolds, in History First Series, Tom Corfe (ed.), Cambridge University Press, 1979)

when some monks worked as gardeners, some as farmers, some as builders, some as fishermen, some as teachers, and some copying manuscripts. The names of religious services are in capital letters on shaded parts of the clock face. There were different kinds of monasteries and all monks did not have exactly the same kind of day.

There is no doubt that every classroom should display a large time-line or time chart on one, easily-seen wall and it should be a permanent tool for teacher and pupils to use in all their work. In addition, each child, even from the age of 6 should have a time-line/chart in the middle of his notebook or file across the double-page spread for reference in relation to the year's work. Children aged 6–8 will need a duplicated

The clock tells the time: 1650

Fig. 4.11 A time clock (from *Why Teach History?*, P. Mays, University of London Press, 1974)

sheet made by the teacher fastened on to the double-page spread. Older juniors can make their own time charts using a ruler and coloured biros. Since time charts have been considered old-fashioned in recent years, inadequate research has gone into the best form of a time chart. As children learn to write on the page from left to right I have found from experience that a horizontal time-line running from left to right is the most effective. The earliest date should start the chart on the left and the present day, or nearer the present day, should be on the far right. Plenty

117

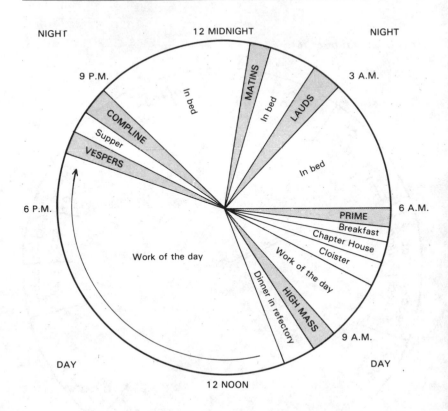

Fig. 4.12 Time clock of a monk's day

of room should be allowed in the depth of the chart, on wall or book page, for illustrations and writing in the older age ranges.

The use of time charts in the years 5–11 varies very much according to age. Time-lines in the infant school must be linked to the past that is being taught, therefore reference should be made to Chapter 3 (pp. 22–29). Family history in the second year seems to be the suitable time to start using a very short life-line of the child's own life from birth to 7, divided into single years thus:

YEARS

I am ── 1 ── 2 ── 3 ── 4 ── 5 ── 6 ── 7

118

Pictures illustrating three or four main events of the child's life could be drawn in the appropriate space, which should allow for drawings. For example, a cradle could depict the birth of a brother/sister and an animal the addition of a dog/cat/tortoise to the household. During the second and third term a class time-line could be made by the teacher large enough to include the local topics and visits made. This would be too intricate for each child to have in his book in addition to his own seven years. They could add pictures to the class time-line if there was enough depth to it. In many cases the class time-line will cover only 100 years (1880–1980) since many areas only yield comparatively recent history for local topics and visits. Thus the 7-year-old would enter the junior school with his own life-line to take with him, having learnt his first understanding of time from a large time-line left in the infant school for future use.

In the junior school, where it is to be hoped that one member of staff will be responsible for history, a more thorough use can be made of time charts. It would seem wise to have a large classroom chart covering the syllabus undertaken and accompanying the class through the four years

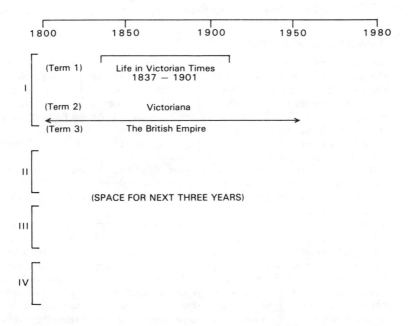

Fig. 4.13 Time chart for the heritage of later English and world history 1800–1980 (7–11 years)

in the school. This should be started simply but be put on a stout roll of paper large enough to accommodate many additions on its life through the school. In addition, each pupil should have a chart on the double-page spread of his notebook for the particular years of the past studied in one year. For example the syllabus *The Heritage of Later English and World History 1800–1980* (p. 33) could use the time chart in Fig. 4.13. In addition each child would have in his notebook separate charts for *Life in Victorian Times* and *The British Empire* adding more detail as the work advanced. During the third and fourth years pupils themselves might make a classroom time chart to supplement and possibly take over from the one started in their first year and just concentrating on the two years' work. It is important for notebooks from previous years to be kept so that children can refer to them in following years.

Time charts are a practical way to learn and a useful teaching aid as well as an 'outcome' or record of children's work. But they are only one aid to teaching and are not an immediate cure for lack of time-concept. They should be a start to the ultimate aim of the history teacher that his pupils should be able to 'move freely and easily in time' (in the words of Lord Briggs). It should also be remembered that other problems besides time beset the history teacher, and time-concept, which only develops gradually, should not be over-emphasized.

Thoughts on time charts

English primary school teachers have expressed a lack of confidence in the use of time charts. Such has been the effect of minimal research on the classroom. There is, in fact, no reason whatever why a classroom time chart should not prove to be a useful, everyday guide for children at any age from 7 to 13. Indeed, such charts can become a colourful aid to children's learning, enabling them to visualize periods of time, one in relation to another, or assist them to span either long eras or short generations at a glance.

Recent research with children aged 7–11 has demonstrated that primary school children are, even without in-school training, adept at recognizing many historical stereotypes and placing these in an accurate sequence. Teachers will find that most children aged 7–9 and afterwards will fairly easily sequence three separate items in time as first, last, and 'one in the middle'. With practice on a time-line this ability, by the age of 12, can be seen to extend itself considerably to the recognition and accurate sequencing of up to 10 or a dozen selected items. Primary school children can master, first sequence, then duration and even at length, relative scale from one period to another. They are, contrary to popular belief, most able at dealing with aeons of time, 'long long ago', as opposed to more recent, closely-knit generations or centuries. Sequencing tests, easily devised by the teacher, will demonstrate that the average child aged 7–9, with practice, will more readily sequence accurately a fossil, a dinosaur, and prehistoric tools, the pyramids and the Crucifixion, than master, backwards, the events of the past two centuries (for example, Concorde, The Flying Scotsman, a 1914 'Tommy', an antique telephone, and Napoleon). The earlier stereotypes are easier to recognize, easier to 'chunk' age by age. It is misleading to assume that children will assimilate a sense of time more confidently if they work backwards, at least beyond the family experience of their grandparents' generations.

When teachers complain that young children 'have no sense of time', this should usually be translated as having 'no sense of *number* associated with time'. The six-year-old who can accurately sequence ten prehistoric tools from a massive palaeolithic hand-axe to a delicate mesolithic microlith will resort to guesswork if he is asked to estimate their ages or their distance 'ago'. The same faulty mathematics will apply until the age of 13, even though the simple processes of place-order, of subtraction and addition have been well mastered in mathematics lessons. Children take some years to understand the association of number with time. Thus, well-meant time-lines drawn up in rigidly numbered intervals or dated partitions will prove to be misleading. Better by far to introduce and develop in the classroom or along the school corridor, down the length of the hall or across the playground, a time-line which is flexible, changeable, and, above all, verbal. This line should be used for a constant reference, so that all work done with any type of historical evidence, whether it be stories, museum objects, textbook extracts, pictures, or documents can be given its proper place in sequence. Its key points, verbally, should be 'now'; 'then'; 'present'; 'past'; 'recent', 'remote', 'long ago'; 'long long ago'; 'in the beginning', etc. To make this type of time-line requires the simplest of materials, preferably a length of clothes line, as long as the dimensions of the teaching space will allow, and some clothes pegs, curtain rings, paper clips, or any device which will permit a symbol or picture to be attached to the line in such a way that it can be easily moved from place to place.

There is a mistaken belief that we can teach chronology by teaching chronologically. Nothing could be further from the truth. Evidence from the past comes at children from all periods and times in a haphazard fashion. No child goes out into the environment and finds houses neatly arranged in chronological order nor sees any other evidence of the past so conveniently ordered. Impressions, anecdotes, pictures, stories, assail him from all parts of the past in random order. His task is to sort and set these into a meaningful chronological sequence; our task is to enable him to do so. The teacher who begins with the earliest item of evidence and painstakingly moves chronologically from period to period fails the child who is absent for a time, changes schools or cannot retain the laborious sequence in his memory. It is far better to offer children short bursts of assorted historical material and require them to practise its rearrangement.

To this end, the most useful device is a ten-picture sequence-card consisting of five to a dozen assorted pictorial stereotypes, each taken from a different historical age. Children can, first, identify each item and discover all they can about it from their history books; second, place

121

each picture in its correct sequential position on the time-line. One such card can best be used among a class divided into five groups of six children each. Each group can then be allocated two of the ten given stereotypes. Their immediate task is simply to order these as 'earlier' and 'later'. Group by group then come to terms with each other on the overall sequence from first to last. If the time-line is conveniently placed along a wall above, first, a length of soft display board and, second, a lower shelf, then as well as placing pictures, the class can add written extracts and solid objects.

The collection of chosen stereotypes should always include at least one very remote item and one very modern article and an illustration from Christ's Life, The Nativity, the Crucifixion, or the Last Supper to establish the 'BC–AD' demarcation. Several pairs of items, which together span almost exactly a century or a millennium, for example, the *Rocket* and the *Flying Scotsman*, Waterloo and Mons, The Crucifixion and Hastings, Hastings and Apollo 13, are also necessary at a later stage. Such intervals can act as markers by which the children will scale their time-line. For example, if from the corner of the room to 'there' takes us to Hastings, then the further distance from Hastings to the Crucifixion must be almost equal. If the distance between the *Rocket* and the *Flying Scotsman* is about a foot, then the distance from 'now' to the Crucifixion must be 20 feet. Given practice, most primary school children will begin to appreciate that there are several ways of scaling the time-line; either we add more and more length at its remotest end or we crowd the recent events more closely together.

The extent to which any teacher involves her class in the essential calculation of age or duration from date is a matter of purely local convenience. Some nine-year-old classes will be ready to undertake the necessary calculations, others will not. Generally speaking, it appears that not enough practice is given in this process, even after the children have mastered the simple rules of mathematics. Primary school children who can cope with the calculations from 100s to units experience insurmountable difficulty if 1000 is added to the place value but the original figures remain the same. (Thus, 980 minus 52 will be relatively easy at 10, 1980 minus 52 may cause confusion.)

Much of the work on time-lines will extend itself into writing, note-taking, individual research, mathematical calculation and the creation of personal time charts, copied into personal notebooks. Some teachers may wish to develop separate lines on different scales; a common feature is to expand one, usually recent, section of the time-line, enlarging it or focusing on to it a separate expansion scale. Similarly, the problems of the past extent of early times, if one once includes a dinosaur, a fossil, or the creation, often leads the teacher into a complex convention of up-scaling the most remote periods at a different level from the recent (copious balls of string, winding tracks and projection beyond the classroom window are some of these devices). One fears that these may only serve to confuse the child; it is better to use a consistent length of wall for all purposes, scaling and re-scaling it as required, rather than endeavouring to make the same scale eternally applicable. Thus, in one term, a 30 foot wall might illustrate the 10-year life time of the child, during the next term might represent the past century and, in the third term, might extend to the life of Christ. During the next school year, one might use the same 30 feet to represent 30 000 years or even three million. Thus, the children will become accustomed to the concepts of time-scale. While it may become convenient in this process to establish certain well-known dates, such as 1980, 1066, AD 33 or 4000 BC such time-marks should not proliferate. Nor should it be necessary for the current time-line to become fossilized and dog-eared by use (this is an argument against the use of lengthy rolls of frieze paper and in favour of the simple clothes line). Children should be encouraged repeatedly to thin out, take down and re-make their classroom line, taking up the most useful time-marks with them to the next class and establishing some of these as the basis for the next year's work.

Frequent discussion of the construction of the line should become a regular part of lessons about the past. Children should be offered their own opportunities to place items as they estimate them; teachers should be prepared to accept some temporary placings in error provided that there are opportunities to discuss and eventually adjust those placings. Oral discussion of the time-line should be a regular feature of the week's work. A glossary of terms such as 'generation', 'decade', 'century', 'millennium', 'before Christ', 'period', and 'age' should be compiled. By the age of 11–13, each child should have become familiar with such terms as 'prehistoric', medieval', 'classical', 'modern', and 'geological'. Generally speaking, the time-line should be developed as a linguistic exercise.

John West
Chief Inspector for Dudley LEA

4.10 Conclusion

How relevant to history that 'time' should be the culmination of a chapter on the classroom operation. Another look at the diagrammatic summary of the chapter in Fig. 4.1 will show that 'time' does dominate half of the two interlinking circles. Primary school teachers seriously interested in teaching the past should spend at least two years in working on the inner circle, the basic methods, building up expertise, resources and generating enthusiasm to colleagues through the excitement and good work done by even an individual class. As the high quality work of this class bubbles out into the rest of the school by display and word of mouth, the second circle may be started. No one teacher or one school will use all the methods in the diagram, but by trial and error the way forward for that school will be discovered. All will be well as long as 'time' and 'evidence' (how do we know?) are of paramount importance in the teacher's thinking.

123

References

1. K. Egan, *Educational Development*, Oxford University Press, 1979, p. 17.
2. J. Fines, 'Trainee teachers of history and infants as learners', *Teaching History*, no. 26, 1980.
3. C. B. Firth, *The Learning of History*, Kegan Paul, 1929.
4. *The Schools Council Project on Gifted Children* has done some interesting work on the Bayeux Tapestry (yet to be published).
5. Obtainable from the Archivist, City Records, Civic Centre, Southampton.
6. P. J. Rogers and R. H. Adams, *Forms of Knowledge, Ways of Knowing and 'Discovery' Learning: Thoughts on 'Discovery Learning'*, Queen's University, Belfast, 1979.
7. *Schools Council Project: Communication Skills 3–11.*
8. A. Blyth *et al.*, *Curriculum Planning in History, Geography and Social Science*, Collins and ESL Bristol, 1975, pp. 113–119.
9. R. J. Unstead, *Teaching History in the Junior School*, A. & C. Black, 1956, pp. 56–58, and 63.
10. The last two examples are taken from R. J. Unstead, ibid., p. 83.
11. J. Fairley, *Patch History and Creativity*, Longmans, 1970, p. 79.
12. M. Le Fevre, 'Introducing history to young children', *Teaching History*, vol. 1, no. 2, 1969.
    J. Salt, 'Approaches to field work in History in the primary school', *Teaching History*, vol. 1, no. 3, 1970.
    D. Hubbard, 'Let's build a castle', *Teaching History*, vol. 2, no. 6, 1971.
    P. Wenham, 'The Leeds and Liverpool canal: the development of a Schools Council project in one education authority', *Teaching History*, vol. 4, no. 16, 1976.
13. T. Corfe (ed.), *History Field Work*, Blond, 1970, p. 37.
14. F. J. Johnson and K. J. Ikin, *History Field Work*, Macmillan, 1974, p. 3.
15. H. Pluckrose, *Let's Use the Locality*, Mills and Boon, 1971, pp. 173–180.
16. E. E. Newton, 'An Evertonian spilling-over', *Teaching History*, vol. 1, no. 4, 1970.
    E. Happer and J. E. Blyth, 'Model-making as an approach to local history in the middle school', *Teaching History*, vol. 1., no. 3, 1970.
17. The words of John West who organized the expedition.
18. E. C. Oakden and M. Sturt, 'The development of the knowledge of time in children', *The British Journal of Psychology*, vol. XII, 1922.

19. Ibid., pp. 335–6.
20. G. Jahoda, 'Children's concepts of time and history', *Educational Review*, vol. 15, no. 2, 1963.
21. M. S. Barnes, *Studies in Historical Method*, D. C. Heath & Co., 1904, p. 101.
22. M. Pollard, *History with Juniors*, Evans, 1973, p. 8.
23. R. Beard, *An Investigation of Concept Formation among Infant School Children*, Ph.D. thesis, London, 1957.
24. N. Martin, P. Williams, J. Wilding, S. Hemmings, and P. Medway, *Understanding Children Talking*, Penguin, 1976.
25. F. Dobson, *A Study of the Concepts of Time, Movement and Speed Among Primary School Children*, M.A. thesis, Southampton, 1967.

5. Sources and Resources

5.1 Introduction

In contrast with the materials and procedures appropriate to science, mathematics, art and craft and music, the nature of history lends itself to reading, discussion, and writing, within the confines of the normal classroom. Therefore, it is essential for the teacher of history to younger children to consciously prepare forms of activity through which children can learn. These are the resources to be discussed in this chapter. What is taught (syllabus) and how it is taught (method) will not be effective without the 'tools of the trade'. 'The classroom operation' is dependent upon at least a minimum of resources.

With money too scarce in the 1980s even to provide an adequate teaching force in the primary schools, emphasis must be put on the better use of resources already acquired and the creation of new resources from cheap and easily obtainable materials. During the 1960s many schools were provided with more material resources than is now possible, but even then the teaching force was not given much assistance in coping with these resources. Teachers' Centres were established by many local education authorities but these were inevitably at a distance from many schools and often closed in the evenings. It was only the young, fit, and highly motivated teacher owning a car who could 'make it' to the Centre at 4 p.m. to take advantage of the brief remaining time available! Yet dependence on Teachers' Centres was particularly important for primary schools, since even in the 'time of plenty' in the 1960s most primary schools could not accumulate appropriate resources of their own, for they lacked the basic capitation allowance required, and the support which secondary schools could more easily command. As L. C. Tayor has honestly written in *Resources for Learning* (Penguin, 1972): 'The major obstacle in any change from a teaching-based to a resource-based system of learning is the *time* [my italics] it takes to produce, to collect, to arrange the required resources.'[1] I should like to add to this, from personal experience, and 'to care for, store, and check' resources.

Therefore in this chapter I am not going to list in detail the ideal resources for teaching history to 5- to 11-year-olds but to talk about practicalities for the 1980s, remembering that history is to be undertaken in a crowded curriculum and that all pr carry an excessive load in preparation and marking. disagree with L. C. Taylor, when in an otherwise excellen of the primary school: 'A single teacher can look after varied learning activities of a class of children throughout ... day and, with enterprise and hard work, supply most of the resources needed.'[2]

How can the past be learnt and enjoyed from slender resources? The outline chart (Fig. 5.1) summarizes my main argument in this chapter. The teacher has a central position as the key resource; in the words of a practising primary teacher: 'In the end, of all the resources at the disposal of a school, the teacher is the most important.' These words start a chapter called 'Human Resources' in *A Handbook of Resources in the Primary School* by Michael Pollard.[3] Therefore the first order resources are closely dependent upon the well-being of the teacher; blackboard, use of paper and note-books, oral work, and the putting up of displays. Other resources depend upon the teacher but to a lesser extent. The second order resources are books of all kinds, source material in books, documents and packs (units), family and oral history. The third order resources are mechanical aids; films, filmstrips, tapes, discs, radio and television programmes. Finally, resources outside school must be considered specifically; museums, field work, Teachers' Centres, in-service courses, and help given by Schools Council projects. The last three categories are useful in themselves but depend for implementation upon the teacher who is the prime resource. Relevant books on resources for learning about the past are *Teaching History 8–13* by George McBride (published by the Teachers' Centre, The Queen's University, Belfast, 1979), particularly Section III 'Resources for teaching history'; *A Handbook of Resources for Primary Schools* by Michael Pollard (Ward Lock Educational, 1976); and *Treasure Chest for Teachers* (Teachers Publishing Co. Ltd, Derbyshire House, Lower Street, Kettering, Northamptonshire, NN16 8BB, 1978).

5.2 First order resource—the teacher

More than most subjects history demands more from the teacher than from any other resource—which may account for it being taught badly in both primary and secondary schools, and also for many primary teachers opting out of teaching it altogether. As in all areas of the curriculum in the primary school the class teacher has a vital role to play; she must know her children individually and be able to maintain reasonable discipline. In addition, for history, she cannot depend much

127

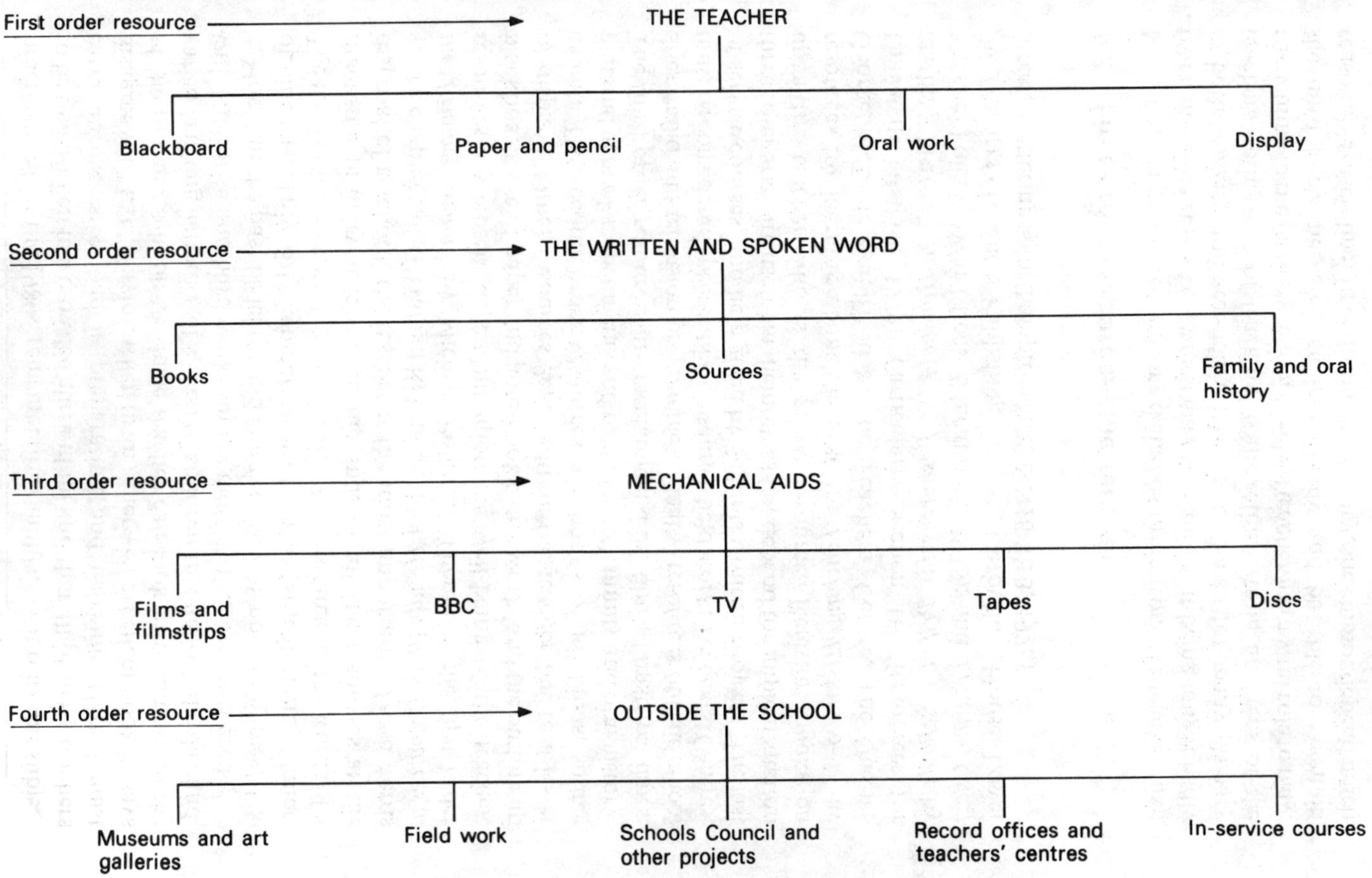

Fig. 5.1 Sources and resources in order of accessibility

First order resource →

THE TEACHER
- Blackboard
- Paper and pencil
- Oral work
- Display

Second order resource

THE WRITTEN AND SPOKEN WORD
- Books
- Sources
- Family and oral history

Third order resource

MECHANICAL AIDS
- Films and filmstrips
- BBC
- TV
- Tapes
- Discs

Fourth order resource

OUTSIDE THE SCHOOL
- Museums and art galleries
- Field work
- Schools Council and other projects
- Record offices and teachers' centres
- In-service courses

upon textbooks in class and is unlikely to have had extensive professional guidance in history as such while at college. Thus she must acquire some information about her syllabus or scheme of work and must be prepared to tell a connected story and explain the events and people of the past in oral exposition and questioning. Therefore, her voice must carry to the back of the classroom and not irritate the children by being monotonous or dull. Many children gain a lifelong interest in the past from the enthusiastic and lively oral work of a primary school teacher. Above all, she must be a good organizer of material to handle the mass of facts of history, selecting the relevant and interesting ones, and to organize to advantage what resources she has collected to use for her lessons.

Closely connected with the teacher, her training and experience, as well as herself, is the blackboard which she has at her disposal. A surprisingly rare mention of this valuable resource is to be found in Pamela May's *Why Teach History?* (University of London Press, 1974). She says of individual aids: 'Strangely enough, the most important is the one that is most frequently forgotten. It is the blackboard.'[4] Therefore headteachers should make a practice of providing one or two roller blackboards to every classroom and should do their best to keep them in good condition and washed down regularly to ensure a black rather than a grey board! Careful organization of the blackboards for a morning's lessons, where possible rolling back work required later, is a sure sign of the efficient teacher. The board may be used for difficult words to spell, for summaries of lessons, for rapid drawing to illustrate, or for building up of a chart (Fig. 5.2). Different coloured chalks may be used for different purposes, yellow and orange standing out more than blue, green, or even red. Although we cannot all work with the dexterity of a Rolf Harris or a Tony Hart our match figures and efforts at ships on the sea evoke appreciative mirth and good learning even if the more artistic children could do better themselves! The teacher can always solicit the help of the artistically-gifted members of the class to fill in her ideas and outline.

Paper and cardboard of all sorts are a staple resource in all teaching and learning. This does not mean that recording by constant writing is recommended but that all children from 5 to 11 should value their history notebooks or files. Children, however young, should not undertake work on pieces of paper to be destroyed or lost. The 6-year-olds I worked with built up some drawing, sentence, or picture to be pasted in, about all our topics and took great pride in their large sugar paper 'books of the past'. These consisted of different coloured paper fastened to make a book, the cover of which they decorated with great

129

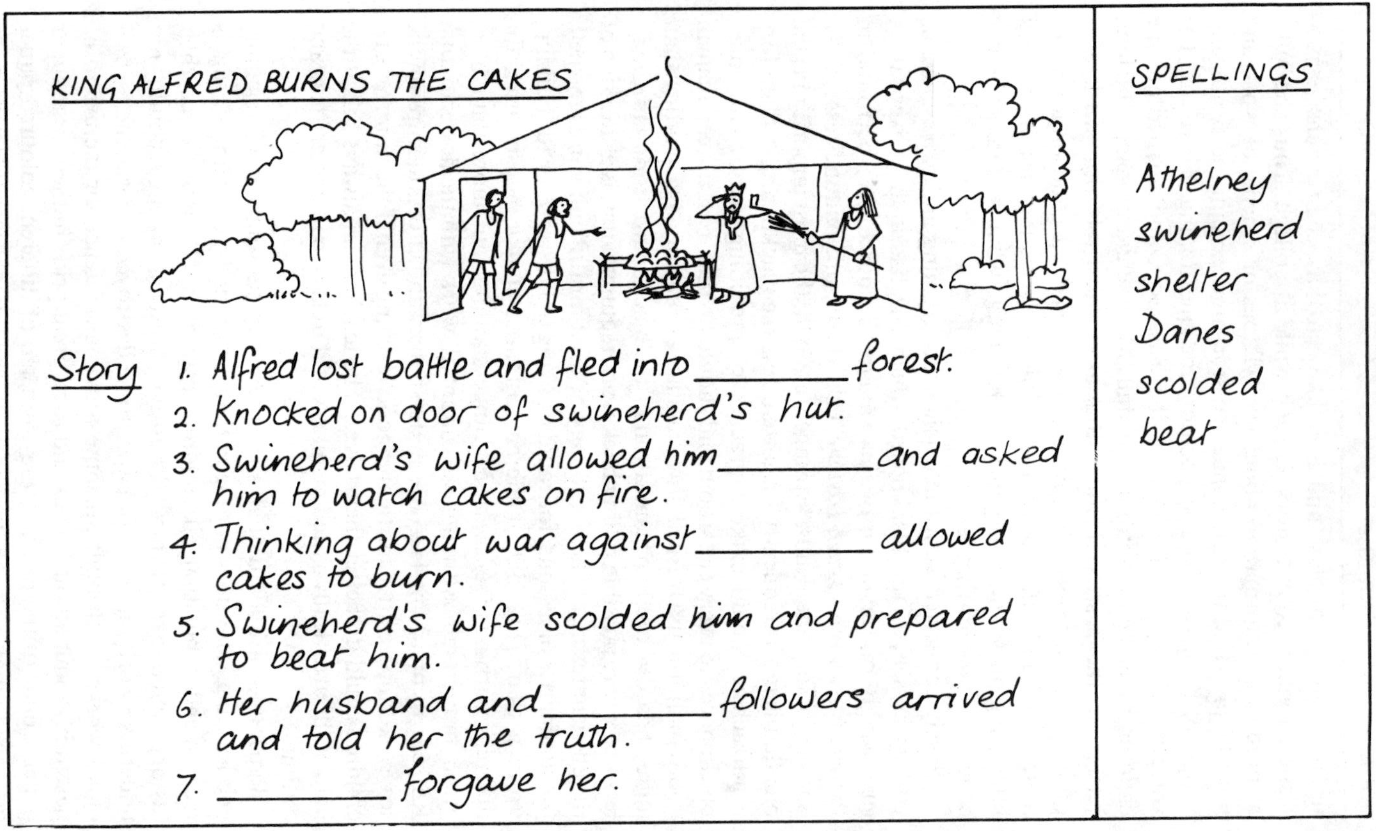

KING ALFRED BURNS THE CAKES

SPELLINGS

Athelney
swineherd
shelter
Danes
scolded
beat

Story

1. Alfred lost battle and fled into _____ forest.
2. Knocked on door of swineherd's hut.
3. Swineherd's wife allowed him _____ and asked him to watch cakes on fire.
4. Thinking about war against _____ allowed cakes to burn.
5. Swineherd's wife scolded him and prepared to beat him.
6. Her husband and _____ followers arrived and told her the truth.
7. _____ forgave her.

Fig. 5.2 How to use the blackboard

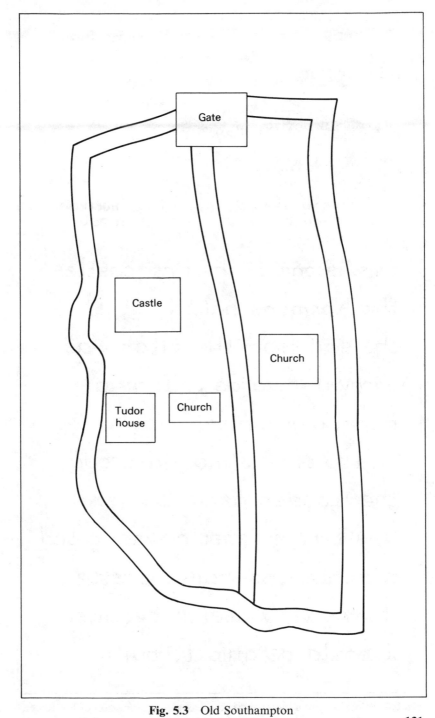

Fig. 5.3 Old Southampton

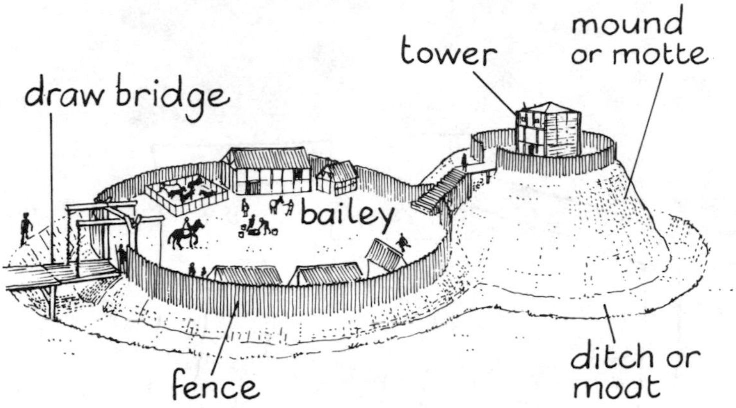

Labels on diagram: draw bridge, tower, mound or motte, bailey, fence, ditch or moat

this is one of the first castles
the Normans built.
the soil from the ditch was
thrown inwards to form a
mound or motte.
on top of this mound stood
the wooden tower.
this type of castle was called
a motte-and-bailey castle.
it was very useful because
it could be quickly built.

Fig. 5.4 Workcard on a motte and bailey castle (by permission of Pat Raper, Cholsey Infants' School)

1. what is the name of this fortress?

2. can you tell me <u>how</u> they were made and <u>why</u>?

3. why do you think they built towers?

4. can you find a book about castles and see what else you can find out?

5. how long would it take you to make a small castle like this?

6. would you like to live in such a castle?

pride. Pat Raper, a gifted Montessori teacher of infants with a real feeling for and knowledge of the past, was responsible for history in her school and each child in every class had large books entitled 'A yesterday book', 'A long ago book' and 'I remember book'. These were built up during the two infant years and each child was responsible for the contents and how it looked. The teacher is also responsible for making and duplicating worksheets, 'missing-word' compositions, charts and diagrams, individual time-lines to paste in the centre of notebooks (until the older juniors make their own), and illustrated workcards. An example of work prepared on paper for 6-year-olds is the plan of 'Old Southampton' (Fig. 5.3). The first letter only of each word would be given to the children to complete the word of the building from work done on the 1611 Speed map of Southampton. An example of a workcard prepared for 6-year-olds by Pat Raper is the folding card on a motte and bailey castle (Fig. 5.4). The teacher also uses deep rolls of white paper to prepare classroom time charts, already discussed. Paper is used regularly for drawings, and card, cardboard, and other materials for display purposes. Other uses of paper of all sorts are too many to list and are obvious to all primary teachers. It is essential to keep a well-organized store-room or cupboard with definite rules to which the children must adhere.

A third first-order function of the teacher is oral expression with the help of the blackboard, pictures, and models. Primary teachers are usually careful to use simple words and to check that children understand their meaning. Recent research on language in the classroom has been applied to the additional difficulties encountered in talking about the past. If infants from lower socio-economic groups are likely to understand only a 'restricted code' of language (according to Basil Bernstein), in their normal communication, they will find talk about the past even more difficult. Jeannette Coltham found that some 9-year-olds thought that the 'ruler of a country' was something to do with the ruler on their desk for measuring. Therefore teachers should explain very carefully the words that they use. As well as talking to the whole class the teacher also uses different methods of talking when helping individual children and groups of children. A teacher who has not been trained to address the class as a whole is very limited as a resource. When teaching history, it is essential to give some stimulus to the class as a whole before starting on individual or group work.

Much has already been said about display as a method and outcome of teaching but in a primary school this depends almost entirely on the initiative of the class teacher. Children should always be encouraged to assist and might take over some displays in the top class, but most ideas and hard work come from the teacher. One cannot imagine a successful classroom without lively and imaginative display using as many children's work as possible. Display should be changed after about two weeks and therefore, if display is an essential resource for learning, the teacher responsible for it is a key factor.

I have emphasized the teacher as a first order resource because all else is pointless without a good teacher. Those who cannot find appropriate other resources or who are irritated by the constant breakdown of the filmstrip projector (not always regularly serviced by the non-existent technician!) need not feel inadequate as teachers of history if they know their work, can handle children, and provide appropriate activity. There has also been a tendency, in spite of the good work of professional associations, to underestimate the importance of the teacher. Michael Pollard believes that class teachers should have outside assistance 'with repairing library books, preparing them for issue, mounting visual aids and making workcards', and 'typing chores in connection with classroom work'.[5] Therefore the other resources that I discuss in this chapter undoubtedly improve the teaching of history, but are not basic essentials. Each teacher must decide what she can manage to do to bring some variety into the teaching of the past. If one method works, keep it and save energy. If you are getting stale, change. You may then find it helpful to try out more of the resources to be discussed later in this chapter.

5.3 Second order resource—the written and spoken word

In history the teacher depends to a large extent on the written word and during the last 20 years she has been given generous support from publishers in the form of textbooks in series, resource books, charts, workcards, historical fiction, and advice about how to use children's families and the spoken words of old people. These all cost money and efforts must now be made to use what is already in the school and what can be carefully acquired to complement what is already in possession.

BOOKS

Michael Pollard devotes half of his very useful little book on resources to books. He presumes that primary schools have libraries, though this is seldom true. Some make use of wide corridors to house a library but this is inadequate for quiet reading and selection of books, and unsafe in these days, especially when doors are unlocked and strangers use the school in the evening. Dependence on small class libraries for topic work, particularly in the upper part of primary schools, is entirely inadequate. All children should be trained gradually to use a library for themselves and 7-year-olds should be introduced to the school library as soon as they enter the junior school. Senior pupils in primary schools should be used in dinner hours (usually too long for children's comfort) to take responsibility in the library and help younger children to find and read books. For many bright 7- and 8-year-olds with reading ages well above their chronological age, a class library is usually quite inadequate. Libraries should contain historical fiction, non-fiction and sets of books useful for 'topic' learning. Children should be encouraged to borrow non-fiction and class teachers could borrow sets of books for the class library for a limited period. Is it too much to hope that some day a scale post will be given to a teacher willing to run the library and that time from teaching will be given for this vital work? Michael Pollard devotes several pages of his book to advice on how to build up a reasonable library of history books as a core stock from which to develop as new publications and finances allow. His basic list is 24 topics as follows:[6]

Prehistoric animals	Communications
The ancient world	(perhaps subdivided)
Prehistoric man	Electricity
The Romans	Inventions
The Saxons	Discoveries
The Normans	Explorers
Children in history	Town life
Clothes	Homes
Entertainment	Country life
Farming	Industry
Fuel	(perhaps subdivided)
Local history	Government
Transport	Sport
(perhaps subdivided)	

He believes these to be basic topics and suggests that some books intended for secondary schools and adults can be very useful for their illustrations. Advice about how to judge the suitability of a book will be given in the section on 'Evaluation' in Chapter 6. If a school has a Parent/Teacher Association much can be done to encourage gifts of books no longer needed at home. In these days of shortage, schools, as well as charitable organizations, might as well gain from unwanted books. Michael Pollard gives advice on mending and preserving books as well as a whole chapter on 'The school library'.

It is a fortunate primary school that can boast a school library, but the staple diet of most children is the 'textbook' or a series of four books published by one firm and written by the same author or authors. Though better than nothing, the 'series of four' has serious limitations. In an original and stimulating article, mainly intended for secondary teachers, Philip Abrams[7], as long ago as 1964, questioned the historical value of textbooks and favoured the use of packs of source material. He rightly believes that of all school subjects, history is bedevilled by the dependence of teachers and class on textbooks and he lists the 'hazards of excessive authority, of meaninglessness and of bias'. Yet the effort to be objective has made many textbooks dull and he praises the works of a well-known writer of the past for juniors: 'Thus, a book with a frankly patriotic intention like R. J. Unstead's "England", is a better tool for the teacher and more stimulating reading for the child than many a more "objective" work.' His belief in source material encourages their use 'at any level, for infants or undergraduates'. To dullness may be added the fact that publishers can dictate the syllabus in a junior school by the sale of large sets of four books (often at a reduced rate for bulk purchase), which saddle the school for many years with one scheme of work. A third limitation is the idea transferred to pupils that one person is the fountain of knowledge in history, an idea more readily gained in schools unable to afford reference books on more detailed topics. A final limitation is that children look at one format, type of illustration, and 'activities' throughout four years.

Yet one has to admit that the four books in one series are normal and if they are there, in practice they must be used. How do we make the most of this unsatisfactory situation? It would be invidious to compare such series, and impossible to analyse the advantages and disadvantages of all series published. Therefore, presuming that 5- to 7-year-old children will not use 'textbooks', I am limiting my review to series specifically written for 7–11 schools, as distinct from middle schools, and to four series in particular; published in 1953 and frequently reprinted since then, R. J. Unstead's *Looking at History*, A. & C. Black; J. D. Bareham and M. Gleave's *Awake to History*, Pergamon, 1964; R. Mitchell and G. Middleton's *Living History*, Holmes McDougall, 1968; Philip Sauvain's *The Story of Britain*, Macmillan, 1980. The dates of publication show that these books are likely to be in use now. All four series are based on British history and their approach is chronological, all include narrative and illustration, and each series has specific additional features absent from the others. In using these books I am not in any way recommending or criticizing them. They happen to be examples I know and which I think are broadly representative of what is used in primary schools.

The narrative or story told in four parts by these books may be used as a resource in various ways. The uninformed teacher may need them for information to form the basis for her lesson and explanation. Or the children themselves may read them, if the worst comes to the worst even round the class. Children can also use the story to answer the activities questions at the end of the chapter. The two more recent series have the narrative printed in two columns for ease of reading, the Pergamon series having a particularly large, clean type-face for easier reading for slower children. A textbook is always useful for reference by the children while the teacher is explaining the work; pictures, words, maps can be easily referred to. Most textbooks have one or two out of four types of illustrations; accurately coloured contemporary reproductions, good photographs, black and white sketches copying contemporary pictures, and crude reconstructions depicting imaginary people and scenes. The last type are the cheapest to produce and therefore are all too common; they are usually too highly coloured and unreal historically. The illustrations in the selected books are a variety of these four types. The Pergamon books have surprisingly few illustrations considering that the books are intended for slow learners. In all cases the manuscript sources, photographs, and sketch-maps are more useful than the imaginary drawings; the latter are particularly unfortunate when depicting people. The Florence Nightingale in one book would be enough to give any sick soldier nightmares rather than comfort! Yet good illustrations remain a tremendously important resource for the teacher. Three of the four series include activities based on the narrative. Some teachers may prefer the A. & C. Black series which omits activities leaving teachers to make up their own. The Pergamon books list ten questions for children to ask one another (good idea) at the end of each topic, therefore these form a short factual test of the chapter. The other two series label this section of the book 'Something to do' although many of the activities involve 'thinking' rather than 'doing'. Rather too many of these suggestions would involve the teachers in more work, providing more detailed source material, and the test tries to cover so much ground that the children cannot gain any detailed information from the books. Very often the teachers would have to prevent attempts to answer some of the vague questions and substitute their own. Therefore teachers should read the activities very carefully and be selective before asking children automatically to answer the questions set. After the first year in the junior school it is advisable to provide different series of textbooks, especially if there is a dearth of reading books, so that children can at least see that the past does not come entirely from one source. This may be done, if two sets are becoming too dilapidated, by selecting two good half-sets and letting pairs of children have one each. This can lead to interesting comparisons by the children but the teacher herself should be careful to know both books. The illustrations in the dilapidated books could be used to make workcards (if ancillary assistance was available) or for children to cut up and paste into their own notebooks. This can also be done with the pictures from old BBC and ITV pamphlets.

Textbook series are only an introduction to wider reading in the third and fourth junior years. Small sets of reference books on detailed topics are essential. They may be kept in the library and brought into the classroom as needed for a month to half a term. Publishers have concentrated on the middle school age range following the lead given by Marjorie Reeves' *Then and There* series published by Longmans, but more help has been given to the 5- to 8-year-olds in the last few years. Reference books are indispensable as preparation for teachers and much more suitable than university-type history books. They are written for individual reading by children and are seldom intended to be read from cover to cover. Most of them have good indexes to be used for topic work and children should be taught how to use reference books effectively. It is also preferable to have at least two different reference books for each topic. Books owned by the school can usually be supplemented by loans from the local education authority library and/or the local branch library. By the third year of the junior school children should be sufficiently motivated to find suitable books themselves from the public library to augment the school collection.

History books for the first school are not published in profusion and many infant school teachers rely on the pictures in junior books to explain the past. Shirley Paice, deputy head of an infants' school, wrote with good sense in the *Times Educational Supplement*,[8] when she showed conclusively that young children do not read non-fiction information books because the books are not suitably written and therefore the children are not helped to do so:

> The aim of much modern education is self-initiated learning. For this one needs an acquaintance, a close friendship even, with books of a particular kind. These can be called reference books, information books, non-fiction of many kinds. This friendship should begin in the earliest years of reading.

She goes on to criticize the inadequacy of information books for this age group, citing Macdonalds' *Starter* series as having the monopoly, and to warn teachers to choose books for the 5- to 8-year-olds much more

139

carefully. 'Until we are prepared to insist on a text which is informed, enthusiastic and lucid, matched by attractive format and accurate illustrations, we get what we deserve, a curate's egg!'

I have found three series eminently suitable for this first school age group and there may be others shortly to be published. Two series published by Longmans are called *As We Were* and *Our Saints*. The first is written by H. Grant Scarfe and has 12 titles ranging from *The Stone Age over 5000 Years Ago* to *An English Sea Port 350 Years Ago*. They are small, light books with a central double-page spread picture in colour, a well-designed coloured picture on every page, and very simple sentences in large writing. *Our Saints* was written by R. J. Hoare and has eight titles including *St Francis*, *St Nicholas* and *St Christopher*. They are both designed in the same artistic way. They may be read to young children as stories and then the children may be allowed to use them for reading and copying the suitable, realistic pictures. In this way a 6- to 7-year-old could successfully read a 'whole history book'. Unfortunately Longmans are not reprinting these books. To some extent they are being replaced by *Into the Past* by Sallie Purkis: four small books about life in 1900 using old photographs and descriptions by old people living at the time.

Nelson's 'Young World' have also published *Tripper* books with good hard backs telling of the adventures of Anne, Tony, and Uncle George in visiting places of interest. *A Trip to a Castle* (1973) by Edward Holmes is more crudely illustrated than the previous books but is accurate historically and written in a lively style. The language and detail need to be read to younger children but 8-year-olds could manage it themselves and there are plenty of large illustrations to learn from and copy.

A third series, published by A. & C. Black and called *Beans*, explains 'the lives of ordinary people both past and present'. Two titles I have found particularly well produced from the historical point of view are *The Blacksmith's House* by Joy James and *Jubilee Terrace* by Christopher Schenk. A real effort is made in the first to help young children to read the handwriting of the seventeenth-century blacksmith's 'inventory' or list of his belongings. Comparison is made all through the book between a seventeenth-century house and a modern house on the same site. *Jubilee Terrace* is also a comparative study but this time of a terrace in Liverpool, now and 100 years ago to celebrate Queen Victoria's jubilee. This series of excellent illustrations and short clear narrative is much to be recommended. These are the sort of books called for by Shirley Paice.

Junior children are more fortunate in their provision; finances and storage space will be the difficulties rather than choice. Again younger juniors have less choice than the top classes. Ginn have published a well-known series, *History Bookshelves*, edited by Catherine Firth starting in 1954. They are intended as reference books to accompany textbooks and six small books on different topics comprise a 'shelf' connected by a topic such as 'From Romans to Normans'. Each shelf has a useful teachers' book. Each book on a specialized topic is illustrated with accurate black and white sketches, manuscript sources, and family trees. These small and scholarly reference books can well be used throughout the junior school. Ginn have also published *Museum Bookshelves* in a similar series to help children to understand the exhibits in a museum and show how they relate to the work done in school. Longmans have brought out one of the most successful series for 7- to 9-year-olds in the *Focus on History* series edited by Ray Mitchell and Geoffrey Middleton, already mentioned in connection with the Holmes McDougall textbooks. This series is a high-quality production of topics in English history from *Stone Age to Iron Age* to *Our Own Century*. The books have an index (good training for 7-year-olds), are profusely illustrated, mainly with black and white photographs and sketches from contemporary manuscripts, and a clear text interspersed by activities relating to the illustrations. The great joy of these reference books is that the illustrations are large and detailed and therefore many types of individual work can be set on them. This series seems to me one of the best possible for younger juniors. A more recent series *History in Focus* is on the same lines as this but in colour and a larger format.

Similar to the *Focus on History* series, but for older juniors, is a series called *The Way It Was* published by W. & R. Chambers. The difference is the greater detail and difficulty of the text and the inclusion of topics in European and Scottish history. Special features are the illustrations, which are all reproductions of contemporary pictures or sketches of them, and the series of questions *at the beginning* of each chapter under three headings—'To think about', 'To find out', and 'To do'. All the books have good indexes and bibliographies but the individuality of different authors (mostly specialist historians) is shown in interesting ways. For example, Gillian Evans in *Pilgrimages and Crusaders* gives a glossary explaining such words as 'holy places', 'patriarch' and 'saracen'; she also starts her book with a most useful, illustrated double-page spread called 'What to look for in medieval pictures'. In spite of their attractive appearance and high standard of scholarship these books are not likely to supplant the cheaper and well-established *Then and There* series edited by the masterly hand of Marjorie Reeves and published by Longmans. When these books began to be published in the 1950s, they gave children so much help through the detail, glossaries,

141

and 'things to do', as well as relevant use of source material, that their shortcomings, seen in 1980, were not noticed. Now the narrative story may seem too packed and the illustrations unambitious and infrequent but they cover most topics in world history interesting to children and have excellent filmstrips to accompany them. It is interesting to read Marjorie Reeves' new book *Why History?* (Longmans, 1980) explaining the philosophy behind this most successful series which has remained popular for over 20 years. 'This deliberately personal book' provides a very full bibliography of books and other resources for teachers and for children from 8 to 15.

It is impossible to even mention the plethora of very good reference books for the 9- to 11-year-olds and teachers cannot go far wrong. I have found three series very useful for my own preparation as well as for children to read. They are *Children in History* by Molly Harrison (Hulton Educational), *Sources of History* (Macmillan—orange covers), and the *Discovery Reference Books* edited by Alys Gregory (University of London Press). Although the illustrations are not very enticing, the detail and scholarship of the subject-matter in all cases has much to be commended. I recommend Molly Harrison's books not only because she was curator of the Geffrye Museum, but because children always want to know about children of other ages. The Macmillan series has a varied list of topics; *Chivalry in the Middle Ages* and *Archery in the Middle Ages* both by E. K. Milliken are good introductions to source material. *Discovering Castles* by Walter Earnshaw provides all one needs to know for detailed topic work on the development of the castle and is supported by excellent plans, sketches, and photographs. Other books in the series are *Discovering Sailing Ships*, *Discovering Roads and Bridges* and *Discovering Heraldry*.

Textbooks and reference books should be regularly used but a third category of the written word demands attention and its use enhances teaching of the past: this is historical fiction. I hesitate to emphasize this use too much since reading any full-length book from cover to cover, even if fiction, is usually only enjoyed by older and abler juniors and it is most often done at home. It also demands interest from the teacher, whose bedtime reading may well not be historical fiction, and considerable teaching skill to use a particular historical novel relevantly in class. Novels are too long for the teacher to read to the children and the historical authenticity must be checked for reliability. Much helpful advice is given in two books already mentioned—Elizabeth Cook's *The Ordinary and the Fabulous* and Ray Lavender's *Myths, Legends and Lore*, and it is interesting that much fiction is based on true history. An analysis of historical fiction is made by M. Barton and K. Davies in *A*

142

Junior History Booklist (Historical Association T.H.27, 1968) but nearly half the pamphlet is of books for teachers to read for themselves. Famous authors are Rosemary Sutcliff (*Eagle of the Ninth*), Cynthia Harnet (*The Woolpack*), Henry Treece (*The Children's Crusade* and *Vikings' Dawn*), C. Walter Hodges (*The Namesake*), Alison Utley (*A Traveller in Time*), Philippa Pearce (*Tom's Midnight Garden*), and Clive King (*Stig of the Dump*). Most of these books are published in cheap paperbacks and it would seem wise to have them in the school library. Make sure that some 10-year-olds are reading them as their current 'reading books' for odd moments in class, and ask them to tell the class about them in short reviews towards the end of term. Perhaps two children could tackle one book and be responsible for a session together, reading out a particularly amusing or colourful paragraph. A list could be put on the library notice-board relating certain novels to certain periods of history. If teachers can read short extracts and stimulate children to read them privately this is probably the most that can be done. Teachers may want to combine English and history lessons and always make a practice of discussing and reading certain novels relevant to the period of history studied. The outline of the history needs to be given before the novel is understood. 'Children are not less interested than grown ups. The problem is that they *know* less. In particular they know less history.'[9]

Teachers who want a short survey of good historical novels should read Helen Cam's pamphlet *Historical Novels* (Historical Association G.48, 1961). A short but illuminating chapter is written by Carolyn Horovitz, 'Dimensions in Time, a critical view of historical fiction' in *Horn Book Reflections* edited by E. W. Field (Boston, 1969). She values the use of historical fiction as a subtle form of teaching 'time' to children—'the historical novel differs from other forms of the novel in its characteristic use of time and place'. She discusses Hilaire Belloc's view that a really good historical novel makes the past seem like the present to the reader.[10] Carolyn Horovitz recommends *The Willow Whistle* by Cornelia Meigs for younger children. This is the story of two children's adventures with Sioux Indian tribes and is presented simply, allowing the teacher to make comparisons between western and Indian civilizations. Historical fiction can bring the past to life for the good intelligent reader but can confuse and antagonize the less able by its intricate detail and specialized vocabulary. Less able children are really better reading a short, clear, and well-illustrated reading book. Older and more able children thrive on historical fiction.

PICTURES, WALLCHARTS AND PERIODICALS

There are few good, large wall pictures for history and fortunate is the teacher who has specialized in art and craft and can build up her own resources, enlarged from good originals. Macmillans sell a set of large coloured pictures of events in English history but the colours are unrealistically stark and children can get tired of having the same sort of picture always before them. *Pictorial Education* (monthly) and *Pictorial Education Special* (published by Evans) provide large pictures which fold out from a centre piece. These usually relate to lesson notes which can be sent free of charge. I have found large paper pictures from the National Portrait Gallery attractive, authentic, and colourful in the right way (e.g., 'Thomas More and his Family Circle', 'Elizabeth I' and 'Richard III'). Ladybird books have just published a chart of Kings and Queens of England which could well be put up in the library as a reference for the whole school. *Pictorial Charts* of Uxbridge have some useful wall illustrations of buildings (e.g., Elizabethan houses) but some of their charts are too full of detail to be useful in the junior school. *Child Education* is useful for the 5- to 8-year-olds but it is doubtful whether historical topics will figure in it frequently. It has yet to be seen whether a new journal, first published in October 1980, and called *Early Childhood* (for those interested in children under 7) will provide suitable historical pictures.[11] If a teacher is hard-working and the school petty cash will extend to it, the 'one-off' national historical event celebrated in the media often provides well-produced wall pictures. The Norman Conquest of 1066 was well represented in 1966 in large pictures, as were the Coronation of Elizabeth II in 1953 and the Silver Jubilee in 1978. These pictures should be backed and preserved and preferably kept flat in a plan chest or hung vertically in a suspender clip if there is absolutely nowhere else to keep them unfolded. For these aids to be really useful it is best to have beavor-boarding at the front of the classroom to use while teaching and to put the pictures in another place in the classroom when a particular topic is completed. An earlier part of this book has been concerned with display (pp. 104–112) which is mainly children's work, but a good beginning is made if the teacher can provide a centre piece to encourage the children themselves to contribute.

Books providing nothing but pictures are difficult to come by. *Britain's Story Told in Pictures* by C. W. Airne (Hope and Sankey) in many volumes, has been supplemented by *Picture Reference Books* (Brockhampton Press, 1968), also published in many volumes. The Airne books were so cheap that they could be cut out by children for their notebooks but the Brockhampton books of photographs and sketches may have tracings made from them, or they can be copied or studied as good reference material. These books are very useful if textbooks are not adequately illustrated. The text at the bottom of the Brockhampton books is much more reliable historically than the Airne books. If we are not always able to prevent our pupils copying exact words from books, they might as well copy correct words.[12]

SOURCES OF HISTORY

The use of textbooks, reference books, and novels is the first way to learn about the past. But the nature of history closely involves time and evidence; therefore teachers should want their pupils to question what they read in textbooks and should encourage them to seek reassurance from original sources, archives, or documents. Since the establishment of national record offices after 1945, and particularly since 1960, publishers, teachers, advisers, HMI, and archivists have cooperated to produce documents for use in schools in one way or another. This use, starting in the secondary schools, has gradually percolated down the age range so that a single challenging and pictorial old map has been used for teaching the past to 6-year-olds.

There is an abundance of advice for teachers from books, articles in *Teaching History*, and handbooks in archive-teaching units and packs. Most of the books on teaching history in the primary school have sections on 'Sources', particularly related to local history and field work but W. B. Stephens' *Teaching Local History* (Manchester University Press, 1977) is the most comprehensive and may be used as a scholarly reference book for all areas of the country. Many examples are taken from primary schools and the notes at the end are exhaustive in references to publications on teaching local history and using source material. It is a pity that the book is so expensive and that no paperback edition has yet been produced. The natural classification of sources is into printed sources and archival sources. The latter differs from the former in that they remain in their contemporary handwriting and in some cases (before about 1700) need 'transcribing' (or translating) into present-day handwriting to be understood. A small selection of these archival sources, being more difficult to find and understand, have been selected and made into archive teaching units or history packs.

PRINTED SOURCES

Primary teachers are likely to overlook compilations of printed documents as being too difficult for 5- to 11-year-olds. Yet there are several very useful collections with introductions and explanations. Basil Blackwell started a series *They Saw It Happen* in the mid-1950s in three volumes of original sources to illustrate English history. They are

145

subtitled 'Anthologies of eye-witness accounts and events in British history' and select key events—'the magic moment'—which altered the course of history in some cases. The short eye-witness accounts are introduced by a concise explanation, and reference to further reading is given in many cases. The influence of eighteenth-century coffee-houses is shown in an extract from a book by a French visitor given in the 1689–1897 volume.

> I have had pointed out to me in several coffee-houses, a couple of lords, a baronet, a shoe-maker, a tailor, a wine-merchant and some others of the same sort, all sitting round the same table and discussing familiarly the news of the court and town. The government's affairs are as much the concern of the people as of the great. Every man has the right to discuss them freely.[13]

A similar compilation, in paperback, is a series called *Portraits and Documents* (Hutchinson). Again they illustrate English history and are helpful to primary teachers because they have good, clear photographs/pictures of important personalities in the centre pages. The extracts are short and are also commented upon by the editors. In the medieval volume, *The Early Middle Ages 871–1216*, Derek Baker includes an extract from the Annals of St Neots giving one version of the words of the swineherd's wife in scolding King Alfred for burning the cakes—'Look man, the cakes are burning, and you do not take the trouble to turn them; when the time for eating them comes, then you are active enough'. The hunger of King Alfred during his wanderings in the marshes of Athelney may well be understood by children when this extract is read to them. A third printed series is the *Picture Source Books of Social History* edited by Molly Harrison and Margaret Bryant (Allen and Unwin), each book covering a century. They have the advantage of using contemporary illustrations, and furniture from the Geffrye Museum, as well as accounts. More compilations of documents are given in *Handbook for History Teachers* edited by W. H. Burston and C. W. Green (Methuen, 1972) but care should be taken to notice the age group intended, as most of the references are appropriate for children over 11 years of age. In all these cases short extracts, as in the case of the coffee-houses, may be duplicated for children but the teacher will have to add what activities arise from the document.

For those who feel restricted by these selected extracts and want to see and use an actual printed original source, there are some very useful easily-obtainable books from which suitable extracts can be taken. J. M. Dent's editions of *The Anglo-Saxon Chronicle* and *The Ecclesiastical History of the English Nation* by the Venerable Bede, a monk of Jarrow

Monastery, are simple accounts of English history up to 1066 and include many vivid accounts of colourful actions through which children can see for themselves what life was like in those far-off days. The martyrdom of St Alban (at Verulamium, now named St Albans in his honour) nearly failed several times through downpours of rain. King Ethelbert of Kent 'sitting in the open air' with his Christian wife Bertha received Augustine and his monks sent by Pope Gregory 'bearing a silver cross for their banner, and the image of our Lord and Saviour painted on a board'. Coifu, the high priest of Northumbria, newly converted to Christianity, mounted King Oswald's stallion to literally strike down with his spear the pagan idols that he had worshipped. These and many other small gems of narrative bring the past to life and can be easily dramatized.

The history of the eighteenth century can be illustrated from *The Journeys of Celia Fiennes* edited by Christopher Morris (Cresset Press, 1959) and Daniel Defoe's *A Tour Throughout the Whole Island of Great Britain*, two volumes (Dent, 1966). These two acute observers give detailed descriptions and their views of localities and so provide wonderful source material for the study of local history. Celia Fiennes' journey by horse from 'Leverpool' (Liverpool) to 'Prescote' (Prescot) is described in this way:

> Thence to Prescote 7 very long miles but pretty good way mostly lanes; there I passed by Mosel (Knowsley), the Earl of Darby's house which looked very nobly with many towers and balls on them; it stands amongst tall trees and looks like a pleasant grove all about it; its an old house runs a large compass of ground; the town of Prescote stands on a high hill, a very pretty neate market town, a large market place and broad streets well pitch'd.[14]

This description of the road in early days on which I travel each day on my way to work, Knowsley House, the present Lord Derby's house, and the market town near my college give added interest and significance to the steady growth of an industrial town (Liverpool) from the eighteenth century to the present day. Children in schools on this road can understand the 'then' and 'now' of their local area through this. In 1724 Daniel Defoe published his well-known contemporary 'guide-book' describing economic and social conditions in England and Scotland before the Industrial Revolution. Teachers can select any area in which they are teaching and find some paragraph of interest with the 'then' and 'now' comparison so helpful to children in starting a discussion. Here is an account by Daniel Defoe of Southampton having lost her medieval trading predominance by the beginning of the eighteenth century:

147

Southampton is a truly antient town, for 'tis in a manner dying of age; the decay of the trade is the real decay of the town; and all the business of moment that is transacted there, is the trade between us and the islands of Jersey and Gurnsey, with a little of the wine trade and much smuggling: The building of ships also is much stop'd of late; however the town is large, has many people in it, a noble fair High-Street, a spacious key, and if its trade should revive, is able to entertain great numbers of people: There is a French church, and no inconsiderable congregation, which was a help to the town, and there are still some merchants who trade to Newfoundland, and to the Streights with fish; but for all other trade, it may be said of Southampton as of other towns, London has eaten it up.[15]

For children in Southampton, innumerable questions may be asked and much useful discussion can arise.

Other well-known travellers' records can similarly illuminate the local scene in different ages: John Wesley's *Journals* for the eighteenth century when industrialization was beginning; William Cobbett's *Rural Rides* for the early nineteenth century; and J. B. Priestley's *English Journey* for the years between the two World Wars.

ARCHIVAL SOURCES AND PACKS

By these are meant information on paper or parchment such as letters, diaries, posters, maps, old books, parish registers, inventories (i.e. lists of property at the end of a person's will), school log books, and old newspapers. Other archival material such as parliamentary papers, legal documents, and those involving Latin and very difficult palaeography (i.e., old handwriting) are not so useful to primary teachers. They are found in Record Offices (both city and county offices), libraries, museums, newspaper offices, and even in the attics of teachers and pupils. Although using archives presents teachers with storage problems and is very time-consuming, the work is rewarding and the older junior years (and early secondary years) seem the ideal time in which to experiment with it as a class activity. The teacher has to be careful to relate the documents to her syllabus and not to get too involved in detail at the expense of seeing the document as illustrating the work as a whole. Carol Wilson and Ken May show how source material can be used well in teaching the History of Liverpool (see pp. 169–174).

Four ways of using archival material may be highlighted as valuable in the 5–11 age range. The first is the use of old maps. The usefulness of the 1611 Speed Map of Southampton with 6-year-olds has already been discussed. More advanced work was done in 1968 by J. M. Salt at Green End Primary School, Burnage (a residential suburb of Manchester), with 8-year-old children using nineteenth- and early twentieth-century maps of Burnage to show the age of and presence of different buildings in their area. Here is Mrs Salt's account of their work.

Visits to Manchester Central Library

A group of 8-year-old children went with their teacher to the Manchester Central Library. Arrangements had been made previously for the original maps of Burnage in 1820, 1845, 1848, 1900, 1926, 1934, and 1960 to be available in the Manchester Room, and for photocopies to be made for further work in the classroom. Each child had cyclostyled sketch maps of the area to be studied, with the present buildings marked.

From the 1820 map, notes were made of the buildings then appearing in the area. These were coloured red on the cyclostyled map. Next the children looked at the 1845 and 1848 maps and noted the buildings which had appeared since the 1820 map. These were filled in on another cyclostyled map in green. The same was done with each map until the children had six maps completed. Finally, on a photocopy of the 1960 map the various colour codes were brought together to show the ages of the different buildings in the area under a colour key.

This gave the children the opportunity to handle and use original documents at the library and to record their findings in a simple form.

It became apparent that Burnage was a small rural community until as late as 1934. The houses were strung out in a ribbon development along Burnage Lane, backed by fields. Until 1900 Burnage did not support a church. The children found that present-day street names related to old farms and features which have since disappeared.

The children were enthusiastic and were stimulated by this visit to make their own enquiries from the few elderly inhabitants who remembered Burnage when it was still farmland. Old books and pamphlets were lent to the children.

A further visit to the library was arranged, at which the 1900 map, 25″ scale, with fields marked, and the tithe schedule, were available. The children took the field numbers from the map and by referring to the schedule were able to find out who owned the land, who used the land and for what purpose, and the rent paid. Most of the land was pasture, meadow, and gardens (conflicting with an old inhabitant who spoke of the fields of corn).

The old maps were of differing scales. This led to a group of children making a scale map of a section of Burnage Lane.

J. M. Salt
Green End Primary School, Burnage

The children thus gained experience in:

1. Use of source material.
2. Making simple records of findings:
   (a) Age of buildings
   (b) Lane use
   (c) Place names.

3. Seeking information from library, school reference books, and local inhabitants on their own initiative.
4. Interpreting their findings in various media:
   (a) Map making
   (b) Individual booklets
   (c) Class books
   (d) Model making
   (e) Pictorial representation in variety of materials.

Liverpool Record Office owns a large-scale original plan of Liverpool in 1650 (Fig. 5.5). This is an excellent aid for teaching local history to 9- to 11-year-olds either as a wall map or, preferably, as a slide. It shows the Pool (hence Liver*pool*), now built over to form the main shopping street, the simple H plan of the main streets (still called by the same names), and the land owned by different Liverpool 'worthies'. In other words, in 1650 Liverpool was a small town dependent on the trade provided by the River Mersey. Comparison with a larger map made by Chadwick in 1725 boasting a very clear index of street names and beautiful depictions of sailing ships in the River Mersey shows the Pool built over and a much more highly complex street formation, but the same street names (Fig. 5.6). The wet dock, the dry dock, and the Custom House are all clear pointers to Liverpool's prosperity in the late eighteenth and nineteenth centuries. Original maps of this quality, used as visual aids or as smaller versions for children to use in pairs, provide endless interest and develop the comparison of 'then' and 'now' in an area known to the children. Sylvia Wheeler used a map of the field system for Bushey in 1800 and the 25 inch OS map of Bushey for 1871 in her work on the social life of Bushey when it was just a Hertfordshire village.[16]

Maps are a particularly valuable original source for children of 8 years upwards but pictures from source material are good learning resources for children from the age of 6. Advertisements for children's magazines are amusing and interesting 'starters' for discussion. In 1884 the magazine cover for *Little Folks* for all boys and girls, 6d. monthly, shows pictures of children, pets, adventures, and games of the late nineteenth century (Fig. 5.7).[17] Although another advertisement refers to boys of 13, older juniors may be sympathetic with the two boys who ran away from Christ's Hospital School in 1817 (Fig. 5.8).[18] Many of these advertisements are a source not only for discussion but for drawing and art work as well as creative writing. Old photographs are always wonderful pictures and more will be said about their use later when discussing family history.

Documents in original handwriting are difficult to handle in junior

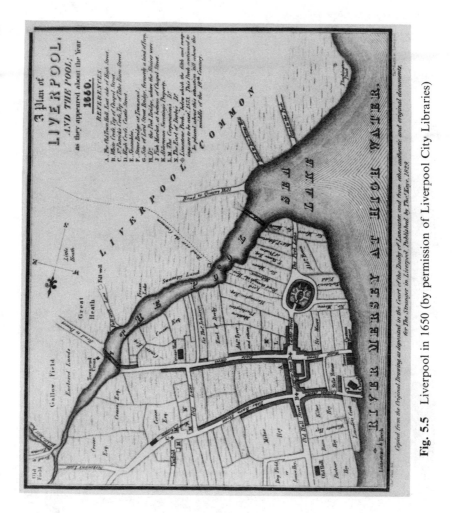

Fig. 5.5 Liverpool in 1650 (by permission of Liverpool City Libraries)

schools when they are dated before 1700, but work has been done successfully with older juniors. For example, the letter from Charles I to Sir William Norris in 1625 demanding a 'forced loan' from him is almost a copperplate hand sent to all those with money, the amount and

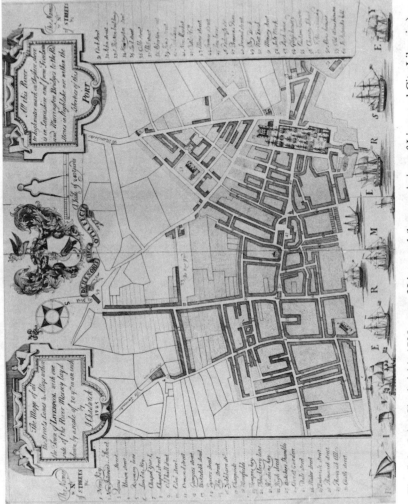

Fig. 5.6 John Chadwick's 1725 map of Liverpool (by permission of Liverpool City Libraries)

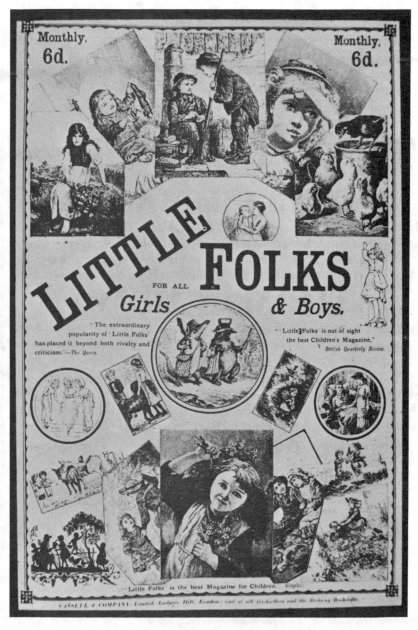

Fig. 5.7 *Little Folks* magazine, 1884

Two Blue Coat Boys.

Absconded,

From Christ's Hospital, Newgate Street, London, on Wednesday last, June the 18th. 1817,

Two Blue Coat Boys,

Answering the following Description :

WILLIAM MASON,

Between 13 and 14 Years of Age, about 5 Feet high, pleasant open Countenance, dark Complection, dark Eyes, round Face—his Two Eye Teeth very prominent, project over the other, so as to appear like Two Tusks when he speaks.

THOMAS HOW,

Between 15 and 16 Years of Age, about 5 Feet high, florid Countenance, has a red Mark on his right Cheek Bone, and his right Arm (when he left London) in a Sling.

Their Shoes and all their Clothes have their respective Names marked on them, they have Two silver Badges on their left Shoulder, as belonging to the KING'S WARD, their Shirts and yellow Stockings, have a large letter K marked on them.

It is supposed they are gone to Exeter, Tiverton, or Plymouth.

Their disconsolate Friends earnestly request any one seeing them will detain them, and give immediate Notice to Mr. HUGGINS, Steward of the Hospital; or to Mr. JOSEPH COOPER, 73, Borough, Southwark—when all reasonable Expences will be thankfully paid by either of the above.

June 23rd. 1817.

ANN KEMMISH, Printer, 17, KING STREET, Borough, London.

13

Fig. 5.8 Runaway schoolboys, 1817 (by permission of the Postmaster General)

BY THE KING.

Rustie and welbeloved, We greet you well. Hauing obserued in the Presidents and customes of former times, That the Kings and Queenes of this our Realme vpon extraordinary occasions haue vsed either to resort to those contributions which arise from the generality of subjects, or to the priuate helpes of some well-affected in particular by way of loane; In the former of which courses as We haue no doubt of the loue and affection of Our people when they shall againe assemble in Parliament, so for the present We are enforced to proceede in the latter course for supply of some portions of Treasure for diuers publique seruices, which without manifold inconueniences to Vs and Our Kingdomes, cannot be deferred: And therefore this being the first time that We haue required any thing in this kind, We doubt not but that We shall receiue such a testimony of good affection from you (among st other of Our subjects) and that with such alacrity and readines as may make the same so much the more acceptable, especially seeing We require but that of some, which few men would deny a friend, and haue a minde resolued to expose all Our earthly fortune for preseruation of the generall; The summe which We require of you by vertue of these presents is _twenty pounds_ which We doe promyse in the name of Vs, our Heires and Successours to repay to you or your Assignes within eighteene moneths after the payment thereof vnto the Collector. The person that We haue appointed to collect, is _Sr Hugh Halsewell Baronitt_ to whose hands we doe require you to send it within twelue dayes after you haue receiued this Privy Seale, which together with the Collectors acquitance, shalbe sufficient warrant vnto the Officers of Our Receipt for the repayment thereof at the time limited. Giuen vnder our Privy Seale at _Hampton Court_ the _twentieth_ day of _December_ in the first yeare of our raigne of England, Scotland, France, and Ireland. 1625.

Ja: Skyller

Fig. 5.9 'By the King': request for a 'forced loan' by Charles I, 1625 (by permission of Liverpool City Libraries)

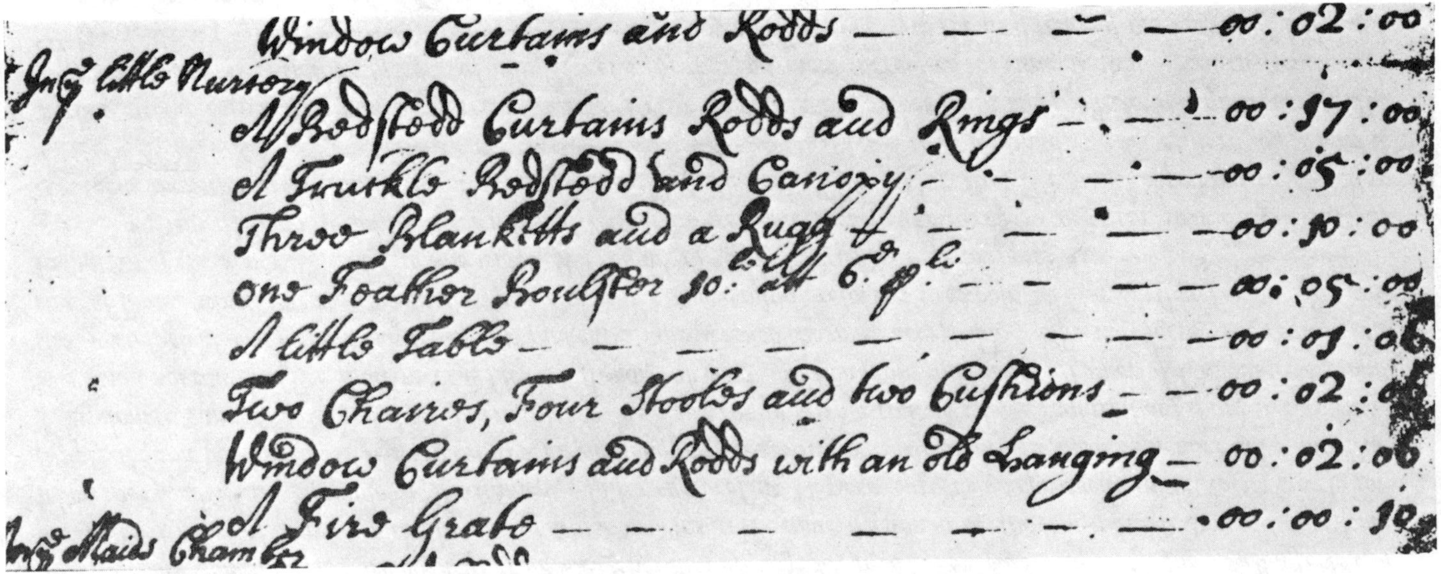

	Window Curtains and Rodds	00:02:00
In ye little Nursery	A Bedstedd Curtains Rodds and Rings	00:17:00
	A Truckle Bedstedd and Canopy	00:05:00
	Three Blanketts and a Rugg	00:10:00
	one Feather Boulster 10: lb at 6. p lb	00:05:00
	A little Table	00:01:00
	Two Chairs, Four Stooles and two Cushions	00:02:00
	Window Curtains and Rodds with an old hanging	00:02:00
In ye Maids Chamber	A Fire Grate	00:00:10

Fig. 5.10 Inventory of the 'Little Nursery', Speke Hall 1700 (by permission of Liverpool City Libraries)

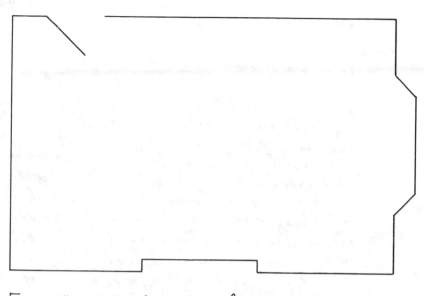

From the 1700 inventory for the Little Nursery, find out the items of furniture and draw them in this plan. Label your items. Add up the items' value and give your final sum.

Fig. 5.11   Plan of the Little Nursery, Speke Hall

collector's name being inserted in another hand (Fig. 5.9). There is an ironic address on the back of the document 'To our trusted and well-beloved Sir Wm. Norris' and a request for quick payment 'with such alacrity and readiness as may make the same so much more acceptable'. There is much here to throw light on the character of Charles I and his lack of intention to repay the loan 'within eighteen months'. This document is easy to transcribe and throws a great deal of light on local and national affairs on the accession of Charles I in 1625.

A seventeenth-century inventory should be tackled one room at a time. Work on the 1700 inventory of 'The little nursery' at Speke Hall can be started by the seven items in the nursery being read without help, then a transcription read as a check (Fig. 5.10). After that the plan of an empty room can be given to each child to draw in the seven items (Fig.

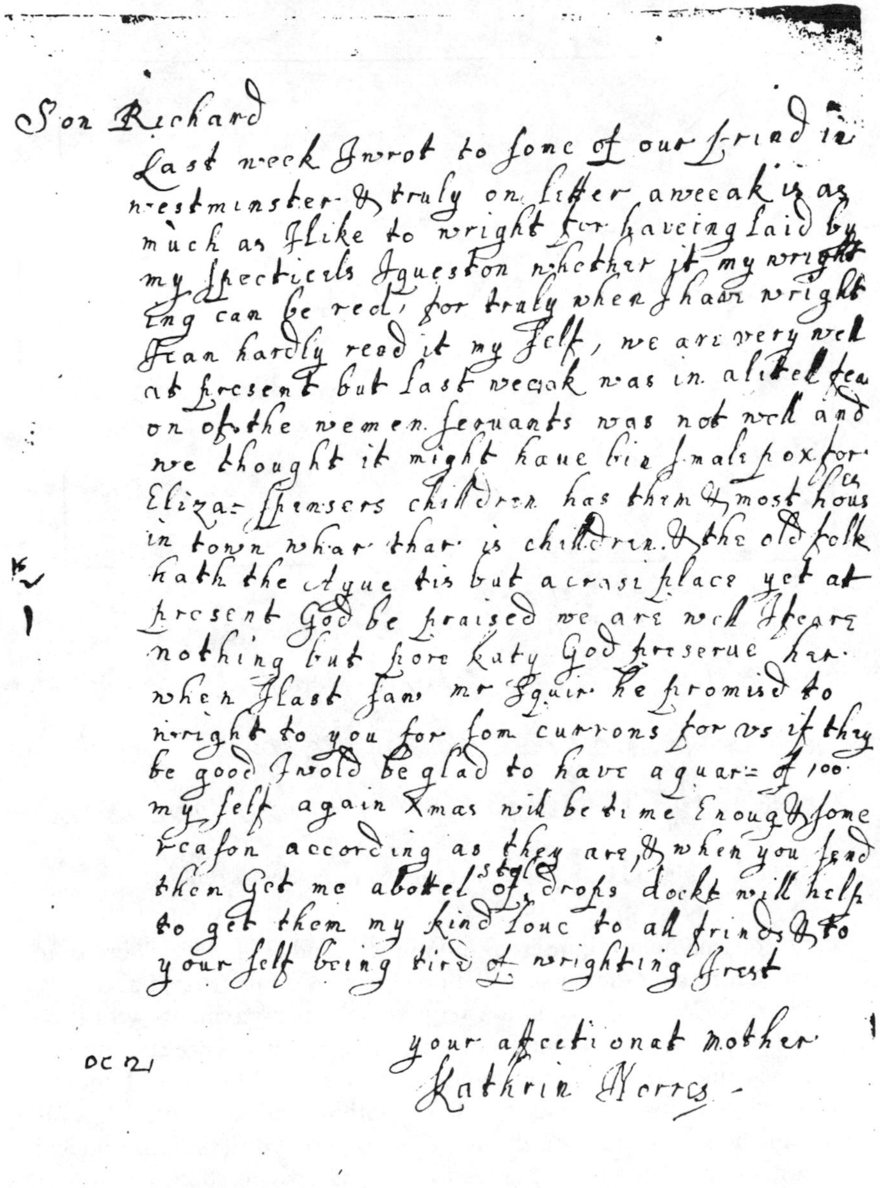

Son Richard

Last week I wrot to sone of our friend in
westminster & truly one liter a week is as
much as I like to wright for haveing laid by
my specticels I queston whether it my wright
ing can be red, for truly when I han wright
I can hardly read it my self, we are very well
at present but last week was in a litel sea
on of the wemen servants was not well and
we thought it might haue bin smale pox for
Eliza: Spensers children has them & most hous
in town whar that is children & the old folk
hath the Ague tis but a crasi place yet at
present God be praised we are well I heare
nothing but hore Katy God preserue her
when I last sau mr Squir he promisd to
wright to you for som currons for us if they
be good I wold be glad to haue a quar= of 100
my self again Xmas will be time Enough some
reason according as they are, & when you send
then Get me a botel of stil drops dockt will help
to get them my kind loue to all frinds & to
your self being tird of wrighting I rest

your affectionat mother
Kathrin Norres -

OC 21

Fig. 5.12 Kathryn Norris's letter to her son, 1705 (by permission of Liverpool
City Libraries)

5.11). Practical, imaginative, and even numerical work develops from this one small piece of source material. A final single document I have used with older juniors is a letter of 1705 from Kathryn Norris of Speke Hall to her son Richard, an apprentice in London. In those days envelopes were not used, the letter was folded and the address written on the back of the letter for the messenger—'This for Mr. Richard Norris at Mr. Alexander Caine's, a merchant in London'. This letter is easy to read without a transcription. The blackboard could be used for comparison of ways of life in 1705 and the 1980s, evidence coming from this letter. Finally, each pupil could write out the letter using present-day punctuation and spelling in order to understand the meaning. Kathryn Norris did not punctuate at all! (Fig. 5.12.)

A very suitable topic for all 5–11 children is classrooms of the past and the most accessible and understood period is the late nineteenth and early twentieth centuries. School log books, inspectors' reports, work done by children, and descriptions of old school buildings abound in record offices and they are usually easy to read, being written in copperplate. The Museum of the History of Education at the University of Leeds, started by W. E. Tate, one of the pioneers of teaching local history, possesses the original of a most enlightening essay written by a 13-year-old girl in 1897. It has such relevance today for those interested in ending discrimination against girls and women, that I shall quote it in full:

I do not like boys. They are so rough and noisy. They think themselves much cleverer than girls but they are mistaken. Girls are much more useful to their mothers than boys. If you see a boy nursing a baby, he does it so clumsily you think all the time he is going to let it drop. Boys make their sisters do all sorts of things, such as clean their boots, brush their clothes, put their playthings—bats, balls, and marbles safely away. When a boy has a toothache he makes a deal more fuss about it than a girl would, and mother has to do a deal of things to make him quiet. Then boys are so fond of play that they cannot find time to come to their meals, and if they are not ready just when they want they make a row about it. The best thing to do is to let them go without, and you may be sure that they will come to the bread and butter, before the bread and butter will go to them. It costs more to keep boys than girls, they wear out their boots so quickly and tear their clothes so dreadfully that the shoe-maker and the tailor are always calling at the house. Girls do not wear out half so many clothes. Folks say girls talk more than boys, but you should hear them at ball or marbles then you would not think so. Well, I suppose there must be boys or we should have no-one to build houses, shoe horses, plough the fields, look after gardens and shops. The nicest boy I know is Willie Murphy, he is a very nice fellow.[19]

159

This very articulate and mature piece of work may be the basis for discussion in a mixed class of top juniors coming from families where the same problems may still be present in 1982. It would perhaps lead to a prepared 'debate' in another session and might even be a talking point at a parents' association meeting.

A fourth area of archival material often under-used is Edwardian and pre-1945 school books and reading books. A particularly valuable collection of children's books from the past is housed in the Education Library at Liverpool University.[20] Although these cannot be duplicated many children can bring them, teachers often possess them, and libraries could supply some from reserved stock. Many of these books have illustrated covers and gilt-edged pages, particularly if they are old school prizes. I have found that an 1892 book called *Stories from English History* by Maria Hack with the subtitle 'during the Middle Ages' provides interesting comparison with children's modern history books. It has eight black and white pictures in 263 pages of text, is divided in chapter into reigns of kings, and the author adopts the narrative style throughout. Two 1890 books—*Tom Brown's Schooldays* 'by an old boy' and *Henry M. Stanley the African Explorer* by Arthur Montefiore also provide detailed narrative and few pictures, but very interesting points of comparison, and a good idea of what late nineteenth-century authors thought young people 'should' read. A 1793 book, picked up cheaply in a second-hand shop in York, throws light on relations between father and son as it is a compilation of letters from a 'nobleman to his son' with the father telling a *History of England in Letters* to his son, a student at Oxford University. This was before the time when a student could study history at Oxford. These letters, which go as far as 1680 in Volume I, can be used in small extracts as the parts of history are learnt in school. They are clearly printed on parchment, easily read, and discussion about family relationships can come from them. This particular book is leather bound. One or two expeditions to second-hand bookshops, particularly in old towns, enables the teacher to build up an adequate resource library of ancient books as sources, to be used as a topic on 'Old books' with a time chart for dates.

So far I have looked at archival material in the form of maps, pictures, and single documents but since the mid-1950s universities, local authorities, record offices, one branch of the Historical Association, and commercial publishers have found a ready market in selecting and editing certain archival materials supported by other materials, and selling them as archive teaching units, history packs or just compilations of documents on certain topics. This was started by Gordon Batho when he was training history graduates at the University of Sheffield. His materials were intended for secondary schools although some of the wall pictures would have been very attractive for younger children (e.g. the large photographs of the houses in which Mary Stuart was imprisoned in England). John West took up this work in Liverpool for junior and secondary children and produced two large boxes of materials as well as large wall pictures in the early 1960s. For about ten years from 1965 to 1975 groups of teachers in schools, teachers in record offices, and authors produced units of materials fitting into folders and therefore more easily carried, used, and stored. But there was still the difficulty of checking each folder for innumerable documents of different sizes, therefore the third stage of development was the A4 folder containing all A4 size documents, pictures, handbooks, and transcriptions. The Essex Record Office has initiated this in its Seax Series of Teaching Portfolios. Since financial difficulties have curtailed many new publications, Teachers' Centres are trying to publish local materials in paperback form. As the printing is usually done at the Teachers' Centre, the booklets are not expensive and schools can buy enough copies for shared class use. This has been done for many years by the Staffordshire Record Office under the leadership of R. A. Lewis, Inspector for Schools. The advent of the photocopying machine has also enabled teachers to use specific materials in one booklet for duplicating enough copies for educational purposes. This financial stringency is also leading to several well-known publishing firms producing 'packs' of booklets, visual aids and workcards instead of individual books (e.g. Cambridge University Press). Care should be taken to adhere to the copyright laws of the day.

So much work has gone into the production of archive units and there have been so many good ones for sale that it would be impossible to describe and analyse even half of them. Many are too difficult for primary children and should be used in the 11–16 age range and even beyond. Yet primary teachers can be selective of those intended for 9–13 use. The teacher should select a unit title within children's understanding and then select certain documents from the unit. The three documents about the Norris family described earlier are part of an archive teaching unit—*A Tudor House: Speke Hall and the Norris Family 1500–1700.* (Liverpool History Unit No. 1. Liverpool Education Committee, 1970.) One of the most attractive I have seen is *Some Kent Children 1594–1875* (Kent Record Office, 1972) edited by Margaret Phillips, the Teacher Adviser in Kent Record Office at Maidstone. The material is divided into separate folders according to the source of the documents; so there is, for example, 'The accounts child', 'A schoolgirl diarist' and 'The inventory child'. Written and visual documents are treated in a most imaginative and lively way, and no child however

161

"Here's a famous menagerie, full of wild beasts,
See this lion with wide open jaws,
Enough to affright one, and yet, I've no doubt,
You might venture to play with it's claws.

"Here a tiger, as tame as a lap-dog, you'll find,
And a fox that will not steal the geese:
So here you must own the old adage is proved,
That wonders are never to cease.

Fig. 5.13 Illustration from a nineteenth-century child's book (from *Some Kent Children*, M. Phillips and by permission of Lord Brabourne and Maidstone Museum)

Fig. 5.14 Eva Knatchbull Hugessen's diary, 1873 (from *Some Kent Children*, M. Phillips and by permission of Lord Brabourne and Maidstone Museum)

young could fail to respond to some part of the unit. Two documents stand out as particularly useful; a page from a nineteenth-century child's book showing children looking at toy animals in a magazine (Fig. 5.13) and the diary of Eva Knatchbull Hugessen, starting 8 January 1873, in her own handwriting (Fig. 5.14). The unit also suggests in outline what work could be done with the materials and provides an excellent bibliography. If all record offices could appoint a teacher/archivist of such calibre records would be used much more in primary schools.

The difficulty of too many loose sheets of varying sizes has to some extent been overcome by the Essex Record Office publications of only A4 sheets in all their folders. *Highways and Byways of Essex* by K. C. Newton (1969) is a combination of 37 documents ranging from a photograph of the Icknield Way in pre-Roman times through the centuries to the Bentall motor car manufactured in Essex between 1904 and 1912, and a pamphlet of historical background for each document. Most relevant of the items are a sketch-map of Roman roads in Essex, part of a 1580–1 account of surveyors of the highway, a sketch of William Kemp, the actor, morris-dancing his way from London to Norwich in 1599, an extract from a pictorial map of Essex made by Oliver in 1696 showing the new 1695 turnpike, and a picture of Mary de Medici leaving Gidea Hall in Essex in 1639. The 1580 account is particularly interesting because it divides those caring for the Essex roads into people who provide carts ('caryages'), labourers who have to do the work themselves, and more wealthy people who pay others to do their work on the roads for them. This is an excellent discussion point for the hierarchy of social classes in 1580 in spite of all being responsible for highway repairs. The information pamphlet provides an excellent bibliography but little practical advice for the non-historian teacher.

Archive units more structured for teaching purposes than those already discussed have been published by the Manchester branch of the Historical Association, the only branch in the country to undertake this from its own funds and due to the initiative of Dr Alys Gregory, the chairman of the branch, who also edited the *Discovery Reference Books* series mentioned on p. 142. Two units have been published and both can be used for 9–11 children because the topics chosen are of perennial interest to children. They are *Orphan Annie* edited by Constance Francis (1969) and *The Princes of Loom Street* edited by Muriel Rosser (1972), both concerned with deprived children and their families in an industrial town in the nineteenth century. Information books of historical quality are included and both units use documents which can easily be read. *Orphan Annie*, about a London orphan Ann Saunderson aged 10, apprenticed to James Pendleton a Manchester tape-weaver, is more

164

useful to the teacher than to the children, as little activity is given for children to undertake from the unit. But the *Handbook* gives excellent information, explaining the documents and the *Research* booklet leads the teacher along with suggestions of how to make workcards appropriate to the documents. Muriel Rosser's unit has one *Handbook* of information but six different coloured cards as 'research cards' from which children can work. These cards cover transport, family living conditions, population and overcrowded towns, education, wages and food, work and leisure. Each card stipulates which documents should be consulted to answer the six questions and Mrs Rosser has cleverly used a particular document only once so that children will not be competing for the same documents to answer their particular workcard. This unit is also the only place where I have seen a clear sketch of 'back-to-back' houses, this time a sketch of two houses in Chorlton-on-Medlock, Manchester. Both these units are scholarly, imaginative, and can be used practically by teachers of the 9–11 primary children.

From the Historical Association contribution I should like to mention the only University School of Education which has published any documentary material since Gordon Batho's Sheffield units (now out of production). Dr Marjorie Cruickshank of Keele University has edited Teaching Units of a less ambitious nature (and therefore cheaper in price) than those already discussed. These have been worked on by local teachers and edited by one or two of their number. A recent issue, *The Darbys and the Dale Company* by Peter Leed and J. J. Waddington-Feather, is a very good basis for study of the Industrial Revolution in industrial archaeology which is becoming more usual in the top classes of junior schools. There is not much documentary material here but helpful information based on the famous Ironbridge Gorge Museum in Shropshire, and worksheets on orange paper for the six original documents. There is no list of contents and no pagination, and therefore children might find the folder confusing. 'Books for younger pupils' is comprehensive and the primary teacher could rely on these for preparation. This Keele unit provides an excellent basis for a whole term's work on the Industrial Revolution as a topic; a visit to Coalbrookdale is very much to be recommended.

Liverpool Education Committee seems to be the only LEA to have financed archive teaching units and its last one was not published for general sale. This may reflect the lack of historians among the advisory staff and even those historians who become advisers are not appointed to stimulate interest and expertise in history in the schools. Liverpool schools have been fortunate to obtain the enthusiastic and voluntary help of Michael Cook, University of Liverpool archivist, who has been the 'spearhead' in getting the three teaching units compiled and published. Dr Marylyn Palmer of Loughborough University, who has researched on the use of documents in teaching history, believes that archives concerned with family, houses, canals, and railways in the locality are most successful with young children.[21] But before the mid-1960s, Liverpool Education Authority did have an adviser, John West, who set about making two boxed units with the help of teachers. The most useful of the two for 9–11 children is the box on *The Liverpool–Prescot–Warrington Turnpike Road 1725–1871* which I experimented with in a local primary school situated on the road (the same road described by Celia Fiennes as 'mostly lanes', quoted more fully on p. 147). The materials were plentiful but we supplemented them with more reading books. The unit's contents formed a natural basis for group work in a 10- to 11-year-old class of nearly 40 children, and included a coach excursion along the actual road, the making of a film (shown to parents), individual folders, and group display at the end. This display included a model of the road and large paintings. A more detailed description of the work may be found in *Teaching History*.[22]

The weight and bulkiness of this unit was overcome in the first Liverpool History Teaching Unit—*A Tudor House: Speke Hall and the Norris Family 1500–1700*,[23] a folder of archival materials, plans, worksheets, and booklets. This appears to be the most highly-structured unit in publication with a handbook showing how each part of the unit can be used in different types of classroom situation; parts may be used as visual and teaching material for oral exposition by the teacher, parts for individual work and parts for group work. All units help to start a good display and this is no exception with its large aerial view of Speke Hall, Yates' map of the area showing 'Speyke', the envelope of photographs specially taken for the unit, and a sketch of the carved overmantel in the Great Parlour depicting the three main families building the present hall. The booklets on brass-rubbing, heraldry, and the detailed information booklet divided into topics which may be studied in groups, all provide ample source material for a large class. It is fortunate for Liverpool schools that an outstanding example of a half-timbered house is so near at hand and that the County Museum is now entrusted with its care by the National Trust.

Another unit, *A Town Under Siege: Liverpool and the Civil War 1642–4* (1978), is suitable for primary children but has not yet been published for general sale.[24] It is concerned with a traumatic and detailed period of Liverpool's history when the town was besieged three times and changed hands from Parliamentarians back to Royalist and then back to Parliamentarians. Three features are particularly useful.

The *Handbook* written by Allan Waplington (formerly of the Schools Council Project *History, Geography and Social Science 8–13*) is linked to new movements in curriculum development by stating the objectives of the unit; to get children to think, to look for, and evaluate evidence and to develop intellectual skills and sympathetic understanding towards the leading characters such as Prince Rupert and Sir John Moore. The *Handbook* gives specialist help to teachers of young children and provides a Civil War game for those interested in simulation and gaming. The *Background Information* booklet provides large A4 maps of England and Lancashire to show how the Liverpool sieges relate to the rest of the war and these are so clear that they can easily be duplicated for use by 8-year-olds upwards. But the most attractive feature for young children is the pamphlet called *Bloodwipes and Tussles* in which everyday life in Liverpool is depicted from the Town Books (municipal records). Leading personalities such as town officials are documented as well as streets, markets, church attendance, school, and local quarrels. The whole pamphlet is illustrated by contemporary sketches and there are questions to be answered on the extracts (given in modern printing). All the documents are transcribed. It is to be hoped that this unit will be published as the topics and contents are most suitable for 8- to 11-year-old children and are a good example of how a siege affected a town in the seventeenth century.

Packs of material have been published without specific intention of being used for teaching purposes. These are collections of information with no handbook for teachers. The most famous are Jackdaw folders, first produced by Jonathan Cape in 1963. Most of them are not suitable for juniors unless they are carefully edited, but they are useful as display and stimulus material rather than learning material. Margaret Devitt wrote a useful companion to Jackdaws—*Learning with Jackdaws* (Cape, 1970)—and she shows in a flowchart how they can be used to relate to each other. Two of the most useful Jackdaws for 5- to 11-year-olds are *The Development of Writing* by Carol Donaghue (No. 47) and *The Tower of London* by David Johnson (No. 62). They are useful resources to be used by all children and both contain very good large wall pictures. During the difficult years for employment from 1975, some job creation schemes have been used by enterprising historians to research and compile packs of local information. Robin Hewitt-Jones of Liverpool Institute of Higher Education has led a team of unemployed historians in producing what he has called SEARCH packets on Liverpool's history. Teachers will find information on many important topics such as the Blue Coat Charity School, Wavertree Mill, and the 1941 blitz of Liverpool. The material is more useful to teachers than children but at

167

times the individual item is appropriate; such as a letter home in copperplate handwriting from a Blue Coat schoolboy about his school visit to Knowsley Park in 1890. It is possible that other areas have also taken this initiative and teachers should enquire in their areas about work of this kind.

Several publishers have put much work into producing packs of booklets, workcards, and visual aids and in these teachers will find the complete antidote to any doubts about schemes, methods, and resources! Many of them contain source material in the form of photographs and some extracts from archival material. Again so much has been produced during the last decade that it is impossible to do justice to much of it, some is now out of print, and some is unsuitable for 5–11 children. Rather than provide a list of authors, titles, publishers, and dates with no comment I shall concentrate on two series, one for younger juniors (and even infants) and the other for older juniors. Both series involve exciting new ideas and are still in print. A. & C. Black under the inspiration of Sue Wagstaff have published *People Around Us* (1978), mainly a social studies course for 8- to 11-year-olds but quite able to be used by 6- and 7-year-olds. Unit 1 is on *Families* and consists of a *Teachers' Guide*, 12 copies of two booklets—*Two Victorian Families* and *Kola's family*—two sets of eight colour photographs showing different kinds of British families and a book of spirit duplicator masters for worksheets. The *Teachers' Guide* is clearly set out and gives detailed and practical ways of teaching from the unit; starting the project, techniques for discussion, techniques for drama, developing the project, and techniques for display and storage. The guide suggests getting children to practise making family trees with the help of the booklets and worksheets. *Two Victorian Families* is ideal for comparison of the life of an upper-middle-class London family and the life of Meg the under housemaid both in her job and in her own home in the country. All the pages are double-page spreads generously illustrated in colour with clear, short sentences describing the pictures. *Kola's Family* is equally imaginative; Kola comes from the Dani tribe in New Guinea. Children of 6 years learning to read are well able to use the pictures and gradually understand the text. *People Around Us* has now been extended to two more units—*Friends* and *Work*—and one large and vigorous Education Authority (ILEA) held a day conference at the Clapham History and Social Sciences' Teachers' Centre in October 1980 to introduce teachers to the units and how to use them. It is refreshing and encouraging to find good historical material being produced that is so suitable for younger children.

The second pack is published by Cambridge University Press and again is ostensibly for 8- to 13-year-olds but much of it is appropriate for 7–8 children. This is a series called *History First* edited by Tom Corfe. It began publication in 1976 and at present has ceased producing new books, with the ninth unit published. The series covers history from the first century BC to the nineteenth century. Each class pack contains three booklets (on a person, a place, and an exciting event), twelve four-page workcards, teacher's notes, a wall picture and a spirit duplicator master for extra copies of the workcards. Older juniors are referred to the *Cambridge History of Mankind* (edited by Trevor Cairns) for more detailed information. To take one example, the pack on *Montezuma* by Don Lincoln provides constructive teacher's notes with extracts from contemporary writings about Aztec Mexico and the Spanish conquerors. The three booklets are short enough for junior children to read to the end and the workcards are stiff and easily wiped to remove marks. In spite of the need for teachers to collect several items safely at the end of a session this series provides all materials needed by the primary teacher with little historical knowledge. My only criticism would be that the illustrations are a little too highly coloured and crude in representation. They do not reach the high standard of the texts. But, as in the A. & C. Black packs, particular attention is paid to *how* the material can be used successfully and the teacher is provided with all resources she needs related to the topic in mind.

The years 5–11 and on to 14 are the ideal ones in which to concentrate on the real stuff of the past before it is subjected to the limitations of examinations. In these years real enjoyment can be experienced by both teacher and children in using different types of source material. This 'involves the ability to steep the class completely, and for protracted periods of time, in the very words and deeds of the subject' comments John West.[25] To do this the teacher needs help from archivists, in-service training, and assistance in school or, where possible, Teachers' Centre to handle the necessary source materials. Teachers should try to familiarize themselves with *one* area of source material for each of the 5–11 years, from old photographs in the infant school to turnpike road accounts in the top class of the junior school. This should be related in some way to the syllabus for that year. In the following two accounts, Carol Wilson and Ken May make skilful use of source material with older juniors in teaching the history of Liverpool.

How I teach the history of Much Woolton in the seventeenth century to 9- to 11-year-olds

I have developed a scheme for teaching local history which could be applied to many areas. The period I cover for Much Woolton, where the school is situated, is from the early seventeenth century to the twentieth century. The work occupies two terms, the first concentrating on the seventeenth century. Just over one hour a week is spent on the basic teaching.

It is possible to discuss only one of its sections here, the introductory one, which involves an examination of local life during the seventeenth century. Of the many sources available for this period I concentrate on Probate and Quarter Sessions records; ten probate inventories and four Quarter Session petitions are used.

A most important task is first of all to motivate the children and to create an interest and curiosity in the subject which will be maintained. A successful way I have developed is to request that the children bring into school objects of any kind which they regard as being 'old'. This always produces a great variety of items ranging from some only a few years old to several of genuine antiquity. They promote discussion and, eventually, classification into categories—'fairly new', 'old', 'very old' and 'very, very old'. We then comment upon how difficult it is to determine whether objects are 'old' or not and usually decide that those not in common use today can be easily recognized as 'old'.

Having developed interest in ideas associated with chronology and change I then show the children photocopies of wills of people who lived in Woolton in the seventeenth century. As with the objects, initial reaction is not directed; pupils are encouraged to examine and draw their own conclusions about age and origin. This leads naturally to a study of palaeography so that they can read the documents for themselves. Each child has a copy of every document and, later, transcriptions of them.

Reading the wills leads to a great deal of discussion about spelling, literacy, and writing styles. It is at this stage that the children try to write with quill pens. They appreciate how difficult it is to form modern letters with them and write about this experience. They find the exercise both enjoyable and instructive.

Next the children are asked to write their own wills, deciding which possessions they would bequeath and to whom they would leave them. These serve as extremely useful comparisons between past and present values and customs.

Once they are reasonably proficient at reading the wills—four class lessons—the children examine inventories. This is after they have made an inventory of their own bedroom, noting all the items belonging to them. We look at these, deciding how useful they could be as evidence to people who found them in a hundred years' time. What would they learn about children in 1980? The pupils then consider which things would not have been included in their parents' day and grandparents' day. It is surprising how acute their observations about change can be.

Following this, groups of children study the inventories, two inventories per group, making lists of things relating to agriculture and 'occupations'. This involves much group discussion and open-ended questions about the way of life of people at the time. The group work lasts for four sessions.

Each group is asked to look at both the will and the inventory and explain how they thought that the person maintained his or her family. This leads to creative writing about life in the seventeenth century. They are able to build up a reasoned picture of what life was probably like for particular family units in Woolton.

To see a little of how the family units fitted into the larger community a further source is introduced, i.e., the Quarter Sessions Rolls. In particular we look at petitions made by distressed people in a variety of circumstances, which gives rise to discussion about the causes of poverty and how the community functioned as a caring society.

Pupils respond to these materials in a number of ways. Imaginative writing and their own dramatic creations are among the rewarding work they produce.

I feel that by using this approach children exercise a number of skills which they will extend and develop in later years. The concepts, so important to any study of history, of time, change, similarity, difference, etc., are dealt with in a meaningful way. They gain an impression of the scale of life in a previous age and are given a more vivid insight into seventeenth-century England than textbooks could provide.

Carol Wilson
Woolton County Primary School, Liverpool

A study of Castlesite in an urban area with 9- to 11-year-olds

Children's enjoyment of history is enhanced when they know it is real, can see where it happened, when romanticism is illustrated with true facts, and when the understanding of the subject under study is within their comprehension. It is for these reasons that I find local history, the more local the better, makes a great contribution to the teaching of the subject, though it is important that it is not isolated from national or international history.

Some 400 metres from the school in Liverpool where I work is a small open space with the evocative name 'Castlesite'. Today the area is bounded by houses on three sides but reserved as an open space because a castle was erected here about the time of the Norman Conquest. National history of the eleventh century conditioning land use in the twentieth century! An ideal subject for a local history study.

A visit to the City of Liverpool Record Office produced some useful information concerning the castle. The VCH* supplied important material concerning the location and environment of the castle, some details of its history and a useful map which included the school, so that by tracings and the use of the OS map scale 1:2500 the exact position of the castle on site could be located. This book was also of obvious use for information and transcriptions of Domesday Book. Another useful booklet which described excavations undertaken at the site in 1927 provided a plan of the castle, a cross-section of the excavations across the inner and outer ditches, diagrams of timbers found lying at the bottom of the ditch and believed to be from a drawbridge, a conjectural drawing of the drawbridge, and a list of other finds including

* VCH = Victoria County History (in this case for Lancashire).

pottery, the leather sole of a shoe, metal, horn, and bone objects found in the ditches.

From the information obtained I planned a work unit on the castle and related subjects for children aged 9+ to 11+. It seems to me that time can be wasted and efforts frequently duplicated in the research and preparation of teaching materials; I therefore planned to put together a unit of work which would be valuable to teachers over a number of years. My aim was to provide background information which teachers could use to plan lessons and pupils' worksheets which would include basic information, maps, diagrams, and tasks to be completed on site or in school. Time required for the work would vary according to the amount of integration with other subjects and the number of aspects covered by each group of children but I considered a minimum of two hours per week for a term to be required. For practical organization at the site and the economical use of resources in school, the work was planned for children to work in groups. I found four groups of from six to eight children to be a workable arrangement but this did not preclude the use of class teaching when appropriate. By using the study during a long period of teaching practice it was possible to have an extra adult to assist and stimulate the children. In the school, which is of open plan design, materials and resources were available to the children on a 'help yourself' basis thus saving children time and teacher frustration.

The materials produced for study consist of pupils' worksheets and a teachers' guide enclosed in a ring binder which includes background information on the building of the castle, the excavation of 1927, maps and diagrams, information regarding the Domesday survey, a list of relevant books in the school library, and of slide sets and film strips, a specimen set of children's worksheets, and a 'Domesday pack'. The worksheets were not designed to be expendable but nevertheless such materials are easily lost or damaged during field work even though enclosed in a plastic sleeve. To ensure a quick method of reproducing additional copies, the originals were typed and diagrams mounted on white A4 card which could be used to produce Xerox copies at the Teachers' Centre. This was found to be a more satisfactory method of reproduction and storage of originals than the use of stencils and ink duplicated copies. It was not intended that the worksheets should be used in their exact form. An enterprising teacher would wish to direct the work to suit the composition of the class.

Before the worksheets were used adequate class teaching about the Normans was given and introductory information explaining the purpose and method of compilation of Domesday Book before this section was undertaken. I found the book *Domesday Rebound* (HMSO 1954) to be helpful and useful for this work.

Teachers will be only too well aware of the problem of children slavishly copying from reference books, which is undoubtedly an unprofitable exercise. A technique I found useful and used in the worksheets was to ask children to use accurate factual information obtained from resource materials in imaginative story writing. Pupils used several books to collect the information but used their own composition and ideas to produce the final piece of work.

THE CONTENTS OF THE WORKSHEETS IN BRIEF

Worksheet 1 (four A4 sheets)

Information provided. Location and building of the castle; scale plan of the castle; sketch of a typical motte and bailey castle; film strips. Normans, Bayeux Tapestry.

Work by children: Use of reference books to study motte and bailey castles and Normans in the mid-eleventh century, use of the information to make sketches of a castle and to write a story about a serf or villein who helped to build the castle, and of a Norman soldier who lived in it; use of the scale plan to mark the dimensions of the outer and inner bailey and the width of ditches in the school playground. (Could the outer bailey be enclosed in our school playground?)

Work Sheet 2 (three A4 sheets and copy of local OS plan (1:2500)) †

Information supplied: Plan showing position of castle and school, cross-section of fosses.

Work by children: Position of castle and school to be traced from plan and superimposed on current OS plan to locate position of castle in relation to road and houses adjacent to site today; use of information discovered to find the exact position of the castle on site; writing of poems about walking on the land where Norman soldiers had tramped; work concerning streams indicated on the map and possible interviews with local residents about any evidence of archaeological remains in the gardens.

Work Sheet 3 (four A4 pages)

Information supplied: Detailed list of finds; maps and diagrams of dig in 1928.

Work by children: Work related to thirteenth-century pottery; imaginative work with correct historical detail derived from the finds of a leather shoe, antler and bones of fourteenth century; plasticine or papier mâché model of castle.

Work Sheet 4 (three A4 sheets)

Information supplied: Details of discovery of timbers from the base of a drawbridge; conjectural drawing of bridge.

Work by children: Further study of finds given in teachers' notes; full-size diagrams to show beams unearthed; model of drawbridge in balsa wood; imaginative story or poem of battle for the possession of drawbridge; further study and work on life in a Norman castle, shields, armour, and weapons.

THE DOMESDAY SURVEY (This could be done in a class group)

Information supplied: A children's 'Domesday pack' including a Xerox copy of the relevant page from Domesday Book; transcript from the VCH; map of the West Derby hundred in 1086; details of Domesday survey; vocabulary; slide set.

Work by children: Study and discussion of Domesday documents; matching present day names of districts of the City with names of manors in the survey; discovering the services rendered by thegns and

† may only be done under licence.

173

villeins to the king; listing crimes and punishments; a 'Domesday survey' of children in the class.

Ken May
West Derby Church of England Primary School, Liverpool

FAMILY AND ORAL HISTORY

A great deal of time has been spent on 'the written word' so far in this chapter and this is one of the problems in the primary school. So many children have reading difficulties that history must be viewed as a spoken/oral subject as well. If emphasis is placed on reading and writing the majority of children will not enjoy the past. In recent years oral history has become a respectable area of historical research[26] and much of it consists of the reminiscences of old people during the last century. This has given the study a natural link with the family history which also depends on using source material, mostly of the last hundred years. Therefore, in this section we consider how primary teachers can use family and oral history in the classroom as an acknowledged professional method of historical enquiry. Oral and family history may be used effectively throughout the 5–11 age range.

Work with 6-year-olds has already been described in an earlier part of this book; in this instance 'life-lines', family trees, and artefacts were used to help the children to reconstitute their families backwards about 60–70 years, to the time of their grandparents (see pp. 26–27). Susan Lynn has continued this work in a London school and describes her experiment in the following way.

How I teach history to five-year-olds

Teaching history to young children means, in my view, introducing them to the skills of historical thinking as well as learning to enjoy the past. These I would define as, first, distinguishing between reality and make-believe (at the common sense rather than at the philosophical level that concerns academic historians); second, ordering a sequence of events; third, relating the sequence to a time scale; and finally, seeing events, people, and their surroundings from the perspective of another point in time.

The problem is to find work that develops these skills and, at the same time, matches the level of development of five-year-olds. When I made the attempt with a group of five children (average age, 5.10), in the second year infant class of an outer-London suburban school one day a week for four weeks, I chose, as the topic, the children's own past lives. Here, I thought, the distinction between reality and make-believe would be meaningful to the children, for they could use their own memories, and incidents reported at home, as well as their observations of their own and friends' younger brothers and sisters (all the children in the group had younger brothers and sisters). Interest in the past could be generated by displays of family photographs, the children's own pictures and cut-out illustrations of babies and young children, tape recording children's memories, and making family trees. I knew that the children could order a sequence and it followed that the sequence in this case would be their own physical growth, and landmarks in their lives, such as the acquisition of skills like walking and talking, the birth of younger brothers and sisters, and so on. I anticipated that relating the sequence to a time scale would not occur spontaneously to the children and that they would have to construct it actively themselves. Each child had a sheet of paper with an 18 inch line drawn horizontally across it. Using a three inch square card, the children marked out six squares below the line, each square representing a year of their lives. Each square was then numbered as shown below:

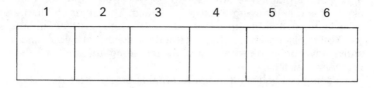

Above each square they drew a picture of themselves to show how they grew bigger each year. To help them grade the heights of the pictures, I gave them a card marked in six sections, the bottom section serving as the height for the baby, the second as the height for age one, and so on.

6
5
4
3
2
1

By writing in each year square something that had happened in that year (or dictating to me when their enthusiasm for putting pencil to paper flagged) they were not only ordering a sequence in relation to a time scale, but also looking at their lives from the perspective of earlier points in time.

How successful was my attempt? The sequence of landmarks in their lives came readily, though it required some initial prompting, especially for years three and four. The time scale did, indeed, prove

175

more difficult. They could not accept that the number at the left of the line of squares should logically be 0 and settled instead for one month. However, they understood that the number at the right end should be six, since, as they said, 'You are five all the time until you are six.' Much more difficult for one of the children was the problem of recording the birth of her one-year-old sister. She could not see that this should go into the 4–5 square and insisted for a time on recording it in the 1–2 square. One source of her difficulty was clearly her fixation on the present age of her sister. However, her subsequent behaviour alerted me to the presence of another problem: an inability to distinguish past and present, compounded by a confusion of identity between herself and her baby sister, which possibly stemmed from a more fundamental inability to distinguish between her own situation or viewpoint and that of another person. Having introduced her baby sister into the scenario, she then began to attribute to herself at age four and five events like teething and having a nappy changed. The other children seemed to have no such difficulties, since they intervened with comments, such as, 'You're talking about Louise (the baby sister), not you', and did not show any confusion after correctly recording the birth of their own brothers or sisters.

To sum up, I believe that the general approach here described could be a useful addition to the repertoire of historical activities in infant classes. It takes a context in which the distinction between reality and make-believe is meaningful to children, and, by concentrating on the skills of historical thinking, it serves as a guide to what might be called historical readiness. It allows particular strengths and weaknesses to be identified and taken into account when planning history-based work. For example, all the children in the group would benefit from more work on time scales, and the weakest member seems to need more practice in distinguishing between different people's situations, without which no real understanding of other people in time or place can occur. The approach is undoubtedly teacher-directed, but I make no apology for that, since, without such direction the practice of skills and diagnosis of difficulties might not have taken place. As far as the children were concerned, the amount of relevant conversation sparked off recall of past events connected both with themselves and with members of their families, and speculation about the future. These results suggest that the children both enjoyed the experience and became more aware of the time dimension in their lives.

Susan Lynn
Polytechnic of the South Bank, London

Help may also be gained by junior teachers mainly from three published sources. One is the work of Sallie Purkis who experimented with children of 7–8 in a Cambridge primary school, another is the work of Brendan Murphy of Wigan working with 10- to 11-year-olds, and finally the extensive work of Don Steel and Lawrence Taylor described in some detail in their book *Family History in Schools* (published by

Phillimore, 1973). Sallie Purkis had a mixed-ability class including five remedial readers and most children found writing more difficult than reading. She started from an old photograph of their school in 1908 found in the local library. In this photograph schoolgirls aged about 13 were gardening as part of the curriculum and the purpose of the project was to find out how these girls, the great-grandmothers of the class, lived in the same area in Edwardian days. Therefore Sallie Purkis sent the children's grandmothers as elderly friends a short list of questions called 'Ask grandma'. The replies enabled the class to build up a picture of Edwardian clothes, washdays, schooldays, shopping days, and general life style. The grandmothers lent artefacts and letters of all sorts and by half term the walls and tables of the classroom were so busy with information and relics of grandmother's day that these ladies were invited to school to talk to the children and look at the display.[27] I hope that this work will be reflected in the new series to be published by Longmans and written by Sallie Purkis—*Into the Past*.

In the same way, a photograph of my maternal grandparents and their four children (the eldest boy had died of meningitis when a baby) taken about 1900 (Fig. 5.15) could form the basis of a family history project with the initiative coming from the teacher and her family. The photograph throws into stark relief the social life of a lower middle-class Edwardian family living near Manchester. The 'best' clothes, particularly of the parents, make this an important and expensive family occasion. My eldest aunt (in the middle) always made the girls' clothes and had put a great effort into her mother's spotted dress. As eldest daughter (given considerable status) she allowed herself a more fancy outfit than her younger sisters (my mother on the right-hand side) and had piled her hair 'on top'. My uncle, in his Eton collar and with a handkerchief suitably placed in his top pocket, has a place of honour near his mother as 'the only son'. He always got more pocket money than his sisters! All look solemn for this splendid occasion although they were a jolly family from my recollections. This may be contrasted with informal family slides in the nineteen-eighties 'then' and 'now'. So much of the past can come out of one good photograph, particularly when supported by 'oral' evidence which I can well remember being told me by my mother. Children are intensely interested in their class teacher and her family. This photograph could lead to children bringing family groups of more recent years, time charts could be made and a topic of 'Family groups—old and new' could be started.

Brendan Murphy experimented mainly with top juniors and therefore more archival work could be undertaken than in Sallie Purkis's class. This involved mostly independent work by children on their own

177

Fig. 5.15 The Craven family c. 1900

families from oral evidence, documentary records (family bibles, birth certificates, parish registers, and school log books), other records (letters, newspapers), material exhibits, pictorial records, and professional evidence from the record office. In the case of these children, four years older than Sallie Purkis's class, great-grandmothers were traced, maps made showing where relations had gone all over England and local maps showing workplaces of relations in the past and present. Children made their own scrapbooks of their families. In this scheme, as Brendan Murphy points out, the teacher has to be very well organized and systematic with so many precious resources about the classroom for a considerable time.[28]

Don Steel and Lawrence Taylor undertook a large-scale research programme on family history in schools near Reading in the late 1960s. The children worked back in three stages through five generations to 1860 starting from 'Who am I?'. The second stage involved parents and the third 'Generation 3, 1918–45', 'Generation 4, 1890–1930' and 'Generation 5, 1865–1900'. They used documents, and evidence through tape recordings of old people's descriptions and many artefacts. Out of 700 children using the scheme only 30 found if difficult to participate because of tensions at home. These children worked on the teacher's family, helped others with their families or collected information from local old people not related to them. The second chapter of Steel and Taylor's book shows how family history may be used as a unifying factor in interdisciplinary work. The natural integration of English, art, drama, geography, mathematics, social studies, and family history is illustrated. One sentence is very encouraging for non-specialists in primary schools:

> Thus history is the natural focal point for work in many subjects, and the reason that it is often taught more interestingly at the Primary level may be that there the teachers are not history specialists. The history they teach is, therefore, more related to other areas of human knowledge and, above all, is concerned not with parties, policies and the balance of power, but with people.[29]

Most of this research was done with children over 11 years of age but four parts of the book are particularly useful to primary teachers. One is the letter sent to parents to show that the work is serious and to guide them in lending artefacts. The second comprises the two accounts by teachers of work done with 7- to 8-year-olds and 8- to 9-year-olds on the 'Who am I?' project and with 9- to 11-year-olds on interdisciplinary work using patches of history at the points 1945, 1914, 1870. These may be found on pp. 153–160 in *Family History in Schools*. The third useful

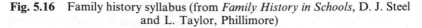

```
┌─────────────────────────────┐         ┌─────────────────────────────┐
│ PHASE I                     │         │ PHASE 2                     │
│                             │         │                             │
│ WHO AM I?                   │         │ INVOLVING THE PARENTS       │
│                             │         │                             │
│ Generation 1 (c.1960–The Future)│     │ Generation 2 (c.1930–date)  │
│                             │         │                             │
│ Unit 1 : My Family          │         │ Unit 6 : Parents' Childhoods│
│ Unit 2 : My Life            │    ──►  │ Unit 7 : World War II: The  │
│ Unit 3 : A Changing World   │         │          Home Front         │
│ Unit 4 : The Future         │         │ Unit 8 : Post-War Britain   │
│ Unit 5 : Evaluation         │         │ Unit 9 : My Family Tree     │
│                             │         │ Unit 10 : Evaluation        │
│                             │         │                             │
└─────────────────────────────┘         └─────────────────────────────┘
            ▲                                       ▲
            │                                       │
            └───────────────────┬───────────────────┘
                                │
┌───────────────────────────────────────────────────────┐
│                                          RESOURCES      │
│                                                         │
│         PRIMARY SOURCES                                 │
│                                                         │
│         Oral evidence        Classroom museum          │
│         Family documents     School records            │
│         Photographs          Maps                      │
│         Newspapers           Genealogical sources      │
│                                                         │
└───────────────────────────────────────────────────────┘
```

Fig. 5.16 Family history syllabus (from *Family History in Schools*, D. J. Steel and L. Taylor, Phillimore)

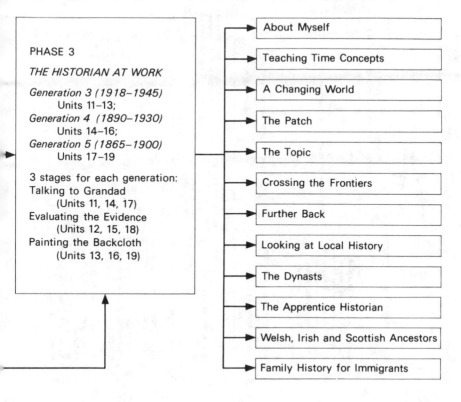

PHASE 3

THE HISTORIAN AT WORK

Generation 3 (1918–1945)
    Units 11–13;
Generation 4 (1890–1930)
    Units 14–16;
Generation 5 (1865–1900)
    Units 17–19

3 stages for each generation:
Talking to Grandad
    (Units 11, 14, 17)
Evaluating the Evidence
    (Units 12, 15, 18)
Painting the Backcloth
    (Units 13, 16, 19)

- About Myself
- Teaching Time Concepts
- A Changing World
- The Patch
- The Topic
- Crossing the Frontiers
- Further Back
- Looking at Local History
- The Dynasts
- The Apprentice Historian
- Welsh, Irish and Scottish Ancestors
- Family History for Immigrants

SECONDARY SOURCES

Resource bank (cards and folders)
Classroom library
Other libraries
Audio-visual aids

181

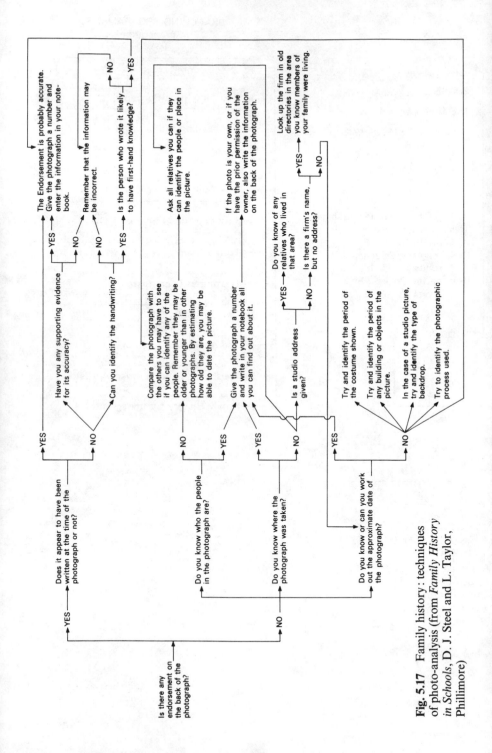

Fig. 5.17 Family history: techniques of photo-analysis (from *Family History in Schools*, D. J. Steel and L. Taylor, Phillimore)

reference is to training primary children to use tape recorders for them to read information found in parish registers which they have not time to write down when visiting a church or record office. They refer to an article written for the *Genealogists' Magazine* on this subject.[30] John Wyman of the University of Kent at Canterbury writes of the need for training both students and children in methods of tape recording themselves and helping old people to record their memories. He also writes of the building up of taped memories to be lent to schools.[31] The last helpful information in *Family History in Schools* is the possible syllabus that a school could follow if it wanted to base work on family history (Fig. 5.16). Phase 1 could form the work for 7- to 8-year-olds, Phase 2 for 8- to 9-year-olds and Phase 3 with some of the branching programmes for the 9- to 11-year-olds. 'Crossing the frontiers' and 'The apprentice historian' are intended for older pupils. 'The dynasts' means applying the family history techniques to families in other periods of the past. For example, the Cecil family from the Tudor age to the present day may be studied quite easily from *The Cecils of Hatfield* by David Cecil (Constable, 1973). If old photographs are the main evidence, teachers will find *Techniques of Photo-Analysis* very useful (Fig. 5.17).

Coventry Community Education Project have recently helped two boys at St Anne's School, Willenhall, to find out about Mr Warr and his life in Willenhall from the beginning of the twentieth century. Mr Warr lent the boys photographs and told them about his long life. He lived in the Toll Bar Cottage about which he said:

> I lived in the old Toll Bar Cottage. It was more or less a square building with two extensions at each end, one with a pantry. It was built on big sand-stone foundations, great big sand stones. There was no concrete flooring, it was a brick floor.
>
> When I was born the front door was a double door so that the toll man, the man taking the tolls, could open the top one and look out, and that is how he could see everything coming. There were windows at each end besides the front as well so they could see all vehicles coming along the road. Well it was altered a bit after I was born, so of course, that is what my parents told me.

The Coventry Community Education Centre made the 'research' done by these two boys into a well-produced pamphlet called *Cameo No. 1: Mr. Warr* from which this extract comes.

All these examples of family and oral history have the great advantage of depending upon human resources in the community, therefore they are cheap in comparison with other resources. They also involve speaking rather than writing which is always an advantage to younger children. They give children pride in their own environment and link

183

them purposefully with other generations. This method can be overdone and I personally would avoid a whole syllabus based on family history.

5.4 Third order resource—mechanical aids

The use of mechanical aids provides an important addition to a teacher's repertoire. However they are nothing more than aids and can be rather capricious, so they should be used with discretion and only when a teacher can rely on technical assistance if necessary. Another problem is that programmes not controlled by a particular teacher can be replaced by others not prepared for. For example, the programme for different years may be given the same title ('Out of the past') but cover completely different topics in the past. Thus the difficulty of all learning dependent upon mechanical aids is the temporary nature of its use. On the other hand 'sound' programmes that are taped can last for three years. In some schools non-specialist teachers have based their entire syllabus on BBC and ITV programmes and their accompanying notes, and have not done any teaching themselves, cutting history out of the curriculum when the programmes end, quite contrary to the intentions of the programme designers. Also, these programmes, though excellent in themselves, do not appear to follow any structure during the year but are 'one-off' topics encouraging teachers to avoid the 'frameworks' we are seeking. Therefore I advocate caution in the use of mechanical aids.

Space prevents discussion of the use of all mechanical aids. Complete filmstrips are not used much now as a whole strip is too long for most 5–11 children and it is clumsy to keep a strip intact and wind it through for the sake of a few frames. Many teachers select suitable frames from a strip and cut the strip up to make about six transparencies for detailed observation and discussion. Longmans make excellent coloured filmstrips to accompany the *Then and There* reference books useful for top juniors but many teachers encourage children to use individual viewers for individual slides which are more useful for topic work. Films are even less useful in the primary school as even the educational ones have usually been made for secondary schools. One educational film I have used frequently on *The Civil War 1642–9* (two reels—Ranks 215 A 17 National Audio-Visual Aids Library, Paxton Place, Gipsy Road, London SE27) is useful with top juniors studying the military campaigns of the period; it should be used preferably for revision rather than actual first teaching. Its animated diagrammatic approach is lively and amusing and explains military movements in a way to be remembered. The showing of old full-length commercial films is useful only for purposes such as an end of term school 'show' if there has been discussion before and after. Films such as *The Six Wives of Henry VIII*, *A Man for All Seasons* (Thomas More) and *Victoria Regina* have all been used for these activities. But all films have to be hired, paid for, and sent back, as well as projected satisfactorily, therefore they are not a good, regular teaching medium, especially in the primary school.

The visual approach has obvious advantages in the primary school but some children also learn well through listening to discs and tapes. Work done on the Elizabethan age would benefit from the playing of Renaissance music on contemporary instruments, especially as so many schools have competent recorder groups. In his *History for Juniors*, already mentioned several times, Michael Pollard has an interesting chapter—'History from traditional culture'—in which he shows how folk songs and songs pertinent to particular areas can be used effectively in primary schools.[32] In his book on resources Michael Pollard has useful general chapters on filmstrip and slides, tape and disc, film, and school broadcasting. Useful addresses may also be gleaned from *Treasure Chest for Teachers*[33] and the *History Teachers' Yearbook*.[34]

The greatest developments during the last ten years have been in BBC sound and television programmes, under the aegis of the School Broadcasting Council of the United Kingdom, those shown by ITA, and also local sound radio. If a school caters for sessions based on television and radio by having a special room, or facilities to move the television to different classrooms, and facilities for tape-recording sound programmes, then the teacher is able to prepare for selected programmes suitable for her year's work. There is no doubt that these programmes are exellent in all respects—preparation, execution, and the production of high-quality teachers' and pupils' booklets. If a school loses a tape, already recorded, a replacement may be bought from the BBC so long as the recording is destroyed after three years.

Younger children are catered for mainly by integrated programmes. A BBC television programme called *Watch* is aimed at 6- to 8-year-olds; the first five programmes in the summer term of 1980 were on 'Moses in Egypt' and the Autumn term 1980 included a programme on 'Guy Fawkes', presumably appropriately near 5 November! The teacher's book is all that could be desired with bibliographies, information, and large illustrations to be duplicated. *Merry go Round* is aimed at the 8–9 age group and was concerned with 'Change through Time' in the Autumn term 1980; this included 'Historical time', 'Ways of telling age' and 'Generation after generation'. These programmes could well be viewed and then applied to the history being studied. BBC radio have prepared a programme called *Springboard* which links with *Merry go Round* and is concerned with such topics as the history of medicine and

185

of the telephone. It is intended for 7- to 9-year-old children; the teacher's booklet in this case is not quite so easy to follow. A BBC television programme, *A Year's Journey*, was popular in 1969 and very useful for environmental studies with top juniors. The booklet ranging from London to an Iron Age village, a castle in Wales (Conway) and Hadrian's Wall, was very well illustrated by excellent photographs and gave plenty of detailed information—some of quite an advanced nature. Let us hope that a similar programme will be devised for schools wanting an integrated approach.

Separate history/geography programmes appear to have replaced *A Year's Journey*. Rhoda Power's early sound programmes, including *How Things Began*, now take the form of a programme called *Man* for 10- to 12-year-olds. These new programmes also have filmstrips employing the resources of 'radiovision'; in 1980–1 they were concerned with 'early man' in various parts of the world. The series *Out of the Past* (BBC television) for 9- to 11-year-olds, was concerned with life in a twelfth-century village, life in a sixteenth-century town and living in the Iron Age. *History Long Ago*, a radio programme, was concerned with British history and has covered such topics as 'the Normans', 'Sea days and sailing ships' and 'the Jacobites'. The programmes are supported by teachers' notes, radiovision notes and a school may also use the Oxford University Press textbooks in the *Oxford Junior History Series* (Books 1–3 *History Long Ago* by Roy Burnell and Books 4 and 5 *History Not So Long Ago* by Peter and Mary Speed).

All the programmes mentioned are transmitted on BBC radio and television. But the Independent Television Companies also provide very useful programmes. In the mid-1970s an integrated studies series from ATV entitled *Exploration Man* included two history study units 'Digging up man' and 'Only yesterday' (tracing the life of a child's grandmother). A series *How We Used to Live* has been a favourite for many years and originated with Yorkshire Television. Starting from Victorian times it has by now reached the early twentieth century with the programmes centring round one family. When I used this programme in school a very useful illustrated booklet of information and follow-up activities was available as well as a poster of Victorian scenes, called a Scrap Book. The viewing of these ten programmes (a term) on ordinary Victorians led among other things to the class bringing Victorian artefacts to form a museum of their own. David Hall, the Educational Officer at Yorkshire Television made a survey of schools using the programmes and found general approval, though the 8-year-olds found some concepts difficult. *History Around You* (Granada) has been popular for the last six years with teachers of 8- to

11-year-olds probably because Allan Waplington (see p. 167) presented them in his lively, happy manner. The programmes aim to introduce children to local field work; they start from Everton football ground, Liverpool, as an urban study and develop into a visit to Winwick Church (near Warrington) and home life in the Second World War. Allan Waplington bases much of his approach on his *Clues, Clues, Clues* pack published by the *Place, Time and Society 8–13 Schools Council Project*. The teachers' books are particularly helpful to teachers new to historical field work. This series is of necessity concerned with particular localities, many in the north-west, therefore teachers need to prepare work to study similar examples in their own areas. Let us hope that when this has been done the series will continue to be repeated.

Local radio is also doing a good job for primary teachers. When Radio Merseyside first started, it developed a useful series on the environment for infants called *Travels with Timothy* and allowed a talk to be given on *A Tudor House: Speke Hall and the Norris Family 1500–1700* when the archive unit was first published by Liverpool Education Authority in 1971 (see p. 166). Radio Solent broadcast a series called *But Why Here?*, environmental studies programmes for 9- to 13-year-olds. Visits in sound were made to places of particular interest such as Southampton, Romsey, and Tichfield which enabled teachers to take pupils on visits after listening to a programme. They also prepared a programme called *Going Places*—for example, Porchester Castle, Winchester Cathedral, and Carisbrooke Castle, with an excellent booklet. The booklets were made at the Curriculum Development Centre at Southampton. Local radio has the advantage over national bodies in providing local history topics and enlisting the help of local teachers in the schools and colleges.

We cannot blame history broadcasts and television programmes for being what appears to be a 'rag-bag' of topics because within their budgeting limits they provide what they think teachers will use, in the light of their general knowledge and reports from field officers. With the topic approach so popular during the last 15 years this type of programme is only to be expected. In the words of Michael Wynne: 'History broadcasts, then, move with the changing curriculum, sometimes following, sometimes leading, and contributing at those points where the special resources of broadcasting seem likely to be most usefully deployed.'[35] It will be fortunate if, in the light of present and future financial restrictions, these resources can continue to be deployed adequately in a field such as history for the primary school.

5.5 Fourth order resource—outside the school

Although resources outside the school are placed as fourth in importance in this chapter, in some ways the teacher has more support from outside the school than inside. Because most large museums and art galleries have excellent education officers, efficient ancillary services, and sometimes an archivist, teachers are helped very practically by their personal assistance, pamphlets, and worksheets as well as the actual exhibits. Provided that the necessary legal conditions are fulfilled, taking children out from a primary school is much less contentious than taking pupils out from a secondary school because the class timetable is the class teacher's business and there is no examination fever. However, expense may now be a difficulty. As well as taking children to museums, field work and brass-rubbing are also excellent learning activities for the study of history. Teachers are also helped by the visits of HMI, LEA advisers (where they exist), Schools Council officers, and publications, as well as visits to record offices, Teachers' Centres, and by in-service courses if they are given time and finances to attend them.

MUSEUMS AND ART GALLERIES

These are the most easily accessible outside agencies and much has been written about them. The overall quality of their educational facilities is so good that it is impossible in a brief space to do justice to their work. More has been written about museums than art galleries, which have developed their educational facilities more recently. General books on museums are more plentiful than books specifically relating museums to the teaching of history, especially where primary schools are concerned. This in itself shows how much museums and art galleries are integrating agencies in the curriculum and how well they may be used for topics and projects. Two names of curators stand out from the point of view of publication. One is Molly Harrison, famous for her work at the Geffrye Museum in Shoreditch, London, and the other is Barbara Winstanley of the Derbyshire Museum Service. Molly Harrison has published widely and her books include *Changing Museums* (Longmans, 1967) and *Museums* ('On Location' Series, Mills and Boon, 1973). The second book is copiously illustrated and perhaps more use for primary teachers. Barbara Winstanley's *Children and Museums* (Blackwell, 1967) is a sound, well-documented book giving illustrations and worksheets and much helpful reference material about museums all over the country. Margaret Bryant wrote an Historical Association pamphlet on *The Museum and the School* (1961) mostly for secondary schools and the BBC published *Museums and Education* (Education Survey 12, HMSO,

1971) of a general nature. The most comprehensive and specifically historical book is John Fairley's *History Teaching through Museums* (Longmans, 1977) in which he analyses types of museums (comprehensive, specialist, folk, open-air, ship, etc.), discusses how visits should be organized and 'work directives' planned, and finally outlines what services the School Museum offers nationally.

As all exhibits in museums are genuine no one collection can be completely comprehensive. The large city museums, such as the County Museum, Liverpool, exhibit a variety of materials ranging from dinosaurs to the Liverpool–Manchester railway engines and coaches. Examples of specialist museums are the Geffrye Museum (English homes), Platt Hall Costume Gallery, Manchester, the Grosvenor Museum at Chester (mainly Roman), the National Portrait Gallery (Old Masters) and the Bethnal Green Museum of Childhood (London). Examples of open-air museums are Fishbourne Roman Palace, Clarke Hall at Wakefield (a seventeenth-century yeoman's house), Ironbridge Gorge Museum in Shropshire, and Singleton Open Air Museum near Chichester. Examples of folk museums are the Castle Museum at York, the American Museum at Claverton, near Bath, and the Abbey Museum, Kirkstall near Leeds. Among ship museums are the *Cutty Sark* at Greenwich, Buckler's Hard Maritime Museum, Hampshire, and of course the *Victory* at Portsmouth. I have seen most of these and think them most suitable for primary children.

The organization of visits requires planning some way ahead, visiting the museum to meet the Education Officer, planning the visit, and buying relevant material for preparation. Most education officers are so efficient that the teacher only has to do as she is told once the museum has been reached. All the usual precautions should be taken for the safety and well-being of the children on a journey. All children should know what their tasks are from preparation in school beforehand and come with clip board (with waterproof cover when not in use) and pencil(s). They should be reminded that all exhibits should be treated very carefully as handling is often allowed in the museum teaching rooms. After an introductory talk by the Education Officer or teacher the children should be divided into groups, each with a child group leader, to look round. It is usually better to limit viewing to one room or area. Infants are capable of doing this if suitable groups are formed, tasks are simple and few, and one area is selected. When visiting the Transport Gallery of the County Museum at Liverpool I had tears from one 6-year-old because she was frightened of the big locomotive engines; comforting her and putting her in the charge of another 6-year-old (hand in hand) led to smiles and jokes by the end of the visit! Children

189

FOOD AND DRINK 6

This is a LATE GEORGIAN lady.
Draw her coffee pot,
her fire and chestnut roaster,
her cup and saucer,
her tea caddy.

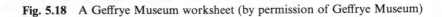

Fig. 5.18 A Geffrye Museum worksheet (by permission of Geffrye Museum)

should be warned when the time of the visit is coming to an end in order to complete their work. A roll call should be taken and one child deputed (preferably by the others) to thank the Museum Officer. It is always courteous to write a 'thank you' letter when these professional people have given their time to a school group.

The workbooks provided for children are an example of quality content and production and they certainly ease the teacher's life and are comparatively cheap to buy. The County Museum at Liverpool produces a neat booklet for younger children called *The Journey* which is taken by Eliza Wallace and her father from Liverpool to Manchester on the newly-opened Liverpool–Manchester railway in 1830. The story runs throughout the booklet with museum exhibits, questions, spaces for drawings, diagrams, and a coach to label from given words and a passage of prose to complete the missing words. The Geffrye Museum provides and sells many teaching resources, one being several worksheets on 'Food and drink', with spaces for drawings of objects found in the period rooms in the museum. Figure 5.18 shows the top part of one worksheet, the rest being spaces for drawing of the coffee pot, fire, chestnut roaster, cup, saucer, and tea caddy.

The Open Air Museum at Singleton excels in its help to teachers. A *Museum Teaching Kit* includes a *Handbook for School Teachers* by Kim Leslie, and *Wander Around Trails* may be bought on 'Windows and doors', 'Medieval timber frame construction', and 'Walling materials and roofs'. In each of these trails, primary teachers are warned that the trails 'are not considered suitable for handing out to children of a junior school age in this form' yet the information, diagrams, and map of the site for each one are so clear that teachers could quickly prepare a trail shortly before the visit. The Singleton Open Air Museum materials are imaginative and provide scholarly information, and the exhibits include a real reconstructed market hall.

Museums and art galleries not only provide visits and materials for children and teachers. They also encourage children to spend time in them in school holidays. In a recent article Peter Dormer[6] gave examples of holiday activities. At the Bethnal Green Museum of Childhood children can play the alphabet game and look for exhibits listed according to the letters of the alphabet. Part of the game is shown in Fig. 5.19.

Peter Dormer also mentions the National Portrait Gallery where a day's Elizabethan music-making has already been described (p. 43). Here children use the portraits as clues to make puppets and portrait blow-ups. Bradford Industrial Museum even organized a family project on photography called 'Snap happy'. The Museum of London runs

A   is for Alphabet, a toy alphabet. Can you find these toys? They are all in the toy
     gallery.

A   is for Aunt Sally.
     Why did you play the game out of doors?

B   is for bricks.
     What could they build?

C   is for clockwork toys.
     Now they are too old to be worked.

D   is for dolls house.
     How many rooms has the largest?

E   is for elephant.
     He is doing tricks with the other circus animals.

Fig. 5.19   Part of an alphabet game (by permission of Bethnall Green Museum)

four-day courses for 40 children at a time on 'Covent Garden market'. In
these imaginative enterprises Peter Dormer sees the education officer
taking a step beyond objects and worksheets. In the same way the
Sudbury Hall Museum, Derbyshire, sells a compact colourful guide for
children which opens out into a board game—'The Entertaining and
Moral Game of Pitfalls and Praises'—to be played with dice and
counters. On a recent visit to Sudbury Hall I found a room packed with
parents and children playing 'bygone' games on an antique table. The
ILEA organize junior children modelling old costumes at Ranger's
House, Blackheath. Although holiday time is not classroom time the
interest children gain from these activities outside school rubs off onto
their work in school.

A final word should be said about museum loan services and John
Fairley's chapter 'School museum services' has up-to-date information
in his useful book on museums. As long ago as 1954 I borrowed Stone
Age tools from Salford Museum for my teaching of early man in a
Salford school; I was handed them in penny numbers to carry in my zip
shopping bag and, although a newcomer to Salford, I must have been
trusted to return them! But even further back, in 1884, the City of
Liverpool Museum was the first loan service, not now continued. City of
Leeds Museum has now built up a large loan collection and this is
reflected in the good work done in history in their first and middle
schools. Some museums lend exhibitions in cases for special occasions in
schools. The Imperial War Museum in London lends materials on the
two World Wars, and the American Museum, near Bath, lends

exhibitions connected with North American history to all country unless they are too fragile to go by rail. Some muse replicas of exhibits which children buy for their collections and so the more expensive items, such as a cuneiform tablet from the British Museum, can form the basis of a school museum. It is these artefacts that can be used as suggested earlier in work with 6-year-olds before they bring their own 'old things'.

This short account of museums and art galleries as resources for teaching and learning history is quite inadequate in comparison with the tremendous support they are to teachers in primary schools. It is almost possible to structure a history syllabus around local museums and art galleries and it is here that original sources so suitable for 5- to 11-year-old children may be found in abundance. This is a safer syllabus than one geared to changing radio and television programmes or family history. From these small beginnings an understanding of history is developed in later years.

RECORD OFFICES AND TEACHERS' CENTRES

A great expansion of city and county record offices took place after the Second World War and many hitherto unseen municipal and family records were at the disposal of schools as well as the general public. Teachers' Centres or Curriculum Development Centres are of more recent growth, being set up from the mid-1960s. Some record offices, such as those at Essex and Kent, were enterprising enough to include a teacher on their staff and these teachers were quite often trained historians. Margaret Phillips of Kent Record Office has already been mentioned as the compiler of the excellent archive unit *Some Kent Children 1594–1875*. Although most record offices are not adequately staffed to help teachers of primary age children, their archivists are as helpful as time allows. Teachers' Centres, on the other hand, are suffering badly in some areas, in spite of the excellent work they have done to help teachers. Some are being closed completely and others joined together.

Teachers should not fear to seek out, when time permits, their local record office, whether it is part of the public library, as at Liverpool, Manchester or York, or in its own building as at Preston (Lancashire Record Office), or housed in another building as the City Office is in the Town Hall at Chester or the County Record Office at The Castle at Chester. Some large museums, particularly in London, have their own archivists as do some universities (for example the University of Liverpool). Archivists are very humble, scholarly, and helpful people though not always very knowledgeable about primary schools. Teachers

193

should look for short, clear, single documents based on a subject relevant to the syllabus and ask for a translation (transcription) from the archivist. This 'starter', in the words of John Fines, can be duplicated and used in class. At one time teachers' groups were created to enable them to gain help from colleagues but most of them have disbanded under pressures, not least the fact that promotion in primary education tends to be associated with other areas of the curriculum. Liverpool Teachers' Archives Study Group made three archive teaching units as a group but the last two units were made by fewer and fewer teachers. This also seems to be happening in other areas. Record offices lend mounted archives to schools, though transport often causes problems. Cheshire County Record Office at one time had a fine collection of original pictures of Civil War leaders in Cheshire with a short account of the part they each played in the war locally. They were mounted on stiff red card and each could be used as a visual aid for teaching or as a display for individual work by top juniors. I have always found the Lancashire Record Office very cooperative in bringing exhibitions to schools with an archivist to explain them to the children. This type of exhibition for one day may be thrown open to the whole of even a large primary school if all children have been told something about it. The Lancashire Record Office also had photocopied for me a large, magnificent document in the form of a letter from Queen Elizabeth I to the Emperor of Cathay; although a late sixteenth-century document, the handwriting is almost copperplate and so clear to read that 9- to 11-year-olds would have no difficulty with the handwriting.

A more obvious resource between 1966 and 1976 has been Teachers' Centres set up by Local Education Authorities. These centres, led by experienced teachers, have provided invaluable resources as well as run in-service courses. Perhaps the most powerful influence for good in an area has been the ILEA History and Social Sciences Teachers' Centre (377 Clapham Road, London SW9 9BT, Tel. 733–2935), until recently led by an enthusiastic historian, Tom Hastie. This centre not only provides in-service courses for both primary and secondary teachers but publishes materials to help teachers of history. The resource unit described earlier, *People Around Us—Work* (published by A. & C. Black) was shown and discussed at ten London Teachers' Centres in October and November 1980, and a residential course based on the same unit was held at Avery Hill College at a later date. A publication, *History in the Primary School: Curriculum Guidelines* written by Howell-Davies, Staff Inspector for History and Social Services, was published during the autumn 1980, and a copy was sent free to all heads of ILEA primary schools. A *Primary Newsletter* was also published in September 1980 concentrating on history and social science. This level of activity is not possible for small authorities.

Dudley Teachers' Centre at Himley Hall has provided especially for the needs of teachers of history, particularly in primary schools. The Centre provides a first-rate warden and plenty of up-to-date equipment for teachers to use in their own way. Teachers' groups meet at the centre to discuss their common needs, and the materials are produced in co-operation, stencils being stored for future use at Himley Hall. These materials include slides, transparencies, and tapes as well as stencils. Packs have been made for example, on archaeology, houses and homes, castles, local churches, arms and armour, and monumental brasses. One of the most ambitious books, of 46 pages, is *Tracing a Medieval Town.* Examples of all the packs are kept in the Centre. The fact that teachers can find such varied material in one centre encourages much more integrated work. John West, Chief Inspector for Dudley, provides the initiative behind this successful venture and his article in *Teaching History* elaborates this brief account.[37] Brian Smith, the Warden of the Chester Teachers' Centre until its closure, worked closely with teachers to produce materials for primary and secondary schools in collaboration with the six other centres in Cheshire. Three out of many valuable booklets are *Chester: a Wall Trail, A Look at Roman Chester* by R. E. Tovey and *The Dee through Chester.* All booklets are well written from the point of view of content, beautifully illustrated by sketches, and most of them provide activities for children. Schools may buy copies very cheaply.

Two other Teachers' Centres should be mentioned. The Curriculum Development Centre at Southampton has produced a small booklet on *Tichfield* (by Charles Cuff), a small compact Hampshire village. The booklet works through the chronology of Tichfield using St Peter's Church, Tichfield Abbey, St Margaret's Priory, Tudor and Georgian houses in the village and the tithe barn. The size of Tichfield is ideal for field work for juniors and this booklet is most attractively produced. Teachers would have to prepare their own activities but the imaginative illustrations make this an easy task. Desmond Lamb, Warden of the In-Service Training Centre at Southport, encourages teachers and college lecturers to help groups of teachers to produce their own tailor-made booklets. In 1973, with the help of Peter Garwood, then of King George V School, Southport, Mr Lamb made an archive teaching unit *Road Travel in Lancashire 1700–1850* mainly for secondary pupils, but some of it could be adapted for top juniors. A more recent venture, initiated by Frank Harris of City of Liverpool College of Higher Education, is to produce a booklet on *The Origins of Southport.* This originated from an

195

in-service course on local history when the teachers involved in primary schools wanted to collect information for their own teaching. It will consist of information, maps, pictures, extracts from source material, and questions to ask pupils.[38]

In-service courses to help primary teachers with history are uncommon but, as already mentioned, Teachers' Centres occasionally run them. Although they usually only run for one day, which does not give time for teachers to actually make resources, many teachers are enabled to exchange ideas and gain impetus to make their own resources, find new materials from others' use, and alter their teaching methods. Other agencies besides local authorities run courses. The Division of Professional Studies at the University of Bristol has organized several day conferences for primary teachers, due to the initiative of one of the lecturers, Ann Low-Beer. She has been able to work closely with the Advisory Service of Avon LEA and the demand for attendance has far exceeded the available places in the 1979–80 session. In several of these courses teachers themselves were actually taught a topic of history as well as methods and resources for the topics being discussed. John Chaffer also runs regular in-service courses for primary teachers at the Bulmershe College of Higher Education near Reading. Apologies are made to many other Teachers' Centres in Britain offering history courses to primary teachers for not describing their efforts.

OTHER OUTSIDE AGENCIES

Much has already been said in Chapter 4 about the resource provided by buildings, streets, and landscape, but more should be said about brass-rubbing as an historical source. Brasses are excellent original source material because they provide evidence of the past in earlier periods of history for which written sources are less accessible. Brass-rubbing also provides the necessary activity for young children. Unfortunately brasses tend to exist in old churches, which are kept locked for security reasons, they have been rubbed too frequently, and quite large payments are asked in some cases for permission to rub. These factors limit their usefulness for primary children, though teachers may find it easier to make the brass-rubbing on their own and use the product with children. I have found that the rubbing of the Childwall brass depicting Henry and Clemence Norris in the fifteenth century and their connection with Speke Hall has brought the study of a Tudor house to life. Two of the most useful publications on brass-rubbing are *Brass Rubbing* by Malcolm Norris (Studio Vista, 1965) and *Discovering Brasses and Brass-Rubbing* by Malcolm Cook (Shire Publications, 1968).[39] The first is a beautifully-produced book fully illustrated and with clear instructions on how to rub brasses as well as specialized information about British and European brasses. Malcolm Norris includes a picture of a brass rubbing of a friar of c 1440 found at Great Amwell, Hertfordshire; it is 16 inches tall and particularly appropriate for young children to rub. He also provides a very full bibliography and a gazetteer of outstanding brasses in Britain. A useful practical article has been written on brass-rubbing from their own teaching experiences by Mary Buckles and Brian Scott.[40] As brasses are immovable they are of restricted use to teachers.

The Schools Council has not given much specific help to teachers about history in the 5–11 age range. The Environmental Studies Project was mainly interested in geography and the *History, Geography and Social Science 8–13 Project* (*Place, Time and Society*) cannot help the 5–8 teachers and was perhaps not specific enough to help the non-specialist in the 8–11 age range. Three of its publications *Clues, Clues, Clues, People on the Move* and *Life in the 1930s* can be used for topic work if appropriate to the syllabus.[41] More help may be gained from this project by teachers who are thinking out their ideas anew and want to interrelate history, geography, and social science. In Chapter 3 of this book on the syllabus Alan Blyth, the original director of the project, has adapted the philosophy of the project to suggesting a syllabus for 7–11 schools (pp. 54–61) (Figs 3.13–16). For those teachers who would like to know more about the project's ideas a small booklet was published by the project team in 1975, *Place, Time and Society—an Introduction*, (published by Collins, ESL, Bristol). Chapter 5—'Subjects as resources'—is particularly useful.

The *Cambridge School Classics Project* has been supported by the Schools Council and the Nuffield Foundation in producing Roman and Greek foundation courses which can be used with older juniors. The units consist of source material (translated) on cards, large and small and in books; there is also a teachers' handbook. The Roman World and the Greek World are separate units. The Greek World also supplies pupils' packs on specialized topics such as *The Gods of Mount Olympus* and *Greek Festivals*.[42] As with the *Place, Time and Society* materials these packs are excellent material for teachers used appropriately to suit their own topic work.

'Outside the School'—a fourth order resource—has endless possibilities but requires teachers to have time to make contacts and arrange visits from school and to school from outside. This means that teachers need to be stable in their jobs and able to develop a repertoire of those special occasions which should be built into the syllabus and repeated to improve their approach.

197

5.6 Conclusion

In a three-stream primary school resources should ideally be in the care of a member of staff with the assistance of at least a part-time technician-cum-secretary. Even if the teacher in charge of history has not that responsibility it is as well to keep all historical resources in one place and for teachers to list their requirements in a notebook for the following week. The teacher responsible for history should work out priorities through looking at the notebook and discussing with colleagues how resource needs can be fulfilled for each term. This is another reason for having a syllabus for all years known to colleagues; their syllabus should be flexible enough to allow for changes in the use of resources. Whenever resources are used they need to be checked and mended at the end of the year. The maintenance of adequate sources and resources for the teaching of history is no mean task and must be built up gradually but the teaching of the past in the primary school is impossible without them.

References

1. L. C. Taylor, *Resources for Learning*, Penguin, 1972, p. 236.
2. Ibid., pp. 235–6.
3. M. Pollard, *A Handbook of Resources in the Primary School*, Ward Lock Educational, 1976, p. 91.
4. P. Mays, *Why Teach History?* University of London Press, 1974, p. 89.
5. M. Pollard, op. cit., p. 93.
6. M. Pollard, op. cit., p. 21.
7. P. Abrams, 'History without textbooks', *Where?* August 1964, p. 15.
8. S. Paice, 'Teaching children not to read', *Times Educational Supplement*, 1 February 1980.
9. H. Burton, 'The writing of historical novels', *Children and Literature* by V. Haviland, Bodley Head, 1973.
10. H. Belloc, 'The character of an historical novel', *One Thing and Another*, Hollis and Carter, 1955.
11. *Early Childhood*, 270b Station Road, Addlestone, Weybridge, Surrey.
12. A useful reference book is G. Williams, *Guide to Sources of Illustrative Material for use in Teaching History*, Historical Association, no. 65, 1967.
13. T. Charles-Edwards and B. Richardson, *They Saw It Happen 1689–1897*, B. Blackwell, 1958, p. 21.

14. C. Morris (ed.), *The Journeys of Celia Fiennes*, Cresset Press, 1947, p. 184.

15. D. Defoe, *A Tour Through the Whole Island of Great Britain*, vol. 1, Dent, 1966, p. 141.

16. S. Wheeler, 'Young Children, Documents and the Locality', *Teaching History*, vol. 1. no. 3, 1970.

17, 18. R. Wood, *Children 1773–1890*, History at Source, Evans, nos. 40 and 13.

19. Quoted in W. B. Stephens, *Teaching Local History*, Manchester University Press, 1977, pp. 130–1.

20. Any enquiry about this collection should be addressed to the Tutor Librarian, Education Library, School of Education, University of Liverpool, P.O. Box 147, Liverpool L69 3BX. (Books cannot be *borrowed* from this collection.)

21. M. Palmer, 'Archive packs for schools: some practical suggestions', *Journal of the Society of Archivists*, vol. 6, no. 3, 1979.

22. J. E. Blyth, 'Archives and source material in the Junior School', *Teaching History*, vol. 1, no. 1, 1969.

23. Out of print but the County Museum, William Brown Street, Liverpool 3, is planning a revised reprint.

24. For a specimen copy apply to M. Cook, University Archives, Senate House, University of Liverpool, P.O. Box 147, Liverpool L69 3BX.

25. J. West, *History, Here and Now*, The Teacher Publishing Co., 1966, p. 21. (See 33 below.)

26. P. Thompson, *The Voice of the Past*, Oxford University Press, 1978.

27. S. Purkis, 'An Experiment in Family History with First Year Juniors', *Teaching History*, vol. 4, no. 15, 1976 and 'Oral History in the Primary School', *History Workshop*, Issue 3, Spring 1977, also *Oral History in Schools* from Department of Sociology, University of Essex, Wivenhoe Park, Colchester, Essex CO4 3SQ.

28. B. Murphy, 'History in the Family', *Teaching History*, vol. 2, no. 5, 1971.

29. D. J. Steel and L. Taylor, *Family History in Schools*, Phillimore, 1973, p. 16.

30. D. J. Steel and L. Taylor, 'Tape recording of Parish Registers' *Genealogists' Magazine*, vol. 16, no. 9, 1971.

31. J. Wyman, 'Oral History and its possibilities in Schools', *Kent Education Gazette*, vol. 52, no. 1.

32. For information about a termly bulletin *Folk in School* edited by M. Pollard contact Topic Records Ltd, 27 Nassington Road, London NW3.

33. Obtainable from The Teacher Publishing Co., Derbyshire House, Lower Street, Kettering, Northants NN16 8BB.
34. Edited by P. J. Harris and obtained from the Historical Association, 59A Kennington Park Road, London SE11.
35. M. Wynne, 'Broadcasting History', *Times Educational Supplement*, 26 April 1968.
36. P. Dormer, 'Worksheets in August', *Times Educational Supplement*, 8 August 1980.
37. J. West, 'The Development of a Local Resources Centre', *Teaching History*, vol. 2, no. 7, 1972.
38. Enquiries to The Warden, In-Service Training Centre, Mornington Hall, Mornington Road, Southport, Lancs PR9 0TS.
39. M. Cook's pamphlet is out of print according to the 1980 Shire Publications catalogue.
40. M. Buckles and B. Scott, 'A Patch Study in a Junior School using Monumental Brasses', *Teaching History*, vol. 3, no. 11, 1974.
41. *Clues, Clues, Clues* (1975), *People on the Move* (1976), *Life in the 1930s* (1977) published by Collins, ESL, Bristol.
42. *The Cambridge School Classics Project*, Cambridge University Press. Help and information may be obtained from M. M. Forrest, Classical Studies Director, CSCP, Faculty of Education, Bristol Polytechnic, Redland Hill, Bristol BS6 6UZ.

6. Assessment, evaluation, and record keeping

6.1 Introduction

If teachers are purposefully concerned with history in primary schools, it follows that they need to know whether their teaching is justified and effective. For this purpose they are bound to engage in three activities which the teaching profession should claim as its own: assessment, evaluation, and record keeping. None of these is easy to carry out, especially in the social subjects where aims and objectives are subtle and complex; but all of them are important, and all of them need to be approached in a way that teachers can manage in the time and with the facilities at their disposal. In defining them, I follow quite closely the terminology used by Keith Cooper in *Evaluation, Assessment and Record-Keeping in History, Geography and Social Science* (Collins/ESL, Bristol, 1976).[1]

Assessment covers how teachers appraise their pupils; how pupils assess themselves and each other; how they assess their teachers; and how the world at large assesses those same teachers. All these are interrelated: children can hardly be learning much if they are unable to say whether they are succeeding. Teachers are aware of all four, and not surprisingly prefer the first two to the last two. It is the first kind of assessment, of pupils by teachers, that will be considered in this chapter.

Evaluation ranges more widely. It is concerned with how far and how well the aims of a scheme are achieved. It takes account of assessment,[2] but also of curriculum processes, teaching methods, and the materials which teachers purchase or devise. If it appears, after honest reappraisal, that a syllabus is not effectively matched[3] to children's capacities, or that worksheets appear to promote copying rather than thinking, then some re-casting of programme and materials alike may be needed. Chapter 5, and Section 6.5 embody some suggestions about evaluation of materials for history teaching; the whole book is intended to help with the evaluation of syllabus.

Record keeping documents assessment and forms a basis for evaluation. It comprises both the informal records kept in order to mark out children's week-by-week development in basic skills, judgement, and empathy, and also the more formal, cumulative records of progress from year to year which eventually constitute some evidence about individual children that may be passed on to a secondary school.

Assessment, evaluation, and record keeping apply of course across the whole curriculum. They will now be considered in relation to history in the successive age-phases of primary education.

6.2   The infant years: 5- to 7-year-olds

During these early years, all children's work is interrelated more firmly even than in later primary education, so minimal assessment of awareness of the past is needed at this stage. The basic skills of reading, writing, and number work are essential to all development and most infant teachers try to make their children curious to find out from books, eager to imagine the past through role-playing, and able to discuss with the teacher and with other children the ideas that they form. Tape recording children's discussions in small groups is an easy form of assessment if one knows the voices of individual children well enough; children also enjoy it immensely. The scheme of work suggested in Section 3.2, page 23, is very flexible and the large books made each year will contain mainly drawings, crayoned pictures, short sentences, a time-line, a simple map or plan, and possibly a short family tree. These books can be prepared for a certain day at the end of the year to be discussed in groups, with the teacher moving from group to group, and the children in each group giving a vote for the best one. Then the teacher could show the class as a whole the books selected and ask for reasons why these have been chosen. This is teacher and pupil assessment and the teacher need only keep a record of the best by putting H (for History) on the child's record card. (Similarly for Geography, Science, etc.) Thus, by 7 years of age two books will have been made and more children are likely to have H by their names.

Figure 6.1 may help infant teachers to keep their eye on assessment throughout the two years or so of the infant school.

Concepts	Skills
1. Age of objects and age of people	1. To observe and gain evidence from pictures, maps, plans, buildings, artefacts
2. Sequence of events	2. To find out and use knowledge of his own family as far back as possible
3. Changes in time	3. To communicate by telling, drawing, or making a plan or map
4. Relationships between people and events	4. To begin to understand the point of view of others

Fig. 6.1   Concepts and skills as objectives in the infant school

Therefore, from the years 5–7 assessment is ongoing and yearly assessment minimal and part of class activity. As so few materials are available in this age range for the past, the only need for evaluation is of pictures and other visual material. Record keeping is also confined to the few children who are particularly interested in the past at this stage. Joan Tough's work, *Communication Skills*, has shown that the best way for teachers to assess children's progress is through talking to them individually or in small groups.[4] It is, however, important to ensure that the new Hs are added where they are deserved, and not just where they are expected. Anyone may develop a liking for history.

6.3 Incidental assessment in the junior school

Although it is possible to assess more comprehensively in the 7–11 than in the 5–7 age range, much of what goes on from day to day and the type of task set by teachers throughout the year is a form of ongoing assessment which is seldom proved wrong, even if supplemented by more formal methods at the end of the year. In *Recording Children's Progress*, Joan Dean writes: 'The outstanding teacher has a highly developed intuitive ability to find clues'[5] (i.e., to children's progress) but it is better, where normal teachers are concerned, to have records from several teachers on one child. In the final report of a DES/Regional course at the University of Liverpool (*History, Geography and Social Science in the Curriculum 5–14—a Workshop Course on the Assessment of Children's Progress*—Autumn 1979) one group of teachers came to the conclusion that the ongoing and seemingly incidental assessment of pupils was the only sure way: 'We are convinced that systematic planning of activities and materials for the pupils we teach is the best way of beginning to diagnose and assess what is going on in the classroom'.[6]

We have already discussed 'systematic planning' of a framework or syllabus (Chapter 3) and the activities and materials needed in order to implement that syllabus (Chapters 4 and 5). Before incidental assessment can be attempted throughout the year it is necessary to find out a particular teacher's aims (general, long-standing, overall ones) and objectives (specific skills carried out by pupils in relation to the syllabus, showing that they have made progress). All the syllabuses discussed in Chapter 3 could have the aims of helping children:

1. to enjoy the past;
2. to understand the importance of a sequence of events, especially in English history;

203

3. to begin to understand concepts such as those of time, power, change/continuity, similarity/difference, then/now, old/new;
4. to begin to use the language of history;
5. to begin to understand people.

Aims 1, 4, and 5 are usually 'caught' from the teacher rather than 'taught' by her. Her use of correct historical language, her explanation, if necessary by use of the blackboard, of the meaning of the more usual words (e.g., century = 100 years), and her sympathetic but dispassionate views about historical characters (e.g., King John and Richard III) will foster aims 4 and 5. The work as a whole and the enthusiasm of the teacher will promote the first aim. Constant discussion and use of time charts will help the second. Concept-formation and concept-attainment are fostered by discussion and questioning, e.g., What did Henry VII, Henry VIII, and Elizabeth I have in common? What did the Romans, the Saxons, and the Normans have in common? In what ways were the Romans different from the Saxons and the Normans? These long-standing aims should be assessed incidentally all the time, and cannot be measured only at the end of the year.

Objectives, or specific skills exercised by children, must be conveyed to children before they undertake a task, and one of these could even be stated by the children at the top of a piece of work. They will be employed throughout the 7–11 years in progressively more difficult tasks, especially in written work and the use of original sources. Here are some objectives to be pursued throughout the junior school. They are arranged in an appropriate order of increasing difficulty.

1. to read a suitable history book from cover to cover;
2. to get information on a specific topic from a history book(s);
3. to make a model, graph, diagram, or sketch-map from written instructions or by looking at a picture;
4. to identify artefacts as to possible use and age;
5. to use evidence of the past from a picture, map, artefact, building, or document;
6. to write a narrative history story;
7. to ask questions systematically;
8. to tell a story orally;
9. to talk analytically about the past.

These skills are practised and improved if the teacher introduces suitable resources into the classroom, sets and marks a variety of written work at the end of each topic in the syllabus, and always encourages sensible discussion at some point in each session. In the later junior years oral assessment may involve entering a different topic on a card for each child, who, after preparation, will talk about that topic for up to five minutes and be prepared to answer questions from the class. I should never favour factual tests, however short, in the junior school since knowledge is a handmaiden of the concepts, skills, and attitudes needed by the historian. The year's work, if taught with variety, will provide enough motivation, feedback, and ongoing assessment until a longer-term check is made at the end of the year.

6.4 Long-term assessment in the junior school

The ongoing assessment of children undertaking a variety of tasks helps the teacher to make a long-term assessment once a year, towards the end of the summer term. This, therefore, will be done four times in all, each child's work being carefully scrutinized each year, with particular emphasis on the last year.

This is where assessment can be closely linked with children's own cumulative record making (see Section 4.5). Books of the past or history notebooks could have the centre double-page spread used for a time-line or chart of the period of the past covered during the year. As the four years pass, this will become more detailed. If a thematic approach is the basic one, the time chart should be constructed accordingly. The rest of the notebook will represent the work first in the form of drawings, charts, and maps, all labelled, and if possible a full sentence written about them. Second, several sentences put together to form a paragraph on one topic, or story told by the teacher, should be another type of work. According to the ability and progress of each child, the written work will vary, but by the final year in the junior school most children should have attempted some of the following types of written work:

1. a short paragraph or account of a past event or person;
2. a longer imaginative eye-witness account from the point of view of one of the participants in an event, e.g., Francis Drake describing how he sent fire-ships into Gravelines harbour to burn the Spanish Armada;
3. a two-paragraph account of a historical character, one paragraph being biased in favour of the character and one against, e.g., Mary Tudor;
4. a comparison of conditions in a past age with present conditions—the 'then and now' approach, e.g., 'A Victorian schoolday' and 'My day at school';
5. a paragraph about a historical character gained from a short

contemporary account, e.g., Samuel Pepys from an extract from his diary;

6. a short piece of documentary evidence to be 'translated' from the period concerned into modern English;

7. a short description of one history book (biography or novel) read during the year, the child writing why he liked it.

Assessing these books made by the children in small groups could take place through the teacher discussing them with the children and giving them one of four grades to be recorded on her record card for the year. The grades could be A for 'very good', B for 'good', C for 'satisfactory', and D for 'not so good'. Most children would reach A, B, or C standard if the work set was appropriate for them. This system has the advantage of children discussing each other's work in the teacher's presence, and in the process learning the essential art of self-assessment, which was referred to earlier as one of the basic aspects of assessment as a whole.

All the four grades from the four junior years would then be inserted on the final record card. It is important to avoid formal tests 'taken in and marked', questionnaires, or too much 'paper work' for the teacher. Assessment should not be external to the children's work, as secondary school examination papers often are. It should relate, like a CSE project, to the work itself.

6.5 Evaluation of syllabuses

The first form of evaluation in primary history is fundamentally important, but is easier to write about than to undertake. As already indicated, it concerns the reconsideration of the suitability of courses. Having struggled to the end of a year, probably concerned with the whole curriculum, teachers are not always bursting with zeal to plan anew, this is particularly true in relation to work with a considerable knowledge content, as history has. So there is a very understandable temptation to repeat, substantially, what has already been achieved. After all, it was not too disastrous, was it? Or alternatively, and perhaps more insidiously, there may be a tendency to abandon parts of it in favour of something apparently enterprising but in fact rather trivial and unproductive. Yet in practice there is a curb on both these tendencies. Teachers do have a fund of common sense which prevents them from indulging in manifest absurdities of the second kind, while it also enables them to make minor adjustments, guided by the outcome of pupil assessment, to their established syllabuses. What is required is a means by which these adjustments can be made systematic.

206

It seems to me that this can be achieved quite quickly when planning a new year's work if the following questions are honestly answered:

1. Which one (or two) pieces of work were least satisfactory with my class in history this year? Why was this? What can I do to remedy it? Or should I abandon this (these) and substitute something better calculated to attain my aims and objectives? And how can I most economically prepare this new work?
2. What do I know (from formal records and informal contacts) about the class that I am to inherit? What history have they already encountered? Are they likely to respond differently when compared with last year's? If so, will this involve making any further changes additional to those suggested under point 1?
3. Who can I consult about the changes I think it necessary to make in response to my thinking about points 1 and 2?
4. What additional equipment shall I need for this new work?
5. What modifications shall I need to make in my methods of teaching in order to carry out the changes arising from my decisions about points 1, 2, 3, and 4?

Put together, this simple evaluation checklist does not involve unrealistic change, not even if it is set alongside comparable changes in the rest of the curriculum. At best, it affords a stimulus; at worst, an investment of effort that may well be more rewarding than the tedium and frustration of unprofitable repetition.

However, this process of evaluation is not something which a teacher should conduct in isolation. It is the responsibility of a head teacher to coordinate the collective evaluation of a school's programme, taking account of a number of related factors. One of these is variety of teaching styles, a matter more likely to be considered seriously now that the work of Neville Bennett[7] and of the ORACLE project[8] is becoming widely known. If Mrs Brown's incisive questioning is followed next year by Mr Black's powers of narrative and then by Miss White's flair for drama and role-playing, a fair balance is likely to result. The outcome is less happy if they all enact rather undemanding, uninspiring, and unrelated variations on the same basic information-giving theme. Again, there is the question of progression in skill acquisition. Suppose that Mrs Brown asks her 7-year-olds:

'And do you think they went to town in cars in those days?'
CHORUS: 'No, Mrs Brown'
then it is reasonable to expect that, two years later, Miss White's role-playing 9-year-olds will be grappling with something subtler, such as the pros and cons of building a railway through a village a century ago. If

instead they are enacting elementary themes as at 7 years and merely changing to a different topic, such as housing, then the whole history sequence calls for some re-evaluation.

How a headteacher can alter such situations is a complex question, beyond the scope of this book. It depends on human relations skills and staff development and may not always be popular with everyone. However, pooling of ideas can only be beneficial and it must be valuable for each teacher to be obliged, even once in a year, to consider his or her own particular syllabus and schemes of work as a part of a larger whole, a component of children's developing experience. The system of official record keeping is habitually regarded in this way. Ideally at least, the same should apply to the evaluation of the curriculum and of its component parts.

6.6 Evaluation of materials

The re-evaluation of the syllabus leads necessarily to re-evaluation of materials. The chief value of this second form of evaluation to the primary teacher is to help her to decide which of the existing stocks to use, and which new books or materials to buy. For few resources are so fruitful that they are applicable to every piece of work, or, for that matter, so bad that they cannot be used profitably for any purpose, even if it is only a means of sharpening children's powers of criticism. Some help for this purpose can be derived from reviews, though these are not much use when the books were published before the teacher was a pupil in a primary school! In such circumstances the help of experienced and knowledgeable colleagues is indispensable, and is one way in which the specialist role suggested in the 1978 survey can be effectively performed.[9] One historian on a staff, whether or not this is the headteacher, can be of great value as a consultant immediately available.

However, individual teachers may be thrown back on their own resources and may find it helpful to use a ready-made instrument for evaluating what is available. An exhaustive evaluation scheme for books for primary and middle schools is given in Fig. 6.2, to be used as a whole or in parts. The blank spaces are left for the teacher to insert either just a tick or a crossed tick, or a cross, and to add comments. The final column on the right-hand side is for the letter G (good), M (moderate), or P (poor), to be decided as a result of the ticks and crosses. Thus, in format, a book might have an attractive layout (tick), poor durability in the form of a paper cover (cross), and the printing clear but not big enough for the age group (crossed tick). The format would therefore have M in the

Author		Price	Level	Use of book: Library – Text – Topic –
Title		Date	Bibliography	Contents page
Publisher		Date of Evaluation	Glossary	Index *

1. TITLE	— Suitability			
2. FORMAT	— Attractive layout — Durability — Printing	**BOOK AS A WHOLE**		
3. LANGUAGE	— Sentence flow — Word difficulty/ease — Explanation — Imaginative stimulus — Beginning and ending chapters			
4. ILLUSTRATIONS (plus maps)	— Clear — Related to text — Varied — Used as evidence	**TOOLS**		
5. EXTRACTS FROM WRITTEN SOURCES	— Suitability — Variety — Used as evidence	**CONTENT**		
6. CONTENT	— Accuracy — Suitability for existing syllabus — Detail generalization			
7. VIEWPOINT	— Bias/objectivity — Point of view	**TOOLS**		
8. HISTORICAL CONCEPTS	— Change/continuity — Time/duration/sequence	**FOR THE**		
9. HUMAN ELEMENTS	— People and their type — Empathy — Power — Conflict/consensus			
10. QUESTIONS AND PUPIL ACTIVITY	— Open — Closed — Skills — Attitudes — Concepts	**CLASSROOM**		
11. FURTHER WORK	— Helping other subjects — Using other resources — Using locality — Bibliography			
ADDITIONAL CRITERIA				
FINAL EVALUATION				

* G = Good   M = Moderate   P = Poor

Fig. 6.2 Evaluation scheme for history books

Section I:
General

Title .... Author ....
Producer .... Publisher ....
Type................................... Cost ....
Index .... Bibliography ....
Glossary............................. Related audio-visual material ....
Age range .... Ability Range ....

Section II: Format	No	Size	Quality	Language
Container				
Documents				
Maps				
Charts				
Photographs				
Illustrations				
Assignment cards				
Information (teacher)				
Information (pupil)				

Section III Questions and activities

A: Comprehension Multiple choice/true false Tabulating Research (find out)	C: Involve other disciplines Involve particular skills (e.g. transcription, translation, palaeography)
B: Imaginative writing Drawing Model-making Drama Visits	D: Then/now comparisons Discussion/opinion Children to pose questions Evaluation (e.g. Why was it made? Of what event did it form part? What form is it in? How reliable is it? What is the overall message or meaning of the document?)
	E: Other

Fig. 6.3 Schedule for archive units and teaching kits (from *History in School No. 1*, C. Hallward, School of Education, Leeds University, 1973)

right-hand column. All the letters would add up to the final evaluation and letter. This evaluation scheme could be kept by the teacher responsible for history and used by all class teachers for a particular series of books.

When describing some of the packs of historical material in Chapter 5, I said that many were too difficult for the primary school except in the top class. In *History in School* (an annual bulletin of the Leeds Area

Topic: Objectives	Workcard									
	1	2	3	4	5	6	7	8	9	10
Finding information										
Curiosity										
Interests of children										
Communicating information										
Interpreting information										
Evaluating evidence										
Concepts and generalizations										
Trying out possible explanations										
Wariness of over-commitment										
Openness to changing ideas										
Small-group relationships										
Wider social relationships										
Empathy										
Personal values										
Use of equipment										
Use of expressive movement										

Fig. 6.4   Evaluative checklist for workcards (adapted from *Evaluation, Assessment and Record-Keeping in History, Geography and Social Science*, Keith Cooper, Collins/ESL, Bristol, 1976)

History Teachers' Group) No. 1, September 1973, Christabel Hallward wrote a useful article: 'Archive units and History kits: an evaluation' and included the schedule shown in Fig. 6.3. This could be used in the same way as the textbook scheme already outlined, with short comments, ticks and crosses.

Keith Cooper has good advice for teachers when making workcards. In order to ensure that a wide range of objectives is covered in the workcards, he suggests the evaluative checklist shown in Fig. 6.4. The objectives are in the left-hand column and each workcard will include only some of these. The point is to ensure that, in any workcard, the possibility should be considered of including objectives other than the intellectual ones.

These three schemes, for books, archive units, and workcards, are not exhaustive as checks on resource materials. Pictures, maps, and wallcharts are also used constantly by teachers and if time allowed, schedules could be made jointly by all class teachers. These might all equally well apply to other areas of the curriculum. The headteacher, or the teacher responsible for history in a primary school, should try to build up useful schedules and to evaluate the main resources used, with the help of colleagues and the children themselves. All of this should constitute an essential part of the evaluation, and re-evaluation, of history teaching in the school.

211

6.7 Record keeping [10]

Assessment and evaluation naturally lead to record keeping if they are to be of use in the future. The important side of this exercise is that it must be simple, efficient, and speedy to execute. Three teachers writing on this topic are well aware of the time this can take. Keith Cooper writes: 'Keeping records takes time. Until the day dawns when teachers have adequate secretarial help, teachers will have to find time from all their other tasks so that their records are adequate and useful.'[11] Joan Dean agrees with this sentiment when she writes: 'Record-keeping is very much the art of the possible, and teachers will vary in the degree to which they find it helpful to make observations on paper.'[12] May Cooper adds to the refrain with: 'Teacher recording uses a tremendous amount of time, which might be better spent in preparatory work.'[13] Joan Dean also warns teachers that assessment and record keeping can encourage the teacher to expect too much from children. Yet with more individual work done in schools, vertical grouping, mixed-ability teaching, cooperative teaching units, and now falling numbers necessitating teaching different age groups together, there is more need than ever for effective records.

Individual record keeping is not to be recommended in history beyond the rough selection of the letter H on the normal record card near the names of children who are good at history. But two ideas may be considered which are not too time consuming. One is a record card for the whole class in history, so that with the syllabus framework, teachers taking the same children the following year will know at a glance what skills have been mastered (or not) as a whole (see Question 2 in Section 6.5). Keith Cooper suggests this in his *Class profile of basic skills* (Fig. 6.5) which may be added to by the teacher responsible for history from the skills already listed (see p. 000).

The other idea is that children should help the teacher by keeping their own records, thus reinforcing their own learning of self-assessment. This is supported by both Joan Dean and May Cooper. Joan Dean knows one school where each child keeps his own record of what work has been done each week, and with which part of the work he needs particular help. Other schools which she mentions keep records of what content of work has been covered, but this is not so necessary if there is a history syllabus. May Cooper starts her 8-year-olds writing their own records for all areas of the curriculum during the last period of each day. From a list on the blackboard, the child selects the work done and adds details about how far he has got with it. He then writes shortly about his feelings in respect of the work and assesses his own performance. The children

Class	J1J	J2F	J3B	J4W
Skills	J1 Mrs Jones	J2 Mr Forsyth	J3 Miss Blake	J4 Mrs Webster
Contents page and index	All class given instruction	Every child now does this well	✓	
Atlas	Briefly introduced to whole class	Most children quite familiar with it	All children happy with use	
Scale	Touched on by a few	Some quite good—no systematic teaching of it	All class given instruction— most have grasped it	

O.S. conventional
  signs
Bar graph
Pie chart
Line graph
Library classification
  system
Portable tape recorder
Slide projector
Camera				

Fig. 6.5 Class profile of basic skills (from *Evaluation, Assessment and Record-Keeping in History, Geography and Social Science*, Keith Cooper, Collins/ESL, Bristol, 1976)

like doing this, and feel more involved with the work as well as providing the teacher with valuable information about the feelings of individual children. This method could be applied to history as one subject, once a month, if the teacher did not want it to cover the whole curriculum.[14]

A combination of a good syllabus, class record card of skills attained, and individual records made each month by each child, may seem the best. If this were done systematically for four years, a very adequate profile of history teaching and learning would emerge by the time the children were 11 years old. It is to be hoped that this could be transmitted to secondary schools, and that the head of the history department there would take notice of it. For if history is adequately considered in the primary school, it should be taken seriously into account by those who plan what is to follow.

References

1. K. Cooper, *Evaluation, Assessment and Record-Keeping in History, Geography and Social Science*, Collins/ESL, Bristol, 1976.
2. For a discussion of the relationship between evaluation and assessment, see Wynn Harlen (ed.), *Evaluation and the Teacher's Role*, Schools Council Research Series, Macmillan Education, 1978, especially her own chapter.
3. See W. Harlen, 'Matching', in Colin Richards (ed.), *Primary Education: issues for the Eighties*, Allen and Unwin, 1980; also *Primary Education in England*, HMSO, 1978, especially Chapter 6.
4. J. Tough, *Listening to Children Talking*, Ward Lock, 1976; *Talking and Learning*, Ward Lock, 1977; *Focus on Meaning*, Allen and Unwin, 1974.
5. J. Dean, *Recording Children's Progress*, Macmillan, 1972, p. 7.
6. Final Report of *History, Geography and Social Science in the Curriculum 5–14—a Workshop Course on the Assessment of Children's Progress*. DES/Regional Course, University of Liverpool School of Education, 1979, p. 25.
7. N. Bennett, *Teaching Styles and Pupil Progress*, Open Books, 1976.
8. M. Galton, B. Simon and P. Croll, *Inside the Primary Classroom*, Routledge and Kegan Paul, 1980.
9. Department of Education and Science, *Primary Education in England*, HMSO, 1978, p. 118.
10. The Schools Council has supported a project on *Record-Keeping in Primary Schools*, an important addition to the literature on this topic.
11. K. Cooper, op. cit., p. 40.
12. J. Dean, op. cit., p. 57.
13. M. Cooper, 'Children as Assessors', *Times Educational Supplement*, 21 July 1978.
14. Ibid.

Suggestions for using the book

The following suggestions may be followed up from the appropriate chapters:

Chapter 2. Background to syllabus construction

1. Having read 2.2 (*Basic principles*) and with your own school in mind, work out a 7–11 syllabus framework, deciding where it should be integrated and where separate history. Take into account what resources you already have and what you can realistically expect to get.
2. With this in mind, work out a 5–7 scheme related to it but avoiding repetition.

Chapter 3. Ideas for constructing a syllabus

Read the lists of skills and concepts in Chapter 6 (p. 202) and write down which your 5–11 syllabus aims to achieve. Be clear in your own mind which skills and concepts run right through the age range, and if not, at which points you start teaching for them. Do not worry if some part of your syllabus is included mainly because it is the part you know most about and you enjoy teaching!

Chapter 4. The classroom operation

1. Make a list of the many different ways in which you already teach history, if you do teach about the past.
2. Select any one history story of your choice and write down a story structured as on p. 67. If you do not know of a suitable story which fits your syllabus, seek help from p. 68 or from Chapter 3, pp. 24–25.
3. Plan any one section of your syllabus for which you have a good large illustration showing how you would start a discussion in your class, using the illustration. What leading questions would you ask? It will help you in framing the questions to think of the answers you might expect.

4. Using Fig. 4.4, *Encouraging Critical Thinking Skills*, choose any personality or event with which you are familiar in your syllabus and draw up a list of 'closed' and 'open' questions leading to critical thinking.

5. Choosing either a *Victorian School* or the *Romans in Britain* find out more about the subject-matter for helping children to build up paragraphs. Suitable books are:

Victorian School

P. F. Speed, *Learning and Teaching in Victorian Times*, Then and There, Longmans.

E. Allen, *Victorian Children*, Black.

R. Wood, *Children 1715–1890*, Evans.

P. H. J. H. Gosden, *How They Were Taught*, Blackwell.

DES, *The Education Act*, (archive teaching unit), HMSO.

G. W. Hogg and J. C. Tyson (eds), *Popular Education 1700–1870*, (archive teaching unit), University of Newcastle upon Tyne.

The Romans in Britain

J. Liversedge, *Roman Britain*, Then and There, Longmans.

P. Fincham, *Roman Britain and the Saxon Shore*, The Way It Was, Chambers.

R. Mitchell, *Roman Britain*, Focus on History, Longmans.

J. M. Jamieson, *The Romans in Britain*, Arnold.

P. Sauvain, *Roman Britain*, Imagining the Past, Macmillan.

6. From instructions in *Activity Methods in History* by John Fairley (pp. 8–11) design a zig-zag concertina-type workbook.

7. Read *Patch Study Examples* (Fig. 4.5) carefully and make your own chart of 'the three stages', using material from your own syllabus.

8. Work out the reading, preparation in class before the field visit, the actual visit, and follow-up work for any one piece of field work relevant to one year in your school. The visit may vary from one afternoon to a week. Confine yourself to what is practicable and assume that it will be raining!

9. Plan out a class time chart and a time chart for a child's notebook for any one year of your school's history syllabus. Take care to avoid too many actual dates on the chart but leave enough space for illustrations so that they do not have to be too scrawled and tiny.

Chapter 5. Sources and resources

1. Using the summary in Fig. 5.1 make a list of all the historical resources possessed by your school. If you do this imaginatively, the list may be longer than you expect.

2. List the textbooks and reading books in your school related to the topics in your syllabus, checking suitability for age range. Duplicate enough copies for all class teachers. The headings on p. 136 will help you with categories. This too may be longer than you expect.
3. Organize a group of your class to undertake dinner-hour help by cutting out illustrations from old books and mounting them on workcards for you to complete. Exclude anyone with unwashed hands!
4. Select a short extract from a contemporary source (e.g., Celia Fiennes' *The Journeys of Celia Fiennes*, ed. C. Morris, Cresset Press) appropriate for a course in your third or fourth year, think out six questions ('closed' and 'open') relating to it and duplicate enough copies for one class. (For this purpose there should be no difficulty about copyright.)
5. Using the extract on *Boys* (p. 159) write down how you would introduce and use it in a mixed top junior class. What discussion, discovery, written, or dramatic work could arise from it? How would you discuss the outcome with your colleagues?
6. Divide your class into groups, let each group bring old family photographs where they can, give each group a set of questions (about people, ages, dates), let them discuss their photographs, and finally make a class frieze putting photographs in date order, with each group writing a short account of their own photographs. This could be done as a one-off exercise to teach time, or as part of work on contemporary history or family history.

Chapter 6. Assessment, evaluation and record keeping

1. As a form of assessment with 6-year-olds, collect three old objects of obviously varying ages, tell a group of infants about them and tape record your half-hour discussion with them about the artefacts and how old they are. Play the tape back while still with the group, and record their comments too. This would provide the basis for assessment.
2. Over a period of time (possibly a summer term) work out a weekly check on the concepts and skills on p. 202 with your 7-year-olds. If they have not been taught any history this will mean constructing learning situations related to the four concepts and four skills upon which you can base your checking. This is less formidable than it sounds. For example, for Concept 4 you could ask each child to write down in what ways *he* has changed in his seven years of life, e.g., height, weight, clothes, skills, colour of hair, etc, (=change in time).

3. Arrange your syllabus in the top class of your junior school in such a way as to find out how many children have acquired how many of the nine objectives named on p. 204. This too is less time consuming than it sounds. It is in fact a necessary piece of evaluation.
4. Select three of the types of written work given on p. 205 and use them with your top class towards the end of the year. Then discuss their work in small groups and assess as suggested on p. 206.
5. Using the *Evaluation Scheme for Books* in Fig. 6.2 evaluate one new history textbook or reading book which you are sampling from a publishing firm. The publishers will be genuinely interested in your comments: that is their kind of evaluation.
6. Check three of your recently-made workcards against the *Evaluative Checklist for Work cards* in Fig. 6.4. If this is done genuinely and the outcome is encouraging, then you can be reasonably sure that the breadth and depth of your history teaching is suitable and will probably go on improving.

These tasks may be undertaken either by the individual or by groups of teachers on an in-service course.

Further reading

General

Primary school in relation to history teaching
ARMSTRONG, M. (1980), *Closely observed Children*, Chameleon.
BLACKIE, J. (1967), *Inside the Primary School*, HMSO.
DEPARTMENT OF EDUCATION AND SCIENCE (1978), *Primary Education in England*, HMSO.
DONALDSON, M. (1978), *Children's Minds*, Fontana.
EGAN, K. (1979), *Educational Development*, Oxford University Press.
MARSHALL, S. (1970), *An Experiment in Education*, Cambridge University Press.
PLUCKROSE, H. (1979), *Children in their Primary Schools*, Pelican.

History teaching
BURSTON, W. H. and GREEN, C. W. (eds) (1972), *Handbook for History Teachers*, (Second Edition), Methuen.
CLARKE, F. (1929), *Foundations of History Teaching*, Oxford University Press.
DYMOND, D. (ed.) (1929), *A Handbook for History Teachers*, Methuen.
FIRTH, C. B. (1929), *The Learning of History*, Kegan Paul.
ILEA (Inner London Education Authority) (1980), *History in the Primary School: Curriculum Guidelines* (from Publishing Centre, ILEA, Highbury Station Rd, London N1 1SB).
JAMIESON, A. (1971), *Practical History Teaching*, Evans.
MAY, T. (1979), *History and the Young Child*, Historical Association Information Leaflet 5 (from Historical Association, 59A Kennington Park Rd, London SE11).
MAYS, P. (1974), *Why Teach History?* University of London Press.
POLLARD, M. (1973), *History with Juniors*, Evans.
REEVES, M. (1980), *Why History?* Longmans.
STRONG, C. F. (1950), *History in the Primary School*, University of London Press.
UNSTEAD, R. J. (1956), *Teaching History in the Junior School*, A. & C. Black.
WEST, J. (1966), *History, Here and Now*, The Teacher Publishing Co.

Ltd (from Derbyshire House, Lower St, Kettering, Northants NN16 8BB).

Chapter 3. Ideas for constructing a syllabus

MORAY HOUSE COLLEGE OF EDUCATION (1965), *History in the Primary School: a Scheme of Work*, Oliver and Boyd.
See also the general history teaching section.

Chapter 4. The classroom operation

General
EARL, A. and R. (1971), *How Shall I Teach History?* Blackwell.
FAIRLEY, J. (1970), *Patch History and Creativity*, Longmans.
FINES, J. (ed.) (1969), *Teachers' Handbook: History*, Blond Educational.

Story-telling
BEST, A. M. (n.d.) *Story-Telling: Notes for Teachers of History in the Junior School*, Historical Association *Teaching of History Leaflet* No. 13.

Art Work and Model Making
FAIRLEY, J. (1967), *Activity Methods in History*, Nelson.
HART, T. (1973), *Fun with Historical Projects*, Kaye and Ward.
MILLIKEN, E. and E. K. (1949), *Handwork Methods in the Teaching of History*, Wheaton.

Time charts
MADELEY, H. (1921), *Time Charts*, Historical Association Pamphlet No. 50.

Local history and field work
CORFE, T. (ed.) (1970), *Teachers' Handbook: History Field Work*, Blond Educational
DOUCH, R. (1967), *Local History and the Teacher*, Routledge and Kegan Paul.
FERGUSON, I. S. and SIMPSON, E. J. (1969), *Teaching Local History*, Oliver and Boyd.
JOHNSON, F. J. and IKIN, K. J. (1974), *History Field Work*, Macmillan.
PLUCKROSE, H. (1971), *Let's Use the Locality*, Mills and Boon.
STEPHENS, W. B. (1977), *Teaching Local History*, Manchester University Press.
TITLEY, P. (1971), *Discovering Local History*, Look and Remember Book 5, Allman and Son.

Chapter 5. Sources and resources

General

MCBRIDE, G. (ed.) (1979), *Teaching History 8–13*, Queen's University, Belfast.

POLLARD, M. (1976), *A Handbook of Resources in the Primary School*, Ward Lock Educational.

TREASURE CHEST FOR TEACHERS (1978), The Teacher Publishing Co.

Illustrations

WILLIAMS, G. (1967), *Guide to Sources of Illustrative Material for Use in Teaching History*, Historical Association No. 65.

Books

BARTON, M. and DAVIES, K. (1968), *A Junior History Booklist*, Historical Association *Teaching of History* Series No. 27.

CAM, H. M. (1961), *Historical Novels*, Historical Association G 48.

Sources

WEST, J. (1971), *Archives for Schools*, The Teacher Publishing Co. Ltd.

Family and oral history

PURKIS, S. (1980), *Oral History in Schools*, Oral History Society (from Department of Sociology, University of Essex, Wivenhoe Park, Colchester, Essex CO4 3SQ).

STEEL, D. J. and TAYLOR, L. (1973), *Family History in Schools*, Phillimore.

Museums

FAIRLEY, J. (1977), *History Teaching through Museums*, Longmans.

Brasses and graves

COOK, M. (1968), *Discovering Brasses and Brass-Rubbing*, Shire.

LINDLEY, K. (1972), *Graves and Graveyards*, Local Search Series, Routledge and Kegan Paul.

NORRIS, M. (1965), *Brass Rubbing*, Studio Vista.

Chapter 6. Assessment, evaluation and record keeping

Assessment

COOPER, K. (1976), *Evaluation, Assessment and Record-Keeping in History, Geography and Social Science*, Collins/ESL, Bristol.

Index

Abrams, P., 137, 198
Activity Methods in History, 85, 104–5, 220
Adams, R. H., 91, 100, 124
Advisers, 38, 188
Airne, C. W., 144
Anglo-Saxon Chronicle, The, 146
Archives, 148–74
Archives for Schools, 221
Architecture, 41
Armstrong, M., 219
Art, 41
Art galleries, 188–93
Art and Craft in Education, 104
Artefacts, 3, 10, 23, 24, 26, 27, 83, 179
As We Were, 140
Assessment, 92, 201, 201–6
Awake to History, 68, 137

Bagenal, M. and A., 41, 42, 43, 108
Baker, D., 146
Barnes, M., 113, 125
Barton, M., 221
Batho, G., 160, 165
Bayeux Tapestry, 73, 108
BBC, 29, 184–7, 188
Beans, 140
Beard, R., 115, 125
Belloc, H., 198
Bennett, N., 207, 214
Bernstein, B., 134
Bethnel Green Museum of Childhood, 189, 191, 192
Blackboard, 44, 84, 85, 87, 106, 127, 129, 130, 134, 159, 212
Blackie, J., 19, 114, 219
Blyth, W. A. L. and J. E., 74, 89, 124, 197, 199
Board of Education, 5, 6
Books, 135–48
Boys and Girls of History, 68
Bramwell, 4, 5
Brassrubbing, 196, 197
    Brassrubbing, 196
    Discovering Brasses and Brassrubbing, 197

Briggs, A., 11, 93, 120
Bristol, University of, 196
Britain's Story Told in Pictures, 144
Bruner, J. S., 18, 26
Bryant, M., 146
Burston, W. H., 146, 219
Burton, H., 198

Callcott, Lady, 4, 5
Cam, H., 143, 221
Cambridge History of Mankind, 169
Cambridge School Classics Project, 197
Canterbury Tales, 42
Centre of interest, 37, 39, 87
Chaffer, J., 196
Changing Museums, 188
Child Education, 144
Children in History, 142
Children and Museums, 188
Children's Minds, 8, 29, 219
Chronology, 14, 21
Churches, 94, 95
Clarke, F., 6, 72, 114, 219
Classical Stories, 24
Closely Observed Children, 219
Cobbett, W., 148
Colleges of Education, 38
Coltham, J. B., 15, 20, 21, 134
Communication Skills, 124, 203
Concepts, 93, 202, 204, 209, 211, 215
Cook, E., 25, 142
Cook, M. (Archivist), 84, 89, 165, 199
Cook, M. (*Discovering Brasses*), 221
Cooper, K., 201, 211, 213, 214, 222
Cooper, M., 212, 214
Corfe, T., 94, 124, 169, 220
Coventry Community Education Project, 183
Critical Thinking, 9, 79
Cruikshank, M., 165
Cumming, R. R., 97

Dance, 41
Darbys of the Dale Company, The, 165
Dates, 85, 113, 216
Davies, K., 201, 221

Day Training Colleges, 5
Dean, J., 203, 212, 214
Defoe, D., 147, 199
Development, line of, 18, 38, 100, 107
Development of Thinking and the Learning of History, The, 20
Devitt, M., 167
Dickinson, A. K., 11, 15, 21
Diorama, 107
Discovery Learning, 37, 47, 76, 77, 91, 100
Discovery Reference Books, 142, 165
Display in the Classroom, 110
Dobson, F., 115, 125
Donaldson, M., 8, 29, 219
Douch, R., 97, 220
Drama, 41–6, 71, 81, 168, 217
Dymond, D., 219

Earl, A. and R., 20, 80, 220
Early Childhood, 144, 198
Early Middle Ages, The, 871–1216, 148
Ecclesiastical History of the English Nation, 146
Educational Development, 61, 63, 66
Educational Objectives for the Study of History: A Suggested Framework, 20
Edwards, A. D., 11
Egan, K., 23, 61, 63, 66, 124, 219
Eggleston, J., 51, 63
Elementary School Work, 5
English Journey, 148
Environment, 18
Environmental studies, 19, 38–41
Environmental Studies 5–13 (Schools Council Project), 7
Environmental Studies 5–13; the use of historical sources, 41
Evaluation, 136, 201, 206–11, 214, 217, 218
Evaluation, Assessment and Record-Keeping in History, Geography and Social Science, 222
Evidence, 2
Experiment in Education, An, 49, 219

Fairley, J., 85, 86, 87, 88, 104, 105, 107, 108, 124, 189, 192, 220, 221
Family history, 13, 23, 26, 27, 36, 83, 174–84, 188
Family History in Schools, 176, 179, 181, 182, 183
Ferguson, I. S., 220
Field work, 9, 10, 19, 39, 93, 98, 101–4, 127
Films, 127, 184
Filmstrips, 127, 184
Fines, J., 15, 21, 63, 67–8, 80, 94, 124, 194

Firth, C. B., 18, 42, 72, 124, 141, 219
Flow-chart, 111
Focus on History, 141
Forster's Education Act, 1870, 4
Foundations of History Teaching, 6
Fox, B., 91–3
Frieze, 106, 108
Fun with Historical Projects, 105, 108

Galton, M., 207, 214
Geffrye Museum, 107, 188, 190, 191
Geographers, 39, 93
Geography, 6, 12, 15, 38, 41, 202
Gibbon, E., 93
Giffins Report, 113
Gleave, M., 137
Gordon, P., 4, 11, 115
Grant-Scarfe, H., 140
Graves and Graveyards, 108
Green, C. W., 146, 219
Gregory, A., 142, 164
Group work, 85–93

Hadow Report (1931), 5
Hallam, R., 3
Hallward, C., 210
Handbook (1959), 6
Handbook for History Teachers (1972), 20, 146
Handbook of Suggestions for Teachers (1927), 5
Handwork Methods in the Teaching of History, 105
Happer, E., 124
Harlen, W., 214
Harris, F., 40, 98, 102–4
Harris, R., 73
Harrison, M., 142, 188
Hart, T., 73, 105, 108, 220
Hastie, T., 194
Heathcote, D., 42, 44, 45, 46, 68
Herodotus, 93
Heroes, 16, 19, 24, 36
Hertzog, R., 61, 63
Hewitt-Jones, R., 167
Highways and Byways of Essex, 164
Hirst, P., 3
Historical Association, 143, 164, 165
Historical novels, 143
History Bookshelves, 141
History of Everyday Things in England, 72, 105
History Field Work, 94, 220
History First, 116, 169

History in Focus, 141
History, Geography and Social Science 8–13, 7, 20, 167
(*See also* Schools Council Project, 187)
History and Handwork for Young Children, 105
History, Here and Now, 18, 219
History with Juniors, 185
History in the Primary School, 15, 219
History in the Primary School: ILEA Curriculum Guidelines, 194, 219
History in the Primary School: A Scheme of Work, 18, 220
History in School, 210
History Teachers' Yearbook, 185
History Teaching Through Museums, 189, 221
History workbooks, 83
History and the Young Child, 219
Holidays, 191
How Shall I Teach History?, 20, 80, 220
Hubbard, D., 124

Ikin, K. J., 94, 124, 220
ILEA, 168, 194, 219
Industrial archaeology, 165
Infants, 8, 22–9, 75–6, 83–4, 86–7, 99, 101–2, 106–7, 115, 118–19, 131–3, 174–6, 189, 202–3
In-service courses, 127, 195, 218
Inside the Primary School, 19
Integration, 18, 30, 37, 38, 46, 49, 51, 93, 185
Interdisciplinary, 179
Introducing the Past, 140, 177
ITV, 29, 186–7

Jackdaws books, 75, 167
Jahoda, G., 113, 125
Jamieson, A., 87, 94, 100, 105, 219
Johnson, F. J., 94, 124, 220
John Wesley's Journals, 149
Journeys of Celia Fiennes, The, 147

Keele, University of, 165
Kent, University of, 183

Ladybird books, 25, 68, 144
Language, 82, 134
Lavender, R., 25, 142
Lawson, D., 4, 11
Le Fevre, M., 124
Learning with Jackdaws, 167
Lee, P. J., 11, 15, 21
Leeds, University of, 159
Let's Make Pictures, 73

Let's Use the Locality, 73, 94, 105
Let's Work Large, 73, 106
Lewis, R. A., 161
Library, 135, 136, 139, 143, 160
Lindley, K., 108, 221
Little Arthur's History of England, 4, 72
Little Folks, 150, 153
Liverpool Education Committee, 161
Liverpool–Prescot–Warrington Turnpike Road, 90, 166
Liverpool, University of:
  archivists, 193
  Education Library, 160
Living History, 137
Local history, 13, 35, 39, 83
Local History and the Teacher, 97, 220
Local radio, 187
Local studies, 28, 29, 131
Lodwick, 3
Looking at History, 137
Low-Beer, A., 196
Lynn, S., 174–6

McBride, G., 127, 221
Macaulay, T. B., 93
Madeley, H., 114, 220
Makin, S., 67, 69–72
Making History—An Approach through Drama, 44
Map That Came to Life, The, 73
Maps, 85–94, 96, 98, 149–52, 164
Marshall, S., 49, 63, 219
Martin, N., 125
May, K., 171–4
Mayflower Park, 28, 45
Mays, P., 105, 106, 115, 129, 198, 219
Merry Company, This, 41, 42, 108
Middle Schools, 9
Middleton, G., 115, 137, 141
Migration, 36
Milliken, E. and E. K., 105, 107, 220
Mitchell, R., 115, 137
Models, 72, 85, 104–12, 134
Montessori, 135
Moray House College of Education, 18, 39, 50, 51, 220
More Boys and Girls of History, 68
Morris, C., 199
Mowl, Dr (F. Saxey), 24, 67, 72
Multi-cultural syllabus, 36
Multi-racial syllabus, 61, 62
Murphy, B., 13, 177, 179, 199
Museums, 23, 43, 94, 127, 188–93
  loan services, 192
Museum Bookshelves, 141
Museums and Education, 188

Museum of the History of Education, 159
Music, 41, 42, 126
Myths, 23, 24
Myths, Legends and Lore, 25
Myths and Legends, 24

National Portrait Gallery, 43, 73, 144, 189
Neighbourhood, 40
Newton, E. E., 13, 124
Norman and Medieval Britain, 115
Norris, M., 221
Notebooks, 108, 121, 122, 127, 129, 134, 205, 216
Nuffield Foundation, 48
Nuffield Junior Science Project, 46–9

Oakden, E. C., 113, 124
Objectives, 202, 204, 218
Oral history, 174
Oral History in Schools, 176–83
Ordinary and the Fabulous, The, 25
Ordnance Survey, 73
Orphan Annie, 164
Osmond, E., 100
Our Saints, 140

Paice, S., 139, 140, 198
Palmer, M., 166, 199
Parent-Teacher Association, 136
Parker, C., 110–12
Parker, F. E., 105
Patch, 20, 36, 38, 51, 80, 87, 88, 91
Patch History and Creativity, 86, 87, 88, 107
People Around Us, 27, 68, 194
Pelling, J., 80–2
Phelps, R., 110
Phillips, M., 161, 162, 163, 193
Photographs, 27, 105, 177, 182, 183, 217
Piaget, J., 3, 113, 115
Pictures, 144–5
Pictorial Charts, 144
Pictorial Education, 73, 106, 144
Pictorial Education Special, 144
Picture Reference Books, 144
Picture Source Books of Social History, 146
Place, Time and Society 8–13, 7, 54
Place, Time and Society 8–13: Curriculum Planning, 55
Playing with Plans, 39
Plowden Report (1967), 6, 12, 15, 37
Pluckrose, H., 73, 105, 106, 124, 219, 220
Practical History Teaching, 87, 94, 100, 105
Preparatory schools, 9

Price, M., 30, 63
Priestley, J. B., 148
Primary Education in England (1978), 7, 12, 55, 214, 219
Princes of Loom Street, The, 164
Projects, 87
Purkis, 177, 199, 221

Quennell, M. and C. H. B., 72, 105
Questions, 76–9, 177, 217

Raper, P., 13, 134
Recording Children's Progress, 203, 214
Record-keeping, 201, 212–13
Record-making, cumulative, 82–5
Record offices, 18, 19, 29, 76, 171, 179, 183, 193–4
Reeves, M., 139, 142, 219
Reference books, 139, 142
Resources for Learning, 126
Resources in the Primary School, A Handbook of, 127, 221
Revised Code of 1861, 4
Road Travel in Lancashire 1700–1850, 195
Rogers, P. J., 3, 11, 76, 91, 100, 124
Role-playing, 43, 111, 112, 202
Rowse, A. L., 93
Rural Rides, 149

Salt, J., 97, 124
Salt, J. M., 148, 149
Sauvain, P., 73, 173
Saxey, F. (Dr Mowl), 24, 67, 72
Scrapbooks, 179
SEARCH packets, 167
Sequence, 2, 84, 112, 120, 121
Schools Council, 7, 127, 197
  Communication Skills (project), 124, 203
  Environmental Studies 5–13 (project), 7, 39
  Gifted Children (project), 124
  History, Geography and Social Science 8–13 (project), 7, 20, 38, 54, 78, 181, 197, 214
  Record Keeping in Primary Schools (project), 214
  Science 5–13 (project), 38, 48, 49
  Social Studies 8–13 (project), 7, 54
Science and History, 47
Science Museum, 107
Scottish Education Department, 48
Simpson, E. J., 220
Simulation and gaming, 167
Skills, 93, 202, 203, 204, 208, 212, 213, 215–17
Social Studies 8–13, 7, 54

Social subjects, 1, 4
Some Kent Children 1594–1875, 161, 162, 163, 193
Sources, 2, 145–74
    archival, 148–74
    printed, 145–8
    Sources of History, 142
Southampton, 28, 76, 77, 131
Speed, J., 76, 77, 134, 148
Steel, D., 13, 179, 181, 182, 199, 221
Stephens, W. B., 97, 145, 199, 220
Storm, M. J., 39
Stories, 22, 23, 24, 27
Story of Britain, The, 73, 137
Story-telling, 64, 65–72, 76, 83
Story-telling: Notes for Teachers of History in the Junior School, 68
Strong, C. F., 15, 16, 114, 219
Studies in Historical Method, 113
Sturt, M., 113, 115, 124
Suggestions for the consideration of teachers and others concerned in the work of public elementary schools (1905), 5

Tableau, 107
Tape-recording, 183, 217
Tate, W. E., 159
Taylor, L., 13, 176, 179, 181, 182, 199, 221
Taylor, L. C., 126, 127, 198
Teachers' centres, 18, 29, 38, 90, 126, 127, 161, 194–6
Teachers' Handbook for Environmental Studies, 39
Teachers' Handbook: History, 80
Teachers' Handbook: History Field Work, 94, 220
Teaching History, 93, 145, 166, 195
Teaching History 8–13, 127
Teaching History in the Junior School, 15, 16
Teaching of History (1952), 6, 17
Teaching Local History, 97, 145
Tests, 205
Textbooks, 137–9, 217
Themes, 38, 39
Thucydides, 93
Then and There books, 91, 139, 141, 185
They Saw It Happen, 145
Thompson, E. P., 93
Thompson, P., 198

Time, 2, 48, 49
Time charts, 6, 16, 65, 82, 112–23, 216
Time Charts, 114
Time lines, 84, 114
Times Educational Supplement, 37, 43, 198,
Titley, P., 221
Topic, 12, 18, 28, 34, 35, 37, 39, 46, 49, 87, 136
Tough, J., 78, 203, 214
Tour throughout the Whole Island of Great Britain, A, 147
Town Under Siege: Liverpool in the Civil War 1642–44, A, 74, 75, 166, 167
Treasure Chest for Teachers, 127, 185, 221
Trevelyan, G. M., 93
Tudor Home Life, 75
Tudor House: Speke Hall and the Norris Family, 1500–1700, A, 89

Understanding Children Talking, 115
Unfolding Past, The, 115
Unstead, R. J., 15, 16, 19, 83, 105, 107, 114, 124, 137–219

Valley Grows Up, A, 100
Vodden, D. F., 39

Waplington, A., 167, 187
Way it Was, The, 141
Wenham, P., 124
Wesley's journals, 148
West, J., 6, 18, 21, 90, 120–3, 161, 166, 199, 219, 221
West, M., 28, 101–2
Wheeler, S., 199
White, A. J., 24
Why History?, 142
Why Teach History?, 68, 105, 129
Williams, G., 198, 221
Wilton, C., 169–71
Winstanley, B., 188
Wood, R., 199
Working Paper No. 39 (Social Studies 8–13), 54
Workbooks, 191
Workcards, 132–3, 211
Worksheets, 85, 94, 134, 173
Wyman, J., 183, 199
Wynne, M., 37